T0354684

# OUT WITH
# JOY

RICHARD R. ROACH, MD, FACP

# OUT WITH
# JOY

## MAKING A PHYSICIAN FROM A CANOE GUIDE

OUT WITH JOY
MAKING A PHYSICIAN FROM A CANOE GUIDE

iUniverse books may be ordered through booksellers or by contacting:

iUniverse
1663 Liberty Drive
Bloomington, IN 47403
www.iuniverse.com
844-349-9409

Because of the dynamic nature of the Internet, any web addresses or links contained in this book may have changed since publication and may no longer be valid. The views expressed in this work are solely those of the author and do not necessarily reflect the views of the publisher, and the publisher hereby disclaims any responsibility for them.

Any people depicted in stock imagery provided by Getty Images are models, and such images are being used for illustrative purposes only. Certain stock imagery © Getty Images.

ISBN: 978-1-6632-6973-7 (sc)
ISBN: 978-1-6632-6974-4 (hc)
ISBN: 978-1-6632-6972-0 (e)

Library of Congress Control Number: 2024926816

Print information available on the last page.

iUniverse rev. date: 01/20/2025

# CONTENTS

Dedicated to my delightful grandchildren,
who asked me to write this:
Tirzah's children, Keziah and Keturah
Temujin's children, Timur, Turner, and Tarek

*You will go out in joy and be led forth in peace; the mountains and hills will burst into song before you, and all the trees of the field will clap their hands.*

*—Isaiah 55:12 NIV*

# INTRODUCTION

Is it possible to thank the people who have influenced a life for seventy-five years? It is not. So, is this just an egotistical presentation? No, it is an acknowledgment of all the people who guided me along the path of life. Some negative influences led me astray, but then someone always brought me back to the right path.

How do I relate to my spiritual journey? A still, small voice told me, "I used one untrained jackass; I can use another." That still, small voice led me through all these adventures.

Why should I write about my life? There are too many things to remember. My grandchildren insist. Is that a good reason?

My grandson says to me, "Tell us another story about your life."

I tell another story, which results in uproarious laughter.

"You're funny," he says.

"Why did you learn French?"

"Because we were illegal aliens in Rwanda."

"That's scary."

My granddaughter asks, "Is that really true, Grandpa?"

"Yes. It happened to me."

"That's unbelievable. You better write that down."

The result of their insistence is my autobiography. However, I've written it not just at my grandchildren's insistence but at the request of my canoe guide friends; my physician partners, nurses, and other health care workers at Southwestern Medical Clinic of

Western Michigan University's School of Medicine; my Malagasy colleagues; and even some of my patients, as well as the guests who lived in our home, Yana and Valentina, Lisa, Fumiko and Paul, and those my wife, Priscilla, cared for as an "adult frame of reference" (they were opposed to the term *baby-sitter*). Each person has so influenced Priscilla and me, for which we can never thank them enough.

Priscilla encouraged me to write. After more than fifty years of marriage, she still thinks I'm funny. She reminds me that our marriage has been much more exciting than she wanted it to be, "so you better write that down."

My brother William and his wife as well as my children, Temujin and Tirzah, and their spouses have read all my novels and insisted that I write my autobiography.

My pediatric partner suggested that I write a textbook on pediatric tropical medicine. "I'm an internist. How can I write a pediatric text?" I asked him.

"Most of the tropical diseases that affect adults, they got when they were children. You have that experience. Write it."

So, I did write nine chapters based on my care for patients in Madagascar. But they would have been incomplete without the help of our residents who had tropical expertise related to diseases with which I had no experience, and they had cared for such patients in their home countries. The result was I became editor in chief of *Tropical Pediatrics: A Public Health Concern of International Proportions* for three editions. That book was used as a text for medical students.

My internal medicine residents provoked me to publish medical research literature as well during my tenure at Western Michigan University (WMU). I am so thankful to them. I never would have published articles without them.

One of my residents kept pulling out a notebook and writing things down during bedside teaching. After several episodes, I snatched her notebook to see what was recorded. Anticipating medical pearls, I was dumbfounded to read what appeared to be nonsense. "What is this?" I asked her.

"Oh, just funny things you say" was the response.

Of my six novels, people ask, "When did you have time to write those?"

"Usually at five a.m.," I reply.

"What in your life caused you to write such stories?"

"How a canoe guide became a physician." That is what *Out with Joy* is all about.

I am so thankful to iUniverse for their willingness to publish my novels and now to assist me in publishing my memoirs.

Reading my memoirs, I hope you have a few laughs and maybe a tear or two. May this be, as they say in Africa, a small, small gift to those who have enriched my life.

—Richard R. Roach, MD, FACP

# 1

## Why Write Memoirs

On a sweet-smelling autumn day, my teenage daughter, Tirzah, and I were paddling a rented canoe down the Dowagiac Creek in Michigan, her in the bow and me in the stern. The riverbank was overgrown with trees. Summer storms had knocked some of them tilting over the river. Around a bend, one tree bent so far over that the channel was like a cave entrance. With a swift current forcing us underneath the bough, I yelled, "Bend down!"

She tried to push the branch out of the way, causing the canoe to rotate on its axis, spinning us into the river. The gunwale rammed my chest as it spun, cracking my rib cage. Gasping for painful breath, I surfaced, delighted that Tirzah suffered no injury. Working together, we stood in the shallows, righted the canoe, and finished our trip without further incident.

Years later, after a chest X-ray to prepare me for coronary artery bypass grafting, my surgeon looked at my film and commented, "When did you break your ribs?" He wanted to hear the whole story.

I'm writing this to let you read the whole story. I consider the leaves of my life by color and texture and, yes, even smell with wonder at their falling in pleasant places.

I've always had trouble remembering dates. A few I remember. My birthday, November 15, the Ides of November 1949, has an ominous ring to it. I was born in the Virginia, Minnesota, hospital, but my parents lived in a basement in Sand Lake, Minnesota. I don't believe there was a town there.

Priscilla, who became my wife, was born before me, August 19, 1948, several months before Israel became a nation. I always teased her that she was older than Israel. At our wedding, people teased her for marrying a baby.

Graduating from the University of Minnesota Medical School was important. At least I remember the month and year, June 1976. There were too many in our graduating class, since the Dakota medical students had come to Minnesota to complete the last two years of their education, so we all got a letter stating that if it wasn't that important to us, we should stay away from the ceremony. Priscilla, our two children, and I were in Madagascar, so it was no problem for us not to attend.

Priscilla and I were married the day after April Fool's Day, so that date is easy to remember. Whenever someone says, "April Fools," I know the next day is our anniversary. My son was born on Mother's Day, and my daughter was born on Valentine's Day, so I can remember those dates as well.

When I looked at my old passport the other day, I saw a myriad of dates that I traveled to various countries. I wouldn't confuse you with those dates, because what I did on each is such a muddle in my head that I am sure I would get incidents mixed up. Therefore, this writing is topical and not chronological. In fact, you could read the chapters in any order you wish, according to the index provided. You might even skip chapters that you don't want to know about.

Writing this at seventy-five-plus years old, I look back at such a colorful tapestry of beautiful events. Priscilla and I have fallen into pleasant places. Whoever reads this may rejoice with us.

# 2

## SPIRITUAL WALK

I'm ashamed to say that I got mixed up with a bad group in Virginia, Minnesota, as a young teen. We played a game on Saturdays where we went down the commercial street in town shoplifting from the stores. We then met at the end of the street and counted the price tags. Whoever's price tags added up to the highest dollar amount won.

One Saturday, as I was going from store to store, I kept hearing sirens. I waited at our usual place at the end of the street and added up my price tags. I was sure to win, but no one else showed up, so I ditched my stuff in a convenient garbage can and went home. I learned that all the others had got caught. Some went to reform school because they were multiple offenders; others, first offenders, were let off by returning their stolen merchandise. That was a wake-up call for me and the first step in my spiritual journey. I told God in my prayers that I wouldn't steal anymore. I read Ephesians 4:28 (NIV):

> *Anyone who has been stealing must steal no longer,*
> *but must work, doing something useful with their own*

*hands, that they may have something to share with*
*those in need.*

I asked God to give my hands something useful to do instead. It has taken a lifetime for that prayer to be answered.

The next step on my walk occurred during a time of severe depression. I was disappointed in myself. Mother added to it by her negative evaluations of my schoolwork: "You should do better." She made me give up my dog because the money I made from my paper route wasn't enough to feed him and she refused to buy him food. I felt worthless and suicidal. One night, I read Luke 19:30–31 (NIV):

> *"Go to the village ahead of you, and as you enter it,*
> *you will find a colt tied there, which no one has ever*
> *ridden. Untie it and bring it here. If anyone asks you,*
> *'Why are you untying it?' say, 'The Lord needs it.'"*

God spoke to me through that verse. "See, Richard? I used one untrained jackass. I can use another." My depression lifted. I belonged to God—not to my mother, not to my teachers—and God would take care of my dog.

The third step involved the church mentorship of some saints once my family moved to Duluth. Mrs. Bjorke, the youth pastor's secretary, had a problem with a Sunday school class. Some of the grade school boys were very disruptive, screaming and teasing the girls. The older woman who was their grade school Bible teacher was struggling with their constant irritating behavior. So Mrs. Bjorke decided to separate the boys and asked me to teach them in a separate room.

As we talked, I got the idea to teach the boys the book of Joshua. I brought my set of toy army men to class, setting them

5

up on the table as the boys worked out the battles in the book. I would read the scripture and have the boys set up the soldiers according to the description. This was the beginning of my interest in teaching the Old Testament. I decided that I would not teach the New Testament until I mastered the Old Testament. Since that time with the obstreperous boys, I've taught every book in the Old Testament, sometimes in churches, sometimes at home, and other times at friends' homes and now by Zoom.

Using my hands to share with those in need relates to my career as a physician. As you will read, the dream of becoming a physician was taken away several times, but God kept telling me, "I have it all under control." That attitude helped me to succeed during college, medical school, and residency, and more important, to see patients as people in need, not as diseases to be diagnosed.

A recent step on my spiritual walk relates to an understanding of a New Testament word. During my study of the Old Testament, I often used my concordance of Hebrew to better understand the text. For personal study, I read the Old Testament fall to spring and spent summer reading the New Testament. I was puzzled by the word *servant* (NIV) in the gospels and Paul's letters. My understanding of Roman society left me unsure of the word's meaning. I discovered that the Greek word means "slave." The word in English translations was changed to *servant* during the European slave trade to sugarcoat the connotation. If Jesus bought me, an untrained jackass, then I am His slave. All I have belongs to Jesus; nothing I merit is mine. My times are in His hands. This has been a source of great comfort and peace.

# 3

## SPORTS

I was never good at any sports that I tried. I always felt clumsy. Growing up in Northern Minnesota, I tried to learn how to ski. There was a small ski resort, Lookout Mountain, just north of Virginia, Minnesota, where my family lived while I was in fourth through sixth grade. It was a great place to learn, as the hills weren't that steep, but I received no lessons. We were basically poor, and lessons cost money. Mother told me to watch the other skiers and learn from them. I watched and tried to imitate them, which was fun, and I didn't mind falling since I was well bundled up for the cold. All my layers cushioned my falls.

After successfully observing, I decided to try my newfound skills on the bunny hill. There was a T-lift to the top of the hill. Being clumsy, I had trouble balancing. I fell off it three times. The person in charge said, "You're holding up other skiers. Just walk up the hill." At the top, I was breathless and collapsed in a soft snowbank. Once rested, I adjusted my skis as I had seen others do and went down the hill. It was great, exhilarating, with the wind whistling past my ears. What I was doing was freestyle schussing,

7

though I didn't discover that until later. Two things that I had not learned observing the other skiers at the lodge: turning, which can slow and control your speed, and stopping.

I was enjoying the acceleration all the way to the lodge, but then I thought, *How do I stop?* And I hit the lodge and flew upside down, up the picture window. I recall seeing a lady on the other side of the window spill hot chocolate down her blouse as my impact jolted her cup out of her hand. I slunk away before she could recognize me. I found my father and we went home.

It was years later that I discovered cross-country skiing. I was never that great at it but survived colliding with some trees without too much brain damage. My children, who were much more coordinated than I, enjoyed cross-country and we had fun as a family. I could teach them the rudimentary skills, but with a lesson or two, they were better than I was. I'm sure they got their coordination from their mother.

I did learn to ice skate, after many bumps and bruises. Never fast enough to play hockey, I still enjoyed the smooth gliding and turns. My friend Burton could skate circles around me backward while I skated as fast as I could forward. I asked him if he was on his high school hockey team. He said that he didn't qualify for the team because he couldn't skate backward as fast as the coach required.

Bicycling seemed easy to my friends, but I always felt wobbly. Dad got me a used bicycle with no gears to learn to ride. I had to use the steps to get onto it, but it was such a tank that smashing into things never hurt it, although I suffered scrapes and bruises. I suppose that I attained mediocrity at riding. While visiting some friends, I got excited when they offered me a bike to ride that was much nicer than mine. We sped down a dirt road together. I was enjoying speeding downhill when, abruptly, the front wheel fell off. The fork of the bike hit the ground, catapulting me into the road headfirst. I have no recollection of what happened next. I was enjoying sweet unconsciousness when I awoke on my friends' couch, propped up in a sitting position with pillows. Everyone was watching television. Maybe my cerebellum got jarred because I always felt out of balance riding a bicycle after that incident.

I love football. In junior high school, I had an opportunity to play. I was big, almost two hundred pounds, and thought I could play center. In my estimation, I was great at hiking the ball, and when the other team hit me, I was a brick wall. When the time came for the coach to choose the team, I was led to understand that there was more to a center's responsibilities than just being a brick wall and hiking the ball. He chose someone else for the center position on the team, so I applied for waterboy. That way, I could practice with the team and go to the games. But again, someone else was chosen.

I asked the coach, "Why wasn't I chosen?"

He said, pointing at a name on the roster, "That boy has more potential."

To this day, I still love watching football. I must have passed some of that enthusiasm to my son because he played in high school and did well for his team. My son said of his experience, "I sacked the quarterback every time the coach said that I could."

I enjoyed basketball. I even played in a church league. However, I could never understand the intricacies of the fouls. So, I usually fouled out early in the game. I practiced my shooting. I did an interesting experiment. I shot the ball ten times, and made two baskets; then I shot a hundred baskets, which took all afternoon because I missed the basket so often. The next day, I shot ten baskets to see if my practicing made any difference. I made two out of ten shots. No improvement. I concluded that practice did not make me perfect.

My son and daughter both played high school basketball. They were good at it and much more coordinated. At the banquet for Tirzah's team, it was said her shooting percentage was the same as that of the team's point star. But she was more hesitant and often fouled out in the middle of games. She practiced with my son and his friends. I understand now that fouls in men's basketball are not the same as fouls in women's basketball, but I don't think she realized that. She always seemed confused as to the referee's calls that she had fouled. She didn't think she had.

Temujin was good at basketball because he was tall and muscular. He played well. He stuck with recreational games throughout high school and college, but never was on a formal team. He played with a group of African American kids and loved it. It's interesting to me that he never knew any of their real names, only nicknames.

I love to swim. My mother wouldn't or couldn't pay for lessons. When she discovered that swimming lessons were offered at Silver Lake, she said, "Go to the lake and sit on the beach. Watch the instructor, and when the lessons are over for the other kids, go do what you saw them do."

With watchful attention, I sat in the sand in my swimming suit, shivering on the beach. That's how I learned to swim that summer. When formal lessons were over, I decided to test my skills and swim to the dock. I was in over my head in both depth and skill. I thought that I was drowning, but somehow, I made it. I sat for a long time on the dock, warming in the sun, before I decided to try to swim back to shore. I jumped as far off the dock as my scrawny legs allowed and somehow made it to the shallow water to walk the rest of the way. Despite that traumatic beginning, I enjoy swimming.

My father was a lifeguard when he was younger, so when he had the opportunity, he improved my rudimentary skills. I took a swimming class in college, but did not ace it because the instructor said, "You have a weak kick." The exam involved the instructor (a beautiful young woman) jumping into the pool and pretending to drown. We were instructed to jump in and rescue her. I think that I was focused on her physique during the rescue and didn't kick as hard as I should have. I completed the rescue, bringing her to safety at the end of the pool, but she still graded me down on my "weak kick." I didn't qualify for a lifeguard certificate.

Later, when I was a canoe guide, I rescued campers who tipped over their canoes in the Boundary Waters Canoe Area (BWCA). I would have liked to inform my college professor of this for an upgrade. I did learn required skills and my kick improved. I have gone swimming in the Atlantic, Pacific, and Indian Oceans as well as the Strait of Malacca, the Irish Straits, the Mozambique Channel, and the Onilahy River, not to mention the hundreds of lakes in the BWCA, Quetico Provincial Park, and the Teslin and Yukon Rivers. When I hurt my sacroiliac joints running, I switched to swimming thirty minutes three to five times a week, which saved my life.

My running career started in residency. A fellow resident asked me to play tennis with him. I was never good at tennis, but he claimed that he wasn't either (he lied), so we ran a couple of blocks to the tennis court. I was exhausted. I realized that I was totally out of shape, so I decided to start running on a regular basis. I was impressed with my improvement. Running was best in the morning because I'm a morning person, and it was quiet. I loved the solitude.

When I finished residency, Priscilla and I moved to Berrien Springs, Michigan. There, I found a nice five-mile route to run. I usually awakened at five o'clock, so I ran then. It was thrilling. The birds chirped, and the leaves on the trees tinkled in the wind. The smell of the earth and the fruit trees blooming and growing was delightful. In the fall, I ran through the neighbor's grape vineyard. The smell of the ripening grapes was intoxicating, like fine wine. I soon understood the so-called runner's high, which occurred for me after the first mile and continued through the completion of my five-mile run. I felt like I could run forever, but I had to get ready for work.

Running was relaxing and gave me time to think through problems. When I had difficult patients as a physician, it was often while running that I resolved the complexities of their diagnoses. And when troubled, I spent time praying through conflicts with my eyes open. But running was not without complications. On several occasions, deer jumped out in front of me, scaring me to death. One jumped out so close to me one morning that I felt its fur with my outstretched hand.

Dogs could be a problem, although not usually at 5:00 a.m. I did run in the afternoon on rare occasions if I had to attend a morning meeting. One afternoon, a dog came running out at me and bit me on the left calf. I have a nice oval-shaped scar to remember the incident. While I was recuperating, I found a copy of Runner Magazine at the library that dealt with dogs. The article suggested calling, "Come," to the dog. As soon as I was adequately healed, I ran that same route, and when I again faced the same dog, I yelled, "Come, boy, come!" It worked like a charm. The dog looked confused and stood still as I ran past him.

My daughter purchased a dog, a big white mixed breed, which she named Princess Ellonwye. She was very intelligent and easily trained. Tirzah suggested that I take her running. Princess heeled perfectly without any instruction, even without a leash. She was a perfect running partner. Her worth became impressive one morning when a pack of five wild dogs jumped out from the bushes, snarling at me. Princess seemed to know which dog was the leader. I certainly had no clue. She jumped at the dog and grabbed it by the throat, thrashing it. The leader gave a mournful yelp. Princess released it, at which all five promptly ran away. That was a wonderful experience. But after that, Princess hated other dogs, so Tirzah could never walk her in the neighborhood when other dogs were present.

My most amazing running experience occurred early one morning, before sunrise. I was running my usual route when alongside the road, in the other lane, some creature started running with me. I tried to analyze its gait. What was this creature? Was it a cat? A rabbit? No, wrong gait. Maybe a weasel? No, it was too big. In any case, the creature ran at my pace for at least a mile. I was still quizzing my brain when the moon came out from behind a cloud to shine on the white stripe down the creature's back. A skunk! I felt adrenaline surging through my muscles. I didn't want to be sprayed. I took off running like I had never done. I knocked five minutes off my five-mile time, a new personal record.

When we moved to Duluth, Minnesota, I continued running. There was a hill near our house that led to a road with a scenic overlook of Lake Superior. One morning, upon reaching the overlook, I was breathless from the climb up the hill. The fresh morning air was refreshing. As I paused to scan the lake, I noticed a brown bear searching for berries in the ditch beside the road. I stopped. The bear was more interested in breakfast than me. As I turned to head home, the experience gave me pause to reconsider my exercise program. I had been running five miles a day, five days a week, for sixteen years. I loved the experience, but my sacroiliac joints were bothering me. The pain was constant even when I wasn't running. It was time to switch to swimming.

The Duluth YMCA had a nice lap pool, which was available after work each day. There, I met some interesting characters and enjoyed their camaraderie. One was the psychologist for the local prison; he swam at the same time each day as I did. After our thirty-minute swim, we would head for the sauna, where we had great conversations. We discussed the inmates' problems in contrast to my patients' problems. He had done a study testing them for learning disabilities. He documented learning disabilities in 90 percent of them.

Another person I encountered at the YMCA was a German hospital radiologist. We spoke German together and became fast friends. He had a limp I noticed in the shower, and quite a scar on his right leg. After we got to know each other over several months, I asked him about how he had got his wound. He said he had been in the Nazi infantry during World War II and got shot in the leg. He laughed and added, "Running away." He received the German equivalent of a purple heart and a military pension.

After the war, he found that all his relatives had been killed, so he qualified as a displaced person and moved to the United States. He received his bachelor's degree from a U.S. university and went on to medical school, where he completed a radiology fellowship, and then joined the U.S. military as a radiologist. On retiring from the military, he received another nice pension. It was then that he began working in radiology at St. Mary's Hospital in Duluth. He never married, so he had plenty of money from his salary and his two pensions. He was quite generous with local charities.

One summer, as a U.S. citizen, he returned to his small town in Germany, where he was overwhelmed with the changes in his community. He found only a couple of old men who still spoke his German dialect, so he had to switch to Hanover German to be understood. He told me wonderful stories of his experiences and became a delightful friend.

My sports career was never impressive until I discovered canoeing. But that is a new chapter.

# 4

## FATHER'S INFLUENCE

My family had huge influences on my decision to be a physician. Some were positive, such as my father's example of caring for people. Other influences were negative, such as when my mother said I would never qualify for medical school. My brother Bob became a minister, my brother Bill became a financial advisor, and my sister loved physics and became a computer nerd. Our family had no other physicians.

Father was a conscientious objector during World War II, but he still felt that he should serve. He always enjoyed cooking, and the recruiter promised him that he could go to cooking school, so he signed up.

After basic training, during which time he earned a marksmanship medal, he was sent to Fort Bragg for training. He went to his first training camp class expecting it to be about cooking. Instead, the instructor discussed how to blow up bridges. Father went to the commanding officer and claimed that there must be some mistake. As a conscientious objector, he had agreed to be a cook. As Father tells it, "The commander tossed his hands in the air and said, 'Demolition, cooking, there isn't much difference.' So, he refused to change my training." However, he was not sent overseas because when he was interviewed, and the interviewer asked, "What would you do if a Nazi came at you with a rifle?" Father responded, "I'd ask him not to shoot me."

"Would you shoot him if a weapon was available?" the interviewer questioned.

Father answered, "No. I'd let him shoot me."

With that answer, they had him defusing bombs, which he did for aircrafts that flew over the Gulf of Mexico looking for Nazi submarines. Very few submarines were discovered. So, every day, he deactivated the bombs that weren't dropped when the planes returned. After the war, he went to Moody Bible Institute, so if he were to be drafted again, he would go as a chaplain instead of a demolition expert.

After his training at Moody Bible Institute, Father became an ordained minister. He met my mother at the Union Gospel Mission, where he preached and she played the piano. They were both interested in mission work, so after they married in Chicago, they moved to Northern Minnesota, where Father chose to minister at logging camps for the American Sunday School Union.

He achieved the rank of master sergeant by the end of World War II. I recently discovered a letter sent to him after the war asking him to apply for officer school. He declined. It might have been better for him if he had gone, since he got drafted again during the Korean War. But who would have guessed that. Besides, he loved ministering at the logging camps.

One time, he showed up at a logging camp chapel and only one logger was in attendance. The camp had closed, and everyone else had packed and left. He preached his planned sermon anyway. Father said that the lone logger was so impressed that the sermon changed his life. When he told me that story, he always added, "So always pay attention to your audience, no matter how few." It was an important lesson for interacting with patients.

At one point, Father was responsible for thirty different chapels. He preached the same sermon four times a Sunday, twice in the morning and twice in the evening. Mother played the foot organ at the chapels, which required vigorous pumping of the foot pedal. She claimed that after the singing, she listened to Father's first sermon but daydreamed during the next three.

When I was born, my parents were living in a basement in Sand Lake, Minnesota. There was no house. There was no town. It was an unincorporated place, named after the lake. My parents expected that someday, they would build a house over the basement. There was running water but no bathroom, only an outhouse.

One evening, when Mother was headed toward the outhouse, Father heard her scream and ran out to see what the problem was. He found she was faced with a skunk in the path. Her screaming scared away the skunk without spray, but after that, Mother refused to go to the outhouse without Father accompanying her.

I do not remember that basement. Father drove by the basement years later to show me where we lived when I was born. It still didn't have a house over it. My poor mother cared for me without bathroom facilities. I recall from her stories that she tried to stay in the Virginia hospital for as long as the physician allowed.

When the Korean War intervened, Father was drafted into the Air Force. I'm sure Mother was pleased to leave the basement. They moved to Air Force base housing, which was a trailer at the end of the runway in Rapid City, South Dakota. The bombers would fly right over our trailer and make it shake like an earthquake. My first childhood memory is running out of the trailer, screaming every time a plane flew over.

During the war, Father was transferred to Las Vegas as a chaplain's assistant. As an ordained minister, he could be a chaplain's assistant, but since he graduated from Moody Bible Institute, not a seminary, the military refused to rank him as a chaplain. I think they gave him the lowest officer rank.

The Air Force developed jet aircrafts during the Korean War. These jets were unwieldy until computers were invented to control them. Even trained pilots from World War II had trouble maintaining stability. The sad result was that many of the experimental jets crashed, which is why the training base was in the desert outside Las Vegas. Father's job as chaplain's assistant involved going to the crash sites, picking up whatever remained of the pilots' bodies, and then going to tell the wives that their husbands had died. I don't think he ever got to preach a sermon, as that was the chaplain's duty.

My only memory of that time is standing on the porch of our house and looking out over the desert, seeing nothing but sand. We must have lived on the outskirts of Las Vegas. Father was disgusted with gambling, so he found the city "boring." He always said, "Las Vegas is the only city in the United States that has no reason to exist."

We moved to the Chicago area, specifically Elmhurst, Illinois, after the war. My parents attended Elmhurst College, where Father received a degree in biology and Mother graduated with a degree in English and a minor in Greek. She was so proficient that she could read the whole book of James in Greek. She was offered a position as a teacher's assistant to the Greek professor while she worked on a master's degree. But she turned down the offer, as my father wished to return to Northern Minnesota to work on his master's degree in botany.

We lived somewhere in Duluth; I am not sure where. Father was fascinated with plants. His master's thesis was on the taxonomy of fungi. His love was shelf fungi, not mushrooms. I still have some of his botany books. The difficulty was that he was selling shoes at Montgomery Ward to make ends meet, as well as preaching at a few churches in St. Louis County.

Unfortunately, working a couple of jobs and going to the University of Minnesota Duluth took its toll on him. He got a C in one of his classes. In those days, you were required to have an A or a B in all graduate classes, or else you lost your master's stipend. Father was offered the opportunity to take the class over, but he would have to get an A to average out to a B in order to continue. Then he lost his shoe salesman job as Montgomery Ward downsized. My parents couldn't pay the rent, so our family became jobless and homeless.

A family in Cotton, Minnesota, heard of our plight. They offered to let us live with them on their two-hundred-acre farm. So the Lorentzens became part of our family. Ellen—I always called her Auntie—was widowed with two teenage children, Rodney and Marcella. I was five years old and didn't understand much, so I considered them my siblings.

Auntie Ellen worked as a nurse, which provided the family income. My father made some money preaching at some of the churches that remained from the logging camp days, prior to the Korean War. Some of those small churches still needed ministers. He provided much-needed help to the congregations.

One of the congregations was on the Nett Lake Indian reservation. I developed friendships with the children who came to the church services. They taught me to eat fishflies (mayflies to anyone else) off the screen door. They did taste like fish. It was a nice snack after the service.

Wahlberg Johnson was the minister, who sometimes invited

Father to come as the guest speaker. She was the only woman I ever met named Wahlberg. She was an amazing woman, an ordained minister, which was unusual in the '50s. And she was not a First Nation person, so she could only live on the reservation if she was sponsored as the pastor to the First Nation church. She was dearly loved because she was so committed to the people at Nett Lake.[1] She served out of her love for the Anishinabek people.

Wahlberg was responsible for building the first church on the reservation. Quite innovative, she put a big potbelly stove right in front of the pulpit. I asked her why, since many other Minnesota churches had a stove in the back so the pulpit view was unobstructed. She told me, "On cold winter Sundays, I stoke up that stove, and everyone wants to sit in the front to stay warm. They listen better to my sermons that way."

She lived in a narrow storage room at the back of the church building until, after years of service, her sponsoring organization decided that a man should be the chapel's pastor instead of a woman. Father was furious at the male chauvinism but took me to Nett Lake to help her pack. With tears in his eyes, Father packed her few possessions from her one room, which was no more than a closet. That night, the tribe met and made Wahlberg a tribe member. Not only was she allowed to stay, but the tribal council moved her to a small home, which they built for her. The man who replaced her lasted three months. She took over the ministry after he left.

Wahlberg subsequently adopted two abandoned girls and raised them to adulthood. When she became disabled, those two girls cared for her. She eventually moved to the Cook Nursing

[1] As a canoe guide, when I met an Anishinabek guide on a portage, I would ask them if they knew Wahlberg. They all did. She was well known not only in Nett Lake but throughout the Anishinabek community, including in Canada.

Home. I received a Christmas card from her every year until one year, the card, sent by one of her adopted daughters, said she had peacefully died at the nursing home. She was a saint in my understanding of the term.

As we were riding home from a fourth sermon one Sunday, I asked my father what denomination we belonged to. He answered, "Whichever denomination will pay for the songbooks." He always mentioned that whoever believed Jesus died for their sins was his Christian brother or sister, no matter their denomination. I never forgot that focus. It allowed me to consider myself nondenominational, which provided important opportunities to speak in Baptist, Pentecostal, Christian Brethren, and Independent Bible churches, and even a Maasai church. I have been the special guest of the cardinal of Madagascar and led a Bible study for Adventist seminarians. And I have been allowed to work at various denominational mission organization hospitals.

During those years living with the Lorentzens, Father made a little money cutting pulpwood. I accompanied him and Rodney into the woods to cut down poplar trees, which were used by paper plants in Cloquet and Duluth. Father and Rodney commanded the chainsaw. My job was to strip off the bark. I would grab one end of the tree and run the length through the forest, stripping off the bark and exposing the slimy xylem. In the winter, we piled the logs onto a sled and pulled it along an iced trail with the tractor. In the summer, we used a wagon.

Mother went to work as a fry cook at the Wilbert, the truck stop restaurant on Highway 53 in Cotton, Minnesota. Rodney told me that she waitressed and cooked. That provided additional income for our mixed family. Rodney loved the brownies my mother would bake for him. But she always hid them somewhere to see if he could find them. He would come home from high school and smell the brownies, and then the search would commence. We got a good laugh from this game. He always found them by smell.

Mother and Auntie Ellen were always best friends. I never heard them argue, and they always appreciated each other's labor to maintain the cash flow. Even when we moved to Virginia, Minnesota, Ellen would stop by for "coffee." She was a very gracious woman to take us into her household.

Ellen's mother, "Grandma Laakso," lived in a small two-room house Ellen's husband built for her before he died. It was just a few feet across the yard from our back door. She called it her coop. She spoke some English but mostly Finnish. She made the best cardamom rolls that I have ever tasted. For years, I have tried to duplicate her recipe, but my attempts do not taste like Grandma's. I think part of her secret was that she was always cold and she heated her house to 80 degrees. I think the yeast in her breads loved that temperature. I always broke into a sweat whenever I visited her to taste the rolls fresh out of the oven.

The chicken coop was three times the size of the coop she lived in. It was large enough that she talked Rodney into walling off a portion of the chicken coop to set up her loom. I still have a rug that she made from my mother's discarded dresses.

We had a bathroom with a toilet, but it was only for adults. Children were required to use the outhouse. Maybe Marcella got to use the bathroom because she was a girl. My sister, Margaret, was born later when we moved to Virginia, Minnesota. Anyway, using the outhouse wasn't too much of a hardship in the summer. But in the winter, it was more challenging. It is not uncommon in Cotton for temperatures to drop to −40 degrees, the temperature where Fahrenheit equals Centigrade. We learned very early, "Palms up, thumbs out," when using the outhouse. That meant sitting on the palms of our mittens with the thumbs facing out so we didn't have to sit on frozen wood. When we were done with our business, we grabbed the thumbs of our mittens as we got up so that they didn't drop in the hole.

Baths were Saturday night. Adults used the tub in the bathroom. We only had cold water, so it was necessary to heat the water on the stove and carry it upstairs to the tub for the adults. For the children, Rodney hauled a feeding trough into the center of the kitchen and half filled it with cold water, adding boiling water off the kitchen stove to the desired temperature.

As a combined family of eight—my two brothers and I, two teenagers, and the three adults—we ate well on the farm. Every year, we had a pig, a beef cow, and thirty to fifty chickens for meat. Several milk cows provided milk and cream. We canned meat as well as froze it. We canned plums off our tree that grew just outside the back door. We had a potato garden and we traded for other vegetables. So, we ate very well.

Every spring, we plowed the potato field, as somehow, it always was full of rocks. Rodney ran the tractor, hauling a flat board behind. I would sit on the board, pick up the rocks the plow unearthed, and put them on the board beside me. When the board was full, we would pile the rocks at the end of the field. I returned to the Cotton farm several years ago at its centennial. The rock pile forming a barrier around the garden is still there and still impressive. Since every year there were more rocks to gather, my childhood imagination believed that the garden grew rocks during the winter and potatoes in the summer.

As an addition to our farm meat supply, Rodney and Father hunted deer. For eleven straight years, they got their limit. Father's marksmanship in the army during World War II served us well, and Rodney was just as good a marksman. Father never bought more than six bullets. Two were for sighting in his rifle, and he saved two for deer hunting and two in case he missed. He never missed in eleven years.

One time, Rodney thought Father missed. He loves to tell this story. Father had been sitting by the Whiteface River, which ran through the property, while Rodney was driving the deer toward him. Rodney is the only person I know who has the skills to stalk deer, which he did on occasions when Father was busy, but it was easier to drive them. When Rodney heard two shots fired, he ran through the woods to where he knew Father was hiding. He found a doe lying on the riverbank and said, "So you missed the first shot?"

Father grinned and replied, "The other deer is floating down the river. The buck always sends the doe over the river first, you know." If Father ever missed a shot, no one ever mentioned it.

We depended on two deer each year to supplement our meat supply. One year, Father and Rodney hunted the whole two-week deer season and never even saw a deer. They were discouraged. On the last day of the hunting season, they had been out all morning without even a sign of a deer before they came back to the house around noon and sat outside on the front porch. Mother had made chocolate chip cookies and brewed a hot pot of coffee, so I brought the coffee and cookies out to them, and we all plunked down in despair. No one said a thing. We were comforted by the smell of coffee and cookies, not to mention the smell of fall air.

Rodney has exceptional hearing, so when a sound came from the woods, just down the road from the house, he alerted Father. They got up off the porch with their rifles raised but saw nothing. Then in a burst of commotion, a doe ran across the driveway, and then a buck ran out of the woods. Father and Rodney both shot. While their rifles were still raised, two wolves came running after the fallen deer. Father and Rodney both shot a wolf. That year, there was a bounty on wolves, and Rodney's and Father's paid for their hunting licenses and for the bullets. We ate well that year, and Rodney made some spending money selling the deer and wolf hides. There was no waste. Rodney always hauled the guts out into the woods to feed the rest of the wolf family.

Over the course of thirty years, Rodney has counted deer every fall. The number of deer that feed in his field have remained constant the entire time. Since the game warden lives down the road from the farm, no one else has ever hunted on Rodney's property.

For three years, we lived with the Lorentzens. I spent first to third grade at Cotton School 100. I don't remember any of the teachers, but I have a pleasant impression of my time there. I do remember the basketball and football games, cheering on our Cotton Cardinals.

I also remember the pine hedgerow that separated the school property from Cotton Covenant Church, where my father sometimes preached. There was no playground, so at recess, we were allowed to wander the school property. We played marbles in the dirt in the fall and spring, and in the winter played king on the mountain on the snowbank the plow left at the end of the parking lot. In the spring, we would also play among the pine trees. Wood ticks drop from pine trees to find creatures to attach to, so we find ourselves covered with wood ticks on us upon our return from recess. Our favorite game was to place the ticks on the teacher when she passed by our desks. I'm sure she always wondered how she got so many wood ticks on her when she didn't even go outside during recess.

Before I started fourth grade, my father was hired by St. Louis County Welfare Department as a social worker. Today, one must have a master's in social work to be hired, but in those days, I guess a degree in biology with a focus on taxonomy of fungi was sufficient. He was assigned the task of liaison between St. Louis County and the First Nation tribes in the county. He was perfect for that position because of his ministry at Nett Lake. Many of the county tribal leaders already knew him.

We moved to Silver Lake Homes in Virginia, Minnesota, which was government-subsidized housing. Despite his work for the county, Father's salary qualified us for government housing and food supplements. On Friday after work, he would leave his office and go downstairs to the distribution outlet to receive our allotment of powdered eggs, cheese, flour, and macaroni. It was all marked "not to be sold." Mother baked cakes with the powdered eggs, and they turned out all right, but never great. She made macaroni and cheese so often that as an adult, I can't tolerate it. It tasted like the box it came in. Even with Kraft macaroni and cheese, I still taste the box, although Kraft is much better than government surplus macaroni and cheese. One time, Mother tried to make scrambled eggs with egg powder. She added the right amount of water and beat the slough with the electric mixer. When she put it in the frying pan, the water evaporated, leaving powder on the bottom of the pan. After that, she only used the egg powder for baking.

When we moved to Virginia, Minnesota, I accompanied Father to the grocery store for the first time. The experience shocked me. The grocer sold meat. I didn't know people could buy meat at a store. I assumed everyone raised their own or bought meat from local farmers. I stood at the counter breathless, my eyes dilated at the piles of meat behind the counter. Here was the smell I recalled from butchering our cow in the shed, but this was in a store.

I attended fourth grade at James Madison Grade School. All I remember about that year is the teacher yelled a lot. I would cover my ears while she yelled at the other students, but never at me. I don't think she taught us anything, but I suppose she did.

My fifth-grade teacher was so nice, and she never raised her voice. Her room was across the hall from the yelling teacher's. When the fourth-grade teacher started her harangue, our fifth-grade teacher would close the classroom door and smile at us, but never said a word. I think I learned a lot that year.

I loved Miss Simmons, the sixth-grade teacher. She was patient and interested in every pupil, the best grade school teacher I ever had. Unfortunately, her career was cut short because she married. In those days, a female schoolteacher was not allowed to teach if she was married. That was an idiotic rule.

One Sunday, either my parents or my brothers and sister were ill, so my parents didn't go to church. I was sent off to the church on my own. It was just a couple of blocks from our house. So I circled back home and got my fishing rod and went to Silver Lake instead. Silver Lake Homes was named after Silver Lake, where I stood shivering on the beach as I learned to swim.

That morning was exceptional for fishing. I caught a dozen bullheads. There was no limit on bullheads, and children under twelve years old did not need a license. In my excitement, I paraded my catch home, admitting that I had skipped church. As a punishment, over the next week, I was required to clean and eat all those bullheads. They weren't that good, sort of muddy tasting, and the stench of fish guts permeated the flesh even after they were cooked. While the family enjoyed macaroni and cheese, I ate bullheads. Out of compassion, when the rest of the family had spaghetti one night, Mother put fried bullheads into tomato sauce and served that as my spaghetti. I think it took a week to eat all my bullheads, so the next Sunday, I was in church.

Because of Father's work with First Nation tribal leaders, whom he loved and admired, we were shunned in Silver Lake Homes. Some days, large Cadillacs would park in front of our house and troops of Anishinabek would come to thank Father for his work. The result was that many of our neighbors, who were prejudiced against Indians (First Nation people), considered us trash. Even some of the children in the neighborhood would yell, "Indian lover!" at me. That made it difficult for my family to make friends in the neighborhood.

But we did have some good neighbors. Mother developed a friendship with the Fleetwood family. Their daughter Doreen was just a bit older than I was, so we became playmates. Mr. Fleetwood worked in the iron mines but was also a good fisherman. That was his connection with my father, who loved fishing.

The Altobellis lived in the next building over, as I recall. Mrs. Altobelli was a fantastic baker and made the best potica I have ever eaten. Years later, she made and donated potica for my and Priscilla's wedding reception. She became one of Mother's best friends in a difficult neighborhood.

The Barto family became our friends because they knew of my father's work and knew Wahlberg Johnson. They were Anishinabek. Ms. Barto once gave me a recipe for wild rice candy. She taught me how to pop wild rice and to caramelize maple syrup, to which the popped rice is added. She laughed as she told me the recipe, which she claimed was nine hundred years old. The Anishinabek used rendered bear grease in the recipe, but butter worked well. She taught me about how wild rice was harvested and parched. To this day, I will only eat wild rice that has been hand parched. I am unwilling to eat the black needles offered as wild rice in the grocery store. That rice is not grown wild and is machine processed.

I've researched the Barto recipe in historical archives and

found that it predates European contact. Ms. Barto also made other Anishinabek specialties that she shared with our family. I do remember that she wrapped moose meat in bear meat "because moose meat can be dry if cooked alone." I don't recall the other recipes. A twelve-year-old remembers candy recipes.

My best friend was Calvin Wong. His family owned the Chinese restaurant in town, where his father was the main chef. After we became good friends at school, he invited me to his house for dinner. Stepping through the door was an interesting experience, as the smell of incense caught my attention.

Calvin lived in an unusual culture. His mother was Catholic, and his father was Buddhist, so there was a Virgin Mary shrine on one side of the living room and a Buddhist shrine on the other side. Incense was often burning at both ends. Calvin and I played together outside until his father came home from the restaurant. That night, the table was loaded with all sorts of Cantonese specialties. When his mother informed his father that I was joining them for dinner, he said he would go get a cheeseburger for me. But when we sat down at the table, Calvin whispered in my ear, "Do you like Chinese food?"

"Yes," I replied.

"Can I have your cheeseburger, then?" he asked me.

I laughed and gave him the cheeseburger, as I enjoyed the glorious Chinese food. I was introduced to chopsticks and developed adequate skills so that later, his parents gifted me with engraved ivory chopsticks, which I still have hidden in my treasures. This was the beginning of a long friendship, as I was frequently invited for dinner after that. I always wondered if Calvin made sure that I was invited so that he could have a cheeseburger.

When Calvin was in college, he visited me in Duluth. I learned then that he had decided to be Buddhist, not Catholic.

Virginia, Minnesota, has lots of other memories for me. Father was a leader in the Boy Scout troop, where I advanced to star ranking before we moved. I even marched in the Memorial Day parade with my troop. I also learned to shoot a rifle. Father required that I take a firearms safety course. I was all right, but not a marksman like my father. My brother Robert developed that skill. He shot a porcupine out of a tree through the eye one time.

I went trout fishing with one of Father's coworkers. Father was a walleye fisherman but thought that I should learn about trout fishing. I was sworn to secrecy as we trampled through the underbrush north of town. There was no trail. My guide told me to keep silent. We crept up on the stream, and he showed me how to cast into the flowing water. We caught several trout that day and fried them up on a small fire among the rocks on the shore of the stream before returning home. To this day, I have no idea where that creek is.

Father maintained his relationship with the Nett Lake Indian reservation; sometimes, he just visited, and sometimes, he preached for Wahlberg Johnson. Later, I learned that when the state widened Highway 53, they discovered an Indian graveyard. Father negotiated an acceptable reburial of the bodies. When they excavated deeper in that area to widen the highway, they ran into an artesian spring, and the whole area flooded overnight. Some of the heavy equipment had to be pulled out of the water and reconditioned. Father thought it was only fitting.

Father did an interesting experiment. He knew of some children raised on the reservation who were going to live with relatives in town to attend public school. He performed IQ tests on the children and then repeated the testing one year later. The tests suggested all the children had increased their IQ by twenty points or more. He concluded, in the early 1960s, that the problem was the test, not the children. There is nothing one can do to increase one's IQ by twenty points in one year. The children had been exposed to a different culture; that was all. He vehemently attacked people who said that Indians were dumb or inferior to whites.

Father did his job so well that he was offered advancement in Duluth, Minnesota, which is still part of St. Louis County. He was asked to start a program for senior adult services. That advancement came with a significant raise, but we had to move to Duluth. Despite his new position and our move, he kept in contact with tribal leaders and Wahlberg Johnson.

# 5

## MOVING TO DULUTH

We moved to a small, smelly apartment on First Street. I never figured out why it smelled like spoiled fruit, but that is my memory of the back steps. My parents were saving money to buy a house, but it took a year.

I attended Washington Junior High School for seventh grade. That was good and bad. The good part was I got As in all my classes except shop, but the bad part was I had trouble making friends. The other boys in my classes resented my grades, and besides, they all knew each other from grade school.

The climax came when we were to write an essay for English class. Our assignment subject was "what I want to do when I grow up." I remembered seeing a horrendous car accident in Chicago when I was preschool age, four or five years old. I saw the bodies and blood spread out on the street and the ambulance personnel trying to resuscitate the victims. Right then, I had decided that I wanted to be a physician. That incident was part of my essay, as was my resolve to be a physician. The teacher was so impressed that she read the essay out loud to the class. That was a mistake.

I heard some of the boys muttering in the back rows. It sounded ominous.

After school, I packed up my stuff to walk home. Just outside the school, I was waylaid by the back-row boys. "You think you're such hot stuff, better than us. You will never be a doctor." They said this and punched and kicked me until I collapsed. They knocked my books into the mud. When they left, I picked up my muddy books, collected what was left of my papers, and walked home. Mother was alarmed at my appearance, but nothing was ever done. I kept my aspirations to myself after that. Anyway, we were never asked to write another essay.

At the end of that first year in Duluth, my parents had saved enough money to buy a house. We moved to Forty-Third Avenue on London Road. Our house was on the poor side of the street. Houses on the rich side faced Lake Superior. Father paid $25,000 for our house, while the house across from ours, owned by the Riches (yes, that was their last name), was worth close to $1 million. Their son was a good-enough friend from school, so I was invited over after school several times. The house seemed like a palace to me, with a fountain in the atrium. They had a cook who made wonderful treats for the family, so the house always smelled sweet and delicious.

Ordean Junior High School was good and bad. The good part was there were so many smart students that I could blend in with the nerds. The bad part was there were so many smart students that I had trouble getting an A in any class. Our Latin teacher was very strict, but I learned to study. I still remember the Gallic Wars, the *Odyssey*, the *Iliad*, and Jason and the Golden Fleece because we had to translate them from the Latin. I learned that English words have roots. My spelling has always been atrocious, but once I discovered that the weird spellings of some English words relate to Latin root words, I could spell English words with Latin roots, as well as medical terms with a Latin base.

The day President Kennedy was assassinated, I was home sick. In Latin, we were allowed to do a special project to improve our grade, so I spent my sick day making a model of the Parthenon. My teacher was very impressed and boosted my grade. I will never forget the day Kennedy was shot, nor will I ever forget the best six-week grade I received in Latin class.

The English teacher was odd. She used so much makeup that we called her Crater-face. When she called on a student, she would say, "Pop right up," at which point we were required to stand at our desk to answer. She had a bad habit of sitting on top of the front-middle desk as she taught, which meant she sat on my desk to teach. No one teased me in that class because they felt sorry for me. She wore the most nauseating perfume. I think it is outdated now, but whenever I met a woman with that same perfume, such as a patient years later, I always instantly developed nausea.

This teacher thought I was a creative writer, so she recommended that I write feature articles for the school newspaper. It was fun to interview teachers, football players, and interesting students to write their stories. I think the paper was published every grading period.

At the same time, I think my parents were struggling financially, maybe because of the house payments. As a result, Mother arranged for me to wash dishes in the school cafeteria so that I got free lunch. In addition, she went to work for St. Louis County as a social worker. Most of her career was spent in Child Protective Services. I think it was very stressful and emotionally exhausting work. She claimed that she knew all the county judges on a first-name basis. She always seemed depressed and grouchy when she came home from work, too tired to fix meals. So, I was commissioned to have supper ready, and on the table, when she arrived home.

That Christmas, I received a cookbook as a present. I still have it and still use the recipes. That is how I quickly learned to cook. I must have been thirteen years old.

My contribution to the family income was to have a paper route. My route was from one block north of Superior Street all the way to London Road and two blocks wide, Forty-Third to Forty-Fifth Avenues. I recall having about seventy-five customers. It gave me spending money, which was mostly spent on dog food for my German shepherd–Husky mix, Smokey.

I enjoyed most of my customers. During winter blizzards, which were common in Duluth, customers would invite me into their atriums to warm up, with an occasional cup of hot chocolate. One customer, Mr. McPherson, was a rascal who never wanted to pay me. He would make me come back several times before he would pay. His house was richly decorated, so I don't think he was short of income; I think he enjoyed being obstreperous. He eventually paid but never on time.

Another customer, Mr. Walston, was always reading the *Wall Street Journal* whenever I came to collect. He would inform me about the latest articles. I asked him one time why he read the *Wall Street Journal*. He said that he read the journal because it had his name on it: *WALl ST jOurNal*. He was comical and always invited me to sit and talk. We had interesting conversations about news and economics.

The rich people on the lakeside of London Road were always kind to me and generous with tips when I collected. I took off my shoes whenever I was invited to tour their homes. They gave me permission to hike down to Lake Superior on their property whenever I wanted. It was a rare privilege because they did not allow other people lake access. Those houses were the last on my route. I loved taking the extra time to go to the shore because of their gracious permission. The lake was calming, and with my paper route completed, I could sit and watch the waves. I was never expected home at a certain time because my parents knew that I had to finish my route.

One cold winter day, −20°F, I went down to the shore and walked out on the ice. I fell through. The first thing I noticed was that the water was warmer than the air, about 38°F. I stayed in the water a few minutes to contemplate what I should do next. I thought out my route home, and when I had it firmly in mind, I climbed out of the water and ran home. By the time I got to my door, my pants were frozen solid like stovepipes. At my knees, the cloth had cracked apart. I put them in the dryer while I took a hot bath to warm up. When Mother came home, she asked what caused the tears on the back of my jeans. I claimed ignorance. "I don't know. It just happened."

One day, I slipped and fell on the sidewalk. I have always been clumsy, but this time, I split my knee open. I could see my kneecap through the wound. Fortunately, I was almost done delivering papers, so despite the blood gushing out of my knee, I finished my route.

When Mother saw the gash in my knee, she took me to the emergency department to get my knee sewn back together. The physician didn't want me to bend my knee until the stitches were out, so I had to walk stiff legged. I would remember this restriction when I gave the same advice to a patient, wondering how it would affect their life. My brother William (Bill) offered to help me deliver papers, so I gave him 10 percent of my daily income for his help. I have forever been thankful for his volunteering. It bonded us together.

At the time, Father enjoyed his job immensely and loved his boss, who said, "You do great work, Richard, but I don't know how to supervise you, because no one has ever done senior adult services before you invented it." Father always had comical stories about his clients' antics. They would, for example, argue with the grocer over the price of eggs and then buy an expensive Cadillac.

Father was invited to help design the senior living center. Meeting with the architect, he insisted that a workshop be added to the design. He described several clients who made birdhouses and sold them to help pay their rent. This was the impetus to encourage the seniors to make crafts. He decided that if they would donate some of the things they made, he would advertise an annual sale. He spoke about this to the editor of the newspaper, who agreed to advertise the sale as a public announcement at no cost to the county. The sale was well attended each year. Father gave a portion of the profits to each of the seniors who donated their crafts, and also used the profits to buy supplies for the next year.

Father negotiated with the Duluth Transit Authority to allow seniors to ride downtown for free. His point was that once they came to town, they would spend money at the local stores, and they would pay to ride the bus home. The local merchants supported his idea. It was effective, but he was chagrined that the sly seniors would go to town for free, and then negotiate with a friend or relative to bring them back.

His job was not all fun, however. When a client died, he was responsible for contacting their relatives. If there were no living relatives, and that was often the case for clients who lived on county subsidies, the county confiscated their possessions to pay back any expenses incurred. It was Father's job to sell what he could to help the county coffers. One old man, a client whom Father enjoyed many long conversations with, died in his ramshackle apartment. Father went to his apartment expecting to put all his possessions in a dumpster, until he found more than $10,000 under his mattress. The county was delighted with the reimbursement.

Father also loved to play Santa Claus. He was hired by JCPenney, who bought him a rather extravagant costume and a throne for one end of the store. But if there were no children in the store, he got bored and would fall asleep. A snoring Santa Claus was not the image the store wanted, so they were going to fire him. But he asked if, rather than sit on the throne, he could walk around the store. Management agreed, and that solved the problem. Many children were scared to go to the throne, but found his manner of walking through the store, greeting them, to be quite charming. JCPenney developed a reputation for having the best Santa in town. They let Father take his costume home at night. He knew many of the children in our neighborhood, and he would ask the parents what their children wanted and then arrange a time to visit. The neighborhood children were in awe of Santa coming to their homes, knowing their names and what they wanted for Christmas without even asking.

My father was the grace of God to me, encouraging me and teaching me to honor people who were different.

## Duluth East High School

I went from Ordean Junior High School to East High School. There were so many smart students among our four hundred classmates that I ranked seventy-fifth at graduation; at least I was in the top 25 percent for college application.

A few teachers made a huge impact on my life and encouraged me to achieve my goals.

## *Herr Gerlach*

I took German for all three years. I don't think Latin was offered, and besides, I'd had enough of Latin. French was offered, but there were mostly haughty girls, cheerleaders, in the class. German was a great choice.

Our teacher was Herr Gerlach. He was from North Dakota, specifically a German community where everyone spoke German. He learned English as a second language in the first grade. During World War II, he was assigned to listen to the radio and transcribe what was aired. He would laugh when asked about his military experience, describing his sedentary duties.

I suppose by today's standards, he was an unconventional teacher. He would probably have had trouble following a legislated curriculum. After he taught the basics, my classmates and I had a delightful time. We spent the first month mastering pronunciation. We were required to read texts out loud that we had no clue what they meant. We were not required to translate. This was an interesting exercise because by the end of the month, we could pronounce any German word correctly. As an adult, I have visited Germany several times, and have no problem being understood there. Native German speakers say that my pronunciation is pretty good. Herr Gerlach's family moved from Hanover, Germany, to North Dakota to avoid the wars, so I suppose he taught us a Hanover dialect, which the Grimm brothers made into standard German.

Next, we learned basic vocabulary, which is an infinite task, but he made it fun. We translated comic strips and children's stories. One day in second year, we found our desks pushed to the wall and chairs set up next to round tables. He brought German treats for us, but we had to order them in German. If we spoke English, he pretended not to understand us.

Another time, we arrived to find German newspapers on our desks. Where he got them, I have no idea. We were given half the hour to read any article, and then in the second half of our class period, we described the events from our chosen articles. It provided new vocabulary and required each of us to explain something in German.

My favorite was reading *Max und Moritz*, a cartoon from the nineteenth century. It is a saucy story in which the two boys cause lots of trouble. Herr Gerlach had to explain to us the German hang-up with noses, as many of the stories involved noses getting pinched or punched or caught in door hinges. As we advanced, we read *Grimms' Fairy Tales* in the original language. We were surprised at how gruesome the tales were compared to the Disney versions. The class agreed that the original versions were much more exciting.

I enjoyed my classmates in German class as we developed a camaraderie. Since no one dropped out, it was the same group for three full years. I think this was because Herr Gerlach was such an amazing teacher. Our respect for him was reflected in our study habits, which resulted in everyone in the class receiving As or Bs, no Cs or lower grades. Today, he would probably be forced to conform to strict curriculum requirements. That would be to his students' loss. He had a huge influence on me, and German became important to me not only in chemistry research but with German patients.

## Mr. Burrows and Mrs. Lurie

My junior year, the school combined Advanced Placement (AP) English and AP History. It was a two-hour class. The two teachers were Mr. Burrows and Mrs. Lurie. Mr. Burrows was British trained with a lovely accent that was easy to listen to. He taught the history of various periods. Mrs. Lurie, the English teacher, taught the literature of the same periods. Even the music teacher was invited at times to teach us songs from each historical period. It was fun and entertaining, and we learned a lot.

Never was history more interesting. Exam questions requested explaining the connections of historical events and the meaning of correlated literature. I don't recall a single question like "What date did this bill pass?" or "What year did so-and-so do such-and-such?" As a result, I got double As and fell in love with history and historical literature. I can still sing some of the songs from the nineteenth century. I learned to be interested in history. My patients' histories always intrigued me.

Years after graduation, I learned that the school board did not allow the combined class to continue. First, it required two hours in the auditorium, which cramped students' schedules (so sad); second, and more important, the other schools in Duluth claimed they could not duplicate the class, so it wasn't fair. I think lowering the standard to mediocrity was a poor decision.

Mrs. Lurie taught the senior year English literature class too. In it, we studied *Beowulf, The Canterbury Tales*, and Shakespeare's *Richard III* and *A Midsummer Night's Dream*. I admired Mrs. Lurie because she did not candy-coat the obscenities, nor did she focus on them. My classmates and I learned a lot about the development of the English language. But the climax for me was her arrangement of a field trip to the Guthrie Theater in Minneapolis to see *Richard*

*III.* Many of the girls were excited about studying Shakespeare until she told us that we were not studying *Romeo and Juliet* "because you all know that story."

I gained so much respect for Mrs. Lurie when the Jewish community in Duluth put on the play *Fiddler on the Roof* and she played the female lead. We also discovered that some of our other teachers were Jewish when we saw them on stage.

## Mr. Kumshaw

Our art teacher, Mr. Kumshaw, was Polish, maybe Jewish, I'm not sure. He was a displaced person during World War II, as all his relatives were killed. He came to the United States, became a citizen, and received a bachelor's degree in fine arts to qualify as our art teacher. He was vehemently patriotic and did not tolerate students saying anything negative about the United States. He privately shared his story with a few of us.

After the Nazis invaded Poland and killed all his family, he *walked* to Paris. Once he arrived, he lived and sometimes slept in the Louvre. He said, "Because it was warm, I found some sneaky places to sleep so the guards wouldn't find me." In the evenings, when the museum closed, he scrounged the garbage cans of the local restaurants for food. He preferred garbage cans from the restaurants where the Nazi officers ate because "they were full of great leftovers." In the morning, he would return to the Louvre.

As a result, Mr. Kumshaw had scrutinized every painting he saw at the Louvre; he could describe the paintings' brushstrokes in exquisite detail as he taught us. He knew the history of the artists without notes and would even describe the layering of pigment on the paintings. He was passionate about art. It had saved his life.

Even in a well-financed school like Duluth East, there never seemed to be enough money for art supplies. I think Mr. Kumshaw personally subsidized our classes. And despite the lack of budget, he received permission to have an art auction to raise money for supplies. He asked the students in the class to donate some of their art. Some students would make or paint things as gifts for parents or friends, but there were plenty of painting disasters that students didn't want and were willing to donate.

I remember one watercolor exercise that I did, which I was about to toss in the garbage. Mr. Kumshaw stopped me. It was on an eight- by ten-inch piece of watercolor paper. "Look at this, Richard," he said. I saw nothing but a mess. "In this upper corner, you have a beautiful blending of colors. It has a feeling." He promptly took scissors and cut out a corner of the paper. "Can I have this for the auction?"

I laughed. "Sure."

This phenomenon repeated itself multiple times with me and other students.

As the auction time drew near, Mr. Kumshaw busied himself making matte frames for all our rejects. Some very talented students had made some amazing pictures just for the auction. One student was even allowed to work on an oil painting; he actually provided the oil paints himself. He was a borderline professional even in high school. I wasn't that good.

At the auction, my castoff was framed and sold for about $12. Many pieces were bought by parents, of course, but the public was invited and was generous in their bidding. The oil painting came up last. It was exquisite, and the bidding went over $500. The student's parents just laughed, but I think the painting doubled the funding for the department.

Students taking second-year art had the opportunity to make things from clay. First, the students were each required to make a slab pot. It was fired and glazed and turned in to Mr. Kumshaw. If he gave it a good grade, the student was allowed to try throwing clay on the wheel. This required some instruction on centering the clay, but Mr. Kumshaw was a master at teaching us how to throw a pot. That is where I first threw pots of my own. I even made a small teapot from the clay, which was sold at the next year's auction.

The next year, my senior year, the school decided to expand the parking lot. The art class windows looked out over the construction area. Mr. Kumshaw became very excited when he saw the deposit of clay that the crew dug up. After the construction crew left, he filled several containers with that clay.

But the parking lot clay was full of stones and sand, so Mr. Kumshaw liquefied the clay and passed it through a series of screens to remove the rocks and gravel. When he was satisfied, he let the clay settle, poured off the supernatant water, and placed the residual material on a marble slab to suck it dry. This process took weeks, but he was finally satisfied. Some of us made slab pots, and he fired them to see what the clay looked like. It was the most beautiful bright red color. In addition, the contaminating sand shone like diamonds when fired.

The rest of the year, when not directly teaching, Mr. Kumshaw used that clay. At first, it tore up his hands because of the sand content, which remained despite passing the clay through his finest screens. As a result, he wouldn't let us throw it on the wheel. "Too dangerous," he said. He used leather gloves when he threw the clay. He formed a three-foot pagoda-shaped birdhouse, composed of three pieces that sat on top of each other. It took him weeks. When it was fired, the clay was so gorgeous that he used only a clear glaze. I know he went through many pairs of leather gloves and still had rough palms from working that clay.

At auction that year, the birdhouse sold for over a thousand dollars. All that money went to buying supplies for the next year. Mr. Kumshaw never kept any of the money. He inspired me to appreciate art. He also taught me to be creative. Medicine is a science but also an art form, so I learned to be creative with my patients and pursue my goals despite hardship.

## Mr. Skogg

I loved science but struggled with physics. I did not get an A in that class; I think I got a B–. Biology was interesting, as I enjoyed dissecting things—easy A. Chemistry my senior year was taught by Mr. Skogg. His magical experiments in the front of the class drew my and my classmates' attention each day. Studying chemical structure under his guidance was like "discovering the fingerprint of God," as he always said. I did well.

One day, he asked to talk to me after class. He told me to consider chemistry in college, since I had done so well. Because he encouraged me, and since my mother didn't think I could get accepted to medical school, I decided to major in chemistry at the University of Minnesota Duluth.

## Finishing High School

A beautiful Jewish classmate caught my attention. I really liked her. She was delightfully intelligent, didn't use a lot of makeup, and maintained a poise that did not require impressing people. We spent a lot of time together. We shared the joys of Israel during the Six-Day War. We sat together, had lunch together, and I fell in love. But on our one and only date, she reminded me, "My father wanted me to tell you that this can't go anywhere." We continued as close friends until graduation. At our ten-year class reunion, I was disappointed that she didn't come. Some of my best friends told me that she still wasn't married. She studied law and became a corporate lawyer in Minneapolis.

My best friend Greg (one of the class's ten valedictorians, and another Jewish friend) died in a car accident that summer, and my other best friend Neil was drafted to fight in Vietnam. As the song "Sunrise, Sunset" from *Fiddler on the Roof* says, life is filled with happiness and tears.

# 6

## MY SIBLINGS

My siblings and I each had our own room at our house on Forty-Third Avenue and London Road. My younger brother Bill's blue room had sports stuff. My sister Margaret's pink room was occupied with stuffed animals. And Bob's room was yellow.

I ended up in the basement because my brothers couldn't get along with each other. Bill would tease Bob, and Bob would retaliate by kicking or pinching Bill. So Mother decided to separate them. My older brother, Bob, got my former room upstairs, and Bill stayed in his upstairs bedroom. Losing my upstairs bedroom, as the oldest, I was demoted (at least that's how I felt) to the basement, but then I hated the color of my bedroom, as the yellow reminded me of urine.

Bob's private room housed over a hundred creatures. His menagerie included fish, frogs, insects, and an assortment of others, so he was required to always keep his door locked. His room opened to the shared upstairs bathroom. Of course, there were still escapees, which Mother usually tolerated. She called him Lover-boy, and he was always her favorite.

One time, Bob found a large water beetle in the creek that ran beside our property. He captured it and kept it in a jar in his room. He left the lid loose "so it could breathe." The water beetle was great at jumping and managed to jump hard enough to knock the lid off the jar. Then, being a water beetle, it began its search for open water. Somehow, it snuck under the locked door, and rejoiced[2] at finding open water in the toilet in the next room.

When Mother went to use the toilet, she didn't notice the water beetle frolicking in the bowl. As she sat down, the water suddenly got dark. That must have frightened the poor thing. It jumped up from the water, pinching Mother in the buttocks. She screamed so loud the water beetle took flight. Bob ran to rescue his water beetle, but Mother had smashed it to death.

Bob's terrarium housed fifty frogs. He counted them. He was neurotic like that. The terrarium had a flimsy plastic lid, and frogs know how to jump. They are quite skilled at that endeavor. And when they jump in unison, they are an unrelenting force. The day Bob forgot to lock his bedroom door, they jumped and knocked off the terrarium's lid.

When we came home from wherever we went that summer day, we discovered frogs all over the house, a true biblical plague. Knowing there were fifty escapees, we counted frogs as we found them under the couch, in the fireplace, in the kitchen, under the dining room table, on the stairs, and in the doorways, contemplating escape. We never did find all fifty, more like thirty or so. Bob said, "Maybe I counted wrong." But he was so analytical, we knew he was bluffing Mother.

Weeks went by. We continued to find frogs dead and decaying everywhere in the house. During that cold winter, we found mummified frogs under the radiators.

---

2 Pardon my anthropomorphism.

Just an aside, understand before I finish telling the frog tale that Mother was not a good cook. Recall that when I was in seventh grade, I made supper every weeknight. She relieved me on weekends. Perhaps she was a bad cook because of all the government surplus ingredients she had when we lived in Silver Lake Homes, or the fact that her mother died suddenly when she was a teen. Maybe she even married my father because he was such a good cook.

Anyway, our kitchen sink had a garbage disposal, which Bill nicknamed Al. Whenever Bill did not like the food Mother served, he would pick up his plate and say, "Mom, I have to feed Al." Either Mother didn't listen, or she didn't understand what he was saying, because it took her quite a while to realize that Bill was putting his food down the garbage disposal.

One day, she caught on, and when Bill picked up his plate to "feed Al," she said, "No, you don't," and started chasing him. Bill was slim, athletic, and fast. Mother was slow because of her weight (about three hundred pounds), so there was no hope of her catching him. Around the kitchen, into the living room, into the TV room, back into the dining room, back into the kitchen, they chased, until Mother was breathless. She never caught him. She wondered out loud what he did with his plate of food. No one answered.

That spring, months later, Mother decided to do some housecleaning. I think she even took some vacation days off work to do it. She decided to start with the closet off the dining room. When she moved a cabinet to dust under it, there she found Bill's plate of food, completely desiccated. She yelled for Bill. He and I both came running. With clenched fists ready to pound my brother, she demanded an explanation. "What do you have to say for yourself, Bill?"

50

Bill bent over in an exaggerated fashion to examine the plate as if he didn't know where he had put it. "But, Mother, the food was poisonous."

"It was not. It was perfectly good food."

Bill pointed at the plate and said, "It was poisonous. Look. It killed the frog."

On the plate was one of Bob's mummified frogs. Mother was chagrined and had to laugh. Bill escaped punishment.

Bob was always interested in the creek beside our house. He had found some small beaver traps that Father got at a garage sale. I am not sure why, or what he thought he would do with them, but Father was fascinated with the contraptions; that was Father. Bob used them to trap rats in the creek. Each rat he captured was carefully measured and weighed, then tabulated in his record books. He then disposed of the rats in the garbage can. My parents were fine with his hobby. Mother did not like rats, and Father thought of it as a biologic research project.

One day, Bob came home from school to find a skunk in a trap of his. The trap must have killed the skunk quite suddenly because it didn't even smell. Bob wasn't interested in skunks, so he deposited it in the garbage can.

Bill was a careful observer. When Bob deposited the skunk in the garbage, Bill took the skunk out. He unrolled some nylon line from Father's fishing pole and tied one end around the skunk's head and the other end to his bicycle. Bill waited at the end of our long driveway with the skunk on the ground. Mother was so prompt that we could anticipate her arrival. When Mother turned the corner, Bill took off on his bicycle, yelling, "Mother, the skunk is after me!"

With an instinct to protect her youngest son, Mother tried to run over the skunk with the car, without running over Bill on the bicycle. Bill swerved and turned. Mother's attempt to run over the skunk appeared quite reckless. Arriving at the garbage can, Bill untied the dead skunk and dropped it in the garbage can. Mother was so mad she started chasing Bill around the outside of the house. But after a few rounds, she was breathless, and she gave up. Besides, we were all laughing so hard that we were breathless too. I think she forgave him, but maybe not.

By this time, Father had accumulated so much vacation time working for the county that if he didn't feel like going to work, he just took a vacation day, which was fine with his supervisor. But Mother had only started working for the county when we moved to London Road, so she had much less vacation and saved it for summer holidays.

One winter day, when Duluth received a foot of snow, Father looked out the window and decided to take a day of vacation. He called Mother's supervisor, Mr. Z, who lived farther down London Road, to ask if he would be willing to pick her up on his way into work. He said that he would be glad to do that.

Despite the foot of snow, a few feet of the sidewalk near the house were clear because of strong winds during the night. However, where the sidewalk dropped to street level with two steps just before reaching London Road, it was filled in with snow, the depth of which was not obvious.

Mother watched out our large picture window that faced the street, and once she saw her supervisor stop, she proceeded out the door. She was wearing boots, but the snow got deeper as she paraded onward. Bill and I were standing at the window watching her. When she took a step, she found herself in thigh-deep snow. "Bill!" she yelled.

Bill slipped on his boots by the door and ran out in his pajamas. He yelled, "I'll save you, Mom!" He got a rope from the shed and threw it to her. But as she lunged for it, he snapped it back. Mother collapsed in a snowbank. He apologized and threw the rope to her again. Again, he jerked the rope back as she tried to grab it. Mother was flailing around in the snowbank; somehow righting herself, she gritted her teeth and repeatedly yelled, "Oh, Bill!"

"Don't worry, Mom," he said, grabbing the snow shovel on the porch. "I'll shovel you out."

He grabbed the snow shovel and, with an elaborate flourish, shoveled Mother out of the snow, still in his pajamas. He shoveled a path all the way to Mr. Z's waiting car. I'm sure they were late for work, but rotund Mr. Z was laughing so hard that nothing came of it.

One day, we learned that when our house was built early in the century, there were no other houses in the area. Our property had been surrounded by a dairy farm, so when the basement was built, it was blasted out with dynamite. The result was that the east wall of my room in the basement was granite, part of the Canadian Shield. The other three walls were concrete blocks. I loved that granite wall.

When *National Geographic* published the paintings on the walls of Lascaux, I was awed. I decided to duplicate three of the animal paintings on my granite wall. It was fun, and I adjusted my bed so that when I sat up in the morning, I faced the buffalo of Lascaux. Nobody ever came to my room, so it was months before anyone discovered what I had done. Father was impressed. Mother wanted the wall repainted white. Father prevailed.

Decades later, after at least three different owners, Priscilla and I stopped at the house. We introduced ourselves and asked the current owners if we could look at the house where I grew up. They were quite gracious and allowed us to investigate. I was most interested in the paintings—whether they were still there. They were, so I took one last look at them. The owners had decided to drywall the basement, but they promised me that they would not erase the paintings, only put drywall over the granite. I suppose the Lascaux buffalo is still there behind a more appropriate plaster wall. Maybe some century, an anthropologist will rediscover it.

# 7

## WORK AS AN ORDERLY

Since Mother decided that I should pay rent as my high school graduation present, I started working at St. Luke's Hospital as an orderly. I loved it right from the start. I was paid $1.75 an hour. The women in my class, called nurses' aides, received $1.50 an hour because they were not required to do heavy lifting or transport patients. We went through a two-week training, which included giving bed baths, changing bed linens, putting in catheters, and fetching whatever a nurse asked for. When we finished our training, we had to take a test. It involved making a bed to specifications, demonstrating on a manikin how to give a bed bath, and carrying out the sterile technique for putting in Foley catheters, male and female.

Having passed the exam, and I recall everyone did, we were sent to our assigned wards. I was sent to the oncology ward. My first patient was Mr. West, who was dying of lung cancer. Some of the other aides had trouble with him because he was grouchy. Once I discovered that he was German, I greeted him in German every day. He was delighted and helped me work on my vocabulary. We got along well. The charge nurse was surprised when he told her that he only wanted me as his caregiver.

Mr. West was quite wealthy, and since he hated hospital food, every day he received catered meals from the Pickwick, the oldest German restaurant in Duluth. As he ate, he was willing to share his story while I cleaned his room. He told me he had been in the German army and was captured by the Czar's Russian army very early in World War I. He was sent to a Siberian prison camp to work. But when the Communists took control, he was released. "They just opened the gates of the prison and told us we were free," he said. He walked from Siberia back to Germany. It took him four years. "I did many bad things to stay alive."

He was conscripted by the Red Army and stayed with them as long as they fed him and were heading west. If the army started heading north, south, or east, he deserted. He was also conscripted by the White Army and fought with them if they were heading west. After four years, he arrived home. Everyone was surprised to see him. His family assumed he had died during the war. He was so paranoid from his tragic experiences that he packed a pistol at meals for years. Tired of European wars, he migrated to the United States, choosing Duluth, Minnesota, as his home. There, he made his wealth in business. And there, I cared for Mr. West until he died.

Not all my patients had such intriguing stories, but I did learn to relate to people who were sick and hurting. I loved hearing patients relate their lives' journeys. I also learned to respect people whom others shunned.

I must have done a good job, because at my three-month evaluation, I was transferred to other floors. Eventually, I was assigned as one of two orderlies for the whole hospital during the evening shift. I got to see various aspects of patient care, from post-surgical patients to cardiology patients.

The hospital did not have in-wall oxygen yet, so patients on oxygen had tanks in their rooms. Orderlies were responsible for delivering the oxygen tanks, which had to be strapped to carriers for transport to each patient's room. I was always apprehensive about those tanks. One day, the other orderly was careless and dropped one. The top valve broke off and it shot like a missile through two walls. No one was hurt, but he was reprimanded. We both learned how dangerous the tanks were.

Heavy rain one spring caused some minor flooding on the ground floor of the hospital. I laughed when I heard about it because it was the urology floor that flooded. All the orderlies were busy transporting the patients to other floors. But one patient urgently needed a Foley catheter before he was transferred. I was told to put the catheter in the patient and then transfer him to another floor. I was nervous, as this was my first catheter placement. I stood in water an inch deep as I went to his bedside.

I prepped and draped the patient's penis as instructed. Following sterile precautions, I started to place the catheter in his urethra. About halfway to the bladder, he suddenly screamed. "Did I do something to hurt you?" I stammered. My hands were shaking. Had I injured him?

"No," he said, "you're fine, but my slippers just floated out the door." We laughed. I finished placing the catheter, with good urine flow that relieved his distended bladder, and then I ran out the door to fetch his slippers before transferring him to a dry floor.

That fall, I needed to switch to part-time work while attending the University of Minnesota Duluth (UMD) as a freshman. I was assigned to the emergency department (ED), which gave the regular orderly every weekend off. He was delighted, and I had a regular weekend position.

Patient care in the ED is not always much fun. Some traumatic events caused me nightmares. I even fainted one time when a man presented with a hatchet stuck in his foot. I carefully took off his boot, cutting it around the hatchet, which remained stuck in his bones. I cleansed the wound as instructed, and then the physician came in to inspect the trauma. All that time, I had maintained my composure, but as the physician removed the hatchet and inspected the wound, I was instructed to stand there in case he needed anything. Hot and flushed, watching the foot laceration and examining the tissue damage as the hatchet was removed, I fainted.

The charge nurse, a former military nurse, comforted me and told me that next time, I should move around the room, not just stand still. I took her advice to heart. I never fainted again, but some traumas, especially extensive burns, required me to "move around a lot."

### Emergency Department Trauma

One couple, still in their wedding garb and traveling to their honeymoon lodge in Northern Wisconsin, were hit head-on by a drunk driver. The groom presented with the ambulance crew in resuscitation. The emergency physician asked me to check the bride, still in her wedding dress. The white lace fabric was covered in blood, and I noticed tissue extruding from her nose. Careful examination revealed it was brain tissue. I went to tell the emergency physician what I found, and he authorized me to call the neurosurgeon. Usually, consults are physician to physician, but after I explained the situation, the neurosurgeon came right away. By that time, the ED team had given up on the groom and pronounced him dead. The bride was taken to surgery, where they found the ethmoid plate fractured. What I had seen from her nose was part of her frontal lobes. Despite a craniotomy to decrease brain swelling, she died later that night.

The ED physician asked me to check on the drunk driver who had killed the couple. The ambulance personnel found him sitting on the hood of his car, singing, "Home on the Range." I tried to examine him. He did have some minor lacerations from flying through his windshield, but nothing that needed stitches. "Leave me alone. I need to sleep," he said. He was quite obnoxious. I turned off the light; he fell back to sleep, and I finished examining him in the dark. No injuries.

Later, the driver was admitted to detox. When he sobered up, he insisted, "I don't have a drinking problem." He was charged with two counts of reckless homicide and whisked off to jail. That experience made me vehement about drunk driving, but compassionate to help patients maintain sobriety.

We seldom have tornadoes in the Duluth area because the mass of Lake Superior makes its own weather. However, we did have a one on the hillside north of Duluth during my orderly years. A frantic father carried his twelve-year-old daughter into the ED. They had been camping when the tornado hit. He described that the tornado grabbed her out of his arms and "tossed her head among the trees like a billiard ball." I held her head as we transferred her to the ED gurney. She was unconscious. Her skull felt like a bag of potato chips. I will never forget that sensation of holding her head in my hands and feeling all the bones crunching against each other. X-ray revealed that every bone in her skull was broken. She died later that day.

## Upsetting Ambulance Attendant

One experience with an ambulance attendant really upset me. He was a tall, muscular man with a machismo attitude. Every time he brought someone to our department, he said something derogatory to me. I gritted my teeth and didn't respond but found him very aggravating. I knew his job was stressful, so I tried to understand. He often grabbed a cup of coffee from the ED lounge without asking. No other ambulance attendant ever did that.

One night, he was particularly rude. I went to the lounge and got a cup of coffee and brought it to him. His demeanor immediately changed. "No one has ever given me anything in my life," he said. After that, he was much kinder to me when he brought people into our department. He didn't share much, but at least he was civil after that incident.

A few weeks later, another ambulance brought him into our ED on a gurney. He had shot himself in the head. Dead on arrival, he had committed suicide. I thanked the Lord that I had not been unkind to him. I sure wanted to be. It was obvious to me that day his life had been very troubled. His nasty attitude only reflected his pain.

## Dr. Fisketti

It was the orderly's responsibility to take bodies to the morgue. One night, I was called to the third floor to transport a body. Dr. Fisketti, an ED physician, was responsible for pronouncing the deaths of patients in the hospital during the night. I found him sitting at the nurses' desk filling out a death certificate. He had already examined the patient. "I heard no heart sounds or breath sounds," he said to me. I was standing at the desk, waiting for him to finish so that I could transport the body, when, suddenly, the patient came out of his room and asked Dr. Fisketti, "How am I?"

Dr. Fisketti crumpled the death certificate in his fist and said, "I guess you're all right."

"Thanks, Doc," the patient said as he reentered his room.

The patient was barrel chested from severe emphysema, which muffled his heart sounds; his thick neck prevented feeling any carotid pulse; and Cheyne-Stokes respirations meant that he was apneic when Dr. Fisketti examined him. As a physician, I always proceeded with caution in pronouncing such patients dead, and I added examining corneal reflexes to my assessment. Even Cheyne-Stokes patients don't like to be poked in the eye, unless they are indeed dead; then they don't mind.

Dr. Fisketti was one of my favorite ED physicians. He was born and raised in Italy before coming to the United States to complete his medical training. In the '60s and '70s, Italian ships often came into the Duluth harbor to buy grain. After the Italian captains discovered that we had an Italian ED physician, they presented their sailors for sick call at St. Luke's. It was not uncommon for as many as twenty Italian sailors to present at once to be examined. That flooded our ED. Dr. Fisketti would start out speaking Italian to the sailors and English to the staff. But when he became frazzled, he would start speaking English to the sailors and Italian to the staff. Then, we would pull him aside and encourage him to relax with a cup of tea before confronting the crew of sailors again. Relaxed, he would return to speaking appropriate languages to sailors and staff.

## Psychiatric Ward Orderly

I found the ED stimulating, exciting, tragic, and meaningful. I worked every Friday and Saturday night while attending university. In the summers between college semesters, I worked full-time in the ED.

One summer, the orderly on the psychiatric ward wanted to take some time off. I was assigned to his duties until he returned. That resulted in two months of working in the psychiatric ward. He must have been very professional because the hospital was so pleased with his work they rehired him as soon as he returned from his "vacation." He explained to me that he had needed to go fishing.

Working on the psychiatric ward afternoon shift, 3:00 to 11:30, was quite different from my experience in the rest of the hospital. The head nurse was compassionate with psychiatric patients and communicated that to her staff. In the evenings, all the patients met in the lunchroom for graham crackers, cheese, and peanut butter. The nurses' aides cleaned the patients' rooms, and the nurses set about administering the evening medications. My responsibility was to join the patients and keep everyone calm, awaiting their evening drugs. "Make sure no one becomes disruptive or combative," the charge nurse said. "You may snack with them to provide a calming influence." Even today, I associate graham crackers, peanut butter, and cheese as a calming snack, but a bit of a crazy one.

I was responsible for making sure all the patients in the locked ward went to bed. I was locked in with the patients until everyone appeared to be asleep. One young woman was in the locked ward because she was suicidal. The charge nurse assigned me to stay with her until she went to bed so she didn't hang herself or do anything else self-destructive. Trained in ballet, she had a routine of dancing before she was willing to lie down, so every night, she did her dance. When the routine was done, she would peacefully go to bed. But if no one attended her dance, she would scream and start destroying her room. She required an audience. I was assigned as the audience for her beautiful, artistic routine.

One time, a large, burly patient tried to escape. He was quite clever, as he would wait until someone came to the ward on the elevator and then, as the doors were closing, would jump inside to leave the ward. I was assigned to halt this behavior. I would go into the elevator and lock it until he left it. But one day, he was quite sneaky getting into the elevator. The head nurse said, "Get in there! Don't let him leave."

I jumped in the elevator. He grabbed me and threw me out. The head nurse yelled, "Get back in there!" I ran back in. He picked me up and threw me out so hard that I smashed into the nurses' desk. The head nurse helped me up and pushed me back into the elevator. "I called security. They will be here soon."

I got tossed out of the elevator four times before security arrived. Despite a few bruises, I tolerated the scuffle. I was thankful when the psychiatric orderly returned from his vacation so that I could go back to the ED.

# 8

## COLLEGE

In the fall of 1967, I started my freshman year at UMD. Due to Mr. Skogg's encouragement and my mother's insistence that I would never be accepted into medical school, I declared my major in chemistry. I loved it right from the start.

Because of the Vietnam War, many students attended college to avoid getting drafted. UMD accepted almost any applicant who was a Minnesota resident, and the rule was that if you flunked out of college, you were eligible for the draft. The college used freshman English as a screening course; it was required of all new students. I was unable to test out of English because my spelling and grammar skills were atrocious, and still are. I had to take the course.

To illustrate how difficult the course was, a young woman I knew from Duluth East High School who had tested out of freshman English decided to take the class as an easy A. And she received a B. I received a B–, for which I was very thankful.

My fun class was German, which I took all four years at UMD. We read German novels and short stories, and discussed them in German. The professors were good, but not as much fun as Herr Gerlach from high school. German was important to my chemistry career because of the research that was done only in German.

Math was another delightful class. I had tested out of the basic courses, so I started taking advanced math. Our obese professor was funny and absent-minded. Several class periods ended with the professor working on the blackboard, telling us we could be excused, and sending us off with the comment, "I think I'll just work through this problem a bit more."

After one weekend blizzard, my classmates and I watched from the math classroom's second-story window as this professor navigated through snowdrifts. The walkways had not yet been shoveled. The rule was that if the professor didn't arrive within fifteen minutes of the start of class, it was considered canceled. One person in the class started timing him. He kept getting caught in the snowdrifts. He was late. We could have left, but watching him navigate through the snow was so entertaining that most of us stayed for class.

I loved my chemistry classes. The professors were exceptional. Dr. Caple, my advisor, noted that I was taking advanced German classes. He asked me to translate an article published in German that related to his research. I must have done well because I became the department translator, since several of the professors were working on research for which there were only German publications.

Freshman chemistry entailed two afternoons of lab work. Our laboratory professor matched up students majoring in nutrition with us chemistry majors because the nutrition students were also required to take freshman chemistry and chemistry lab. As partners, we did our experiments together, wrote the results in a single document, and both got the same grade. The experiments were both qualitative (What was the unknown substance?) and quantitative (How much product did you get?).

My nutrition major partner was particularly beautiful, slim, and petite with a gorgeous figure and an adorable face. She was so attractive that she made me nervous. And she always smelled good from expensive perfume. It took every bit of my willpower to focus on our experiments each session and not be distracted. This was a struggle, but we worked together. She was not much of a chemist, so she took notes, documenting our experiments and detailing our results. She had beautiful handwriting. At the end of the quarter, she thanked me because she was pleased she received a much better grade than she had anticipated. That was nice. I planned to ask her out on a date the last day of lab.

That last day, a beautiful, warm spring day, we only had to clean our equipment and turn it in. If nothing was broken, we would receive back our lab deposit of $35. I started cleaning up our equipment without my partner because she was late. I had finished with all our equipment except an Erlenmeyer flask, which is cleaned with a mixture of sulfuric and hydrochloric acids. Once I cleaned that, we would get our full deposit returned.

It was then that my partner flitted into the laboratory like a butterfly, wearing a tiny, shimmering acetate top with matching very short shorts. She startled me, asking, "Anything I need to do?"

Shaking, I dropped the Erlenmeyer flask. The flask didn't break, but as it hit the floor, the acid splashed onto her outfit. It dissolved. Before my blinking eyes, her shimmering acetate fell to the floor as a tiny piece of carbon. (Acetate is a small chain carbon chemical, which the cleaning solution instantly dissolved.) She stood shocked in a bra and panties. She screamed, grabbed her stuff, and ran to the bathroom.

She reappeared in her shorts and T-shirt from her athletic class. The flask was very clean and unbroken, so we received our full deposit. I offered to give her my part of the deposit for ruining her outfit, but she refused and left. My thoughts of dating her never materialized, as I never saw her again. After that required class, all the nutrition students avoided the chemistry building.

Being a chemistry major had perks. For example, we had priority over other students for classes that were required for our major, so we never had to worry that a class we needed was full. In addition, after taking all the required chemistry courses, a minor in mathematics was automatic. I was still in my junior year when I had completed all the requirements, and had priority for elective classes, most of which were sought after by freshmen who had not decided on a major.

I suppose that I could have graduated early, but I wanted to take some electives for fun. As a senior, when I could register before freshmen and sophomores, I enjoyed my electives, including classes in art, geography, child psychology, anthropology, and comparative anatomy. The end of my junior year and my senior year were like vacations.

The other dubious advantage of being a chemistry major was that many hippy generation students wanted to be friends. Several times, the following scenario occurred. While I was eating lunch alone in the cafeteria, some unknown young woman would sit next to me. The conversation went something like this: "Hi, I'm Heather. I'm majoring in sociology. I heard that you're majoring in chemistry. Is that right?"

I would swallow a bite of sandwich while gazing at an attractive, braless sociology major who smelled of sandalwood, and then reply, "Yes, I'm majoring in chemistry."

"Neat," she would say, resting her chin on her hand. "I like you.

You're special with all that chemistry knowledge. Tell me about it. Can you make things?"

"Better living through chemistry," I usually said.

After more small talk came the climax question. She would come closer and whisper in my ear, "Can you make LSD for me?"

I could have, as it was not that complex of a chemical, but I wouldn't, so that usually ended the conversation and our relationship. But these young sociology or psychology majors would still smile and greet me in the hall. I suppose that they were hopeful.

When I was a sophomore, my advisor, Dr. Caple, invited me to work in his lab for my required research. He described a chemical, benzonorbornadiene,[3] which has a beautiful structure, including a benzene ring with an attached carbon double-bond bridge. His purpose in studying this chemical was to show that an electron could be simultaneously shared by three carbon atoms. To prove his hypothesis, he required several chemical reactions with various chemicals at the double-bond structure. Given sufficient reactions, it would logically follow that the only way these reactions could occur would be if the electron was shared with all three carbons. As mentioned, the only other research of this chemical was published in German, so I had to carefully read that provided research to focus on the assigned experiments.

It was fun and artistic work because all our products came in a rainbow of colors. Whatever was attached to the double bond changed the color of the chemical. All of us who were working in Dr. Caple's lab kept samples of our products on a glass shelf according to the rainbow. We displayed them on a glass shelf so the afternoon sunlight could shine through, creating an artistic display.

[3] The chemical had no known use then, but varenicline, the smoking-cessation drug, was developed from the structure.

Dr. Caple would inspect our product, analyzing by spectrometry and magnetic resonance to prove what the chemical and the byproducts were. Then he would choose the next step in the process toward proving his hypothesis. He did publish his results, which he presented at several national scientific conferences.

The only dangerous part of this research was that lithium was required as a catalyst to force the reactions. Lithium metal reacts violently with water, producing a salt (LiOH), and in the process releases hydrogen in an exothermic reaction that immediately explodes in a blaze. The chunk of lithium in the lab was kept in a container of oil to avoid exposure to even the water vapor in the air. It weighed enough, according to the calculations of several members of the laboratory, to explode all of Lake Superior. It was a big chunk. We used just a tiny scraping to catalyze our experiments.

One afternoon, after I completed my experiment and put my product in a tiny vial, I added it to the shelf of our rainbow products and carried on cleaning up. The cleanup process required safe disposal of the lithium, which in this case was a tiny crumb at the bottom of my beaker. I took out the printed protocol and followed each step very carefully. These steps first involved adding alcohol, with which the lithium only mildly reacts. Next step: add water mixed with alcohol in various ratios. I did each step according to the protocol. Nothing bad was happening. I went over the steps to make sure that I had followed them properly. I took a glass rod and crunched the crumb at the bottom of my beaker. Nothing bad happened.

The last step of the protocol was to dispose of it down the drain, assuming all the lithium had turned into salt (LiOH). I dumped the whole mess, and a four-foot flame jumped out of the drain! I shook!

After I stopped hyperventilating and caught my breath, I looked around the lab. Nothing appeared to be broken or damaged. I collapsed on a bench, thanking God that I—and more important, Dr. Caple's third-floor lab—was intact.

I gathered my books and notes, and scuttled down the stairs to the first floor to go home. The first-floor freshman lab was in total chaos as I passed. One of the students, who fled out the door, told me that artesian fountains had suddenly sprung out of every drain in the lab. No one was hurt. Everyone was busy mopping up the sewage. The instructor was scratching his bald head, wondering what caused the sudden increased pressure in the plumbing. I slunk home after that.

Despite my mother's prophecy, I took the required courses for premed that were outside my chemistry major requirements: biology and comparative anatomy. They were relaxing and not particularly challenging. I enjoyed comparative anatomy most because in it, I learned that ontogeny replicates phylogeny. What a mouthful, but what it means is that as a human fetus develops, it replicates the evolutionary process. It is very useful, as birth defects in humans relate to incomplete development along that evolutionary pathway. If one understands phylogeny, then birth defects become logical outcomes of incomplete ontogeny.

I almost lost my dream of becoming a physician in taking physics. I couldn't wrap my mind around the process and the interaction of the formulae. The disaster was even more devastating because the physics class, fortunately only one, was required for my chemistry major. Our grade was dependent on a midterm and a final exam, nothing else. I flunked the midterm, with a bright red F on top of my exam sheet. I was despondent. What could I do? If I had to take the course over, the grades would be averaged, but I doubted that I could do much better. I recalled my father's experience with his graduate course. It gave me nightmares.

The physics lab was worse than the didactic sessions. We were supposed to have the professor inspect our experiments before we ran them. Watching and timing a ball rolling down an incline plane was no problem. But as the lab progressed, the experiments became more complicated. One experiment involved an electrical system. I carefully set it up according to the instructions in the manual, and I asked to sign it out. The professor—who had no body hair, including eyebrows, because of his research with radioactive substances—yelled at me, "What are you trying to do, blow up my lab?" To this day, I have no clue what I did wrong. But he assigned me to work with a classmate, a physics major, for the rest of the lab, who redeemed my laboratory grade.

The final exam was very difficult. I still remember one of the questions: "Describe the wave motion of a train going down the tracks." Nothing more was given. I had no idea that a train had a wave motion. We were supposed to supply the weight of the train, the speed of the train, and anything else required for the formulae. I had no idea how much a train weighed, much less how fast it went, and had no notion of how to calculate the wave motion. I recall writing down some formulae that I thought applied, but never answered the question.

A miracle happened. The professor said all the class had done so poorly in the midterm that our grade would be whatever we got on the final exam. Then he returned our final exam papers. I found he had given me credit for writing down the applicable formulae, but as I recall, I hadn't really completed any question. I saw a giant C at the top of my paper and took a deep breath. I passed! Since he didn't count the F from my midterm exam, I received a C for the class. My dream was salvaged.

Physical chemistry wasn't much better. It was all about electron clouds, valences, and nuclear theory. Our professor was an Oxford professor who had worked on neutralizing mustard gas (the chemical warfare used in the First World War) in case the Nazis used it in the Second World War. He was a kindly old gentleman with a delightful British accent. That didn't help my understanding of the mysteries of the atom. I still have the class's book because it was the only chemistry class I took where no matter how much I studied, I still couldn't completely understand. I got the lowest B in the class. I've looked through the book periodically and still don't understand it.

I enjoyed organic chemistry. I had to study hard but always aced the tests. I have talked to other chemistry majors from other universities who hated organic because they were required to memorize seemingly infinite reactions and recite them for the exams. Our classes over three quarters were nothing like that. Dr. Carlson focused on why reactions happened, how things reacted, what properties different organic compounds had, and why a chemical was polar or nonpolar. This approach prepared me for toxicology and pharmacology in medical school because I could look at an organic structure and predict how it would react in biological systems.

Later, as a physician, I irritated drug sales representatives because I always asked them to draw the structure of their new drug. If they couldn't, I would tell them to come back to my office when they could. Some returned drawing their new drug; most never returned.

I will never forget my last organic chemistry class. It was inspiring. There was a glitch in the system at the end of my junior year. The quarter ended on a Tuesday, but exams for all my chemistry classes at UMD were finished on the Friday before. Dr. Carlson told us that we weren't required to come to class the following Monday, but if we were willing, he would prepare a special lecture. Most of our class showed up, and I'm glad that I did. His lecture was on the chemistry of a cake. He had the chemical structure of all the ingredients on the board as we entered. Then throughout the hour, he demonstrated the chemical reactions that occurred with baking. Flour (a long chain carbon), butter (a conjugated lipid), sugar (a carbohydrate), et cetera, baked together with all types of organic reactions became a single molecule. "When you cut a cake," he explained, "you are busting up a single molecule." We were all on the edges of our chairs; you could hardly hear anyone breathing. Then he pulled out a surprise from under his podium: cake for everyone. Too bad those nutrition majors hadn't taken the class.

After completing all my requirements for a chemistry major and mathematics minor, I had three quarters left for elective courses: art, geography, and child psychology. I even tried to minor in art, which required only two more classes, but the head of the department said, "No chemistry major is getting a minor in my department." He resented the As that I received in my previous art classes.

I remember one project that particularly galled him. We were supposed to make three or four three-dimensional, identical objects out of paper that could be repeated to form complex patterns. I chose an organic chemical structure. When I presented my paper objects to my professor, she was delighted and gave me an A for the project. Later, she asked me how I developed the repeating structure. I explained my structure represented a common carbon chain structure. Unfortunately, she told the head of the department, and he demanded that she downgrade my project to a C because I had used a chemical structure. But she didn't. He vented his anger by refusing to allow me to take the two upper-division art courses required for a minor in art.

Anthropology, specifically the study of North American Indians, was the most fascinating elective. Professor Smith, who hadn't yet received his doctorate because of some administrative glitch, gave the lectures. He had lived with the Chipewyan in Canada for four years as part of his PhD research. As he taught, he would give examples from his field experience. His class was so exciting that the auditorium filled up for each session.

In those days, the university administration took attendance in almost no class; the exceptions were chemistry and physics. A student only needed to take the required exams to get a grade. Many students would study the text or someone's notes if they considered the professor boring and show up only for the exam. The result was anyone could audit any class—that is, attend the class but not get credit if they weren't registered. No one ever audited a chemistry class.

Professor Smith's class usually had three hundred attendees, but less than half were registered students. Those of us registered discovered how few we were at the midterm. Fewer than a hundred students took that exam. The others came because his class was so interesting.

Forty percent of our grade was based on a term paper. In mine, I compared Sioux religion to Anishinabek religion. The two tribes were neighbors and rivals aboriginally, but Sioux religion related to plains geography consistent with Cheyenne and Kiowa theology, while Anishinabek religion related to woodland geography based on Eastern Woodlands tribes' Iroquois Confederacy theology. Professor Smith loved it. I aced the exam and received an A for his most enjoyable class.

My other electives were swimming, fishing, geography, and

child psychology. Compared with chemistry, they were just plain fun, although, as mentioned, my kick wasn't good enough for my professor, and I didn't catch a fish on the field trip. Both these experiences downgraded my expected grade, based on the A of my written exams, to a B.

UMD was good for me. The tuition was reasonable, and working at the hospital as an orderly paid for tuition, books, and rent, even when I moved away from Mother's apron strings.

The year before I graduated, there was a job fair for chemistry majors. Everyone was offered a job. The year I graduated, there was no job fair. We were told that the job market for chemistry majors was saturated. No employer needed any chemists that year. How I survived is another chapter.

# 9

## CANOEING

When I learned to paddle a canoe, I shouldn't have. Father took me out on a weekend canoe trip with a coworker. We had a side-mounted ten-horse motor on our canoe, as did Father's friend and his son. We went to an island in the east end of the Boundary Waters Canoe Area (BWCA). I don't recall that we caught a lot of fish, but we had a good time camping. I enjoyed cooking over the open fire. I remember roasting marshmallows and making s'mores. After a good night's sleep, we awoke Sunday morning to a howling wind facing us from the direction we needed to paddle to the landing. No one seemed that concerned because we had the motors.

I come by my clumsiness naturally. Father and I loaded our canoe, and then he attempted to climb into the stern, which was balanced on a few rocks. Over it went, motor and all. The water-logged motor refused to start once we righted the canoe. Our friends took off, claiming they would send someone after us if we didn't show up. Some comfort that was! Father and I started out, and I paddled in the bow, facing the wind. Then it started to rain.

We were not only paddling the canoe but dragging a dead

motor on our side. In retrospect, it might have been easier to take the motor off and put it in the bottom of the canoe, but Father hoped that it would dry in the wind and kept trying to start it. The rain pelted us. What had been less than a two-hour jaunt to the island became a four-hour death-defying paddle against wind and whitecaps smacking me in the face.

We arrived at the resort exhausted, cold, probably hypothermic, hungry, and delirious. Father's friend had gone home but told the resort owner that we were coming. When we arrived looking like drowned rats, this resort owner offered us hot chili, hot chocolate, and a hot shower, all at no cost.

I learned several lessons from that trip.

- Kind people exist who provide free chili, hot chocolate, and a hot shower to those in need.
- Don't depend on someone who doesn't stick by you when you are in need; Father's friend and his son could have towed us behind their canoe.
- Always have someone stabilize a canoe before you climb in.
- Push your muscles to their limit to survive.
- Learn important paddling skills.
- Don't bother bringing a motor on a canoe trip. Motors are for motorboats.
- When you are cold, hungry, and miserable, hot chili tastes the best.

It took a while before I was willing to go on another canoe trip, but when I did, the paddling skills learned during hardship came right back. I even learned to stern the canoe with some degree of expertise. I went on InterVarsity Christian Fellowship trips in college and short paddles around the lakes in our area. Then my friend Daniel asked me to go down the Little Fork River.

## *The Little Fork River*

My friends Tom and Mark and my best friend, Daniel, wanted to canoe the Yukon River during the summer between our junior and senior years of college. They decided it would be wise to canoe the Little Fork River as a test run.

We started in Cook, Minnesota. There are no towns on the river until it forks into the Rainy River on the U.S.–Canadian border because the river flows on the east side of the Indian reservation. The trip through the wilderness of the reservation was important because when canoeing the Yukon, we would have no access to resupply. We had to make decisions about portaging, as there were no marked portages. We couldn't abandon the trip with a hike to the road, as it was miles through dense forest. All these factors would prepare us for the Yukon River.

The trip down the Little Fork River was wet. It rained the whole time. Our sleeping bags were so wet they never dried the whole trip. We renamed them the "amniotic sacs." Because of constant rain, we never saw the sun or the moon the whole trip. It was dreary but forced us to depend on each other physically and emotionally.

We made many good decisions about campsites, learned to start a fire in the rain, and cared for each other. We made one bad decision. Arriving at a waterfall, we got out of our canoes to scan the situation. It was only about a four-foot drop from the top of the falls to the water below. A canoe is seventeen feet, so we reasoned that we could go over the falls without portaging. Tom and Mark said that Dan and I should go first. If we made it safely, they would follow. If not, they would find a way to portage their canoe. There was no portage trail marked. For safety, we took all our gear out of the canoe.

We scouted it out again. There were two car-sized boulders at the bottom of the falls. We decided to go over the falls and make a sharp turn into the V channel on the left of the large rocks. Confident with our plan, we got back in our canoe. Dan was in the bow; I was in the stern. Over the falls we went. My last memory was seeing Dan straight below me. We both lost consciousness.

Mark and Tom told us what they observed. Below the falls, it must have been much deeper than we anticipated because, as they related, Dan and I, including the canoe, completely disappeared, submerged at the base of the falls. They were horrified. Then, we popped up between the two car-sized rocks at the bottom, still in the frozen posture from when we went over the falls. Mark and Tom portaged their canoe and our gear. Everything was wet, but it had been raining for five days already and our submerged state didn't make things any worse. They were glad we were alive. I vowed not to canoe over waterfalls anymore.

We all laughed each night as we set up the tent. The stakes could be pushed into the soggy ground with no effort. We had to put rocks on top of them to prevent them from pulling out during the night. Each night, we cheered to find another campsite with "good pounding ground," which required no pounding at all—just a flick of a finger and the stake was submerged in muck.

The night we made it to the campsite at the confluence with the Rainy River, it stopped raining. The moon was visible that night. Its bright glare scared us. We hadn't seen it for ten days. We had a good, hot, dry meal in International Falls the next day, splurging at the best restaurant we could find. We had learned many valuable survival lessons that prepared us for the Yukon. Now, we just needed to chart our way down the Yukon River.

## Trip down the Yukon

What follows is based on my diary, which I wrote each day of the trip. Some of my partners disagree with the description of these events, but what was written during the trip holds more weight than their fragile, incomplete memories.

A lot of planning went into the trip. We had maps of the entire region. We laid them out across the living room floor and into the dining room of Daniel's home. That allowed us to make a very important decision. We chose to canoe the Teslin River to the Yukon rather than start at Whitehorse. Those who start in Whitehorse, the largest city in the Yukon, canoe through Lake Laberge.

This caused some dissent among the group. On the one hand, the Teslin flowed between mountain peaks and was likely to be very picturesque. On the other hand, we would miss Lake Laberge, where Sam McGee was cremated in Robert Service's poem. Although that part of the trip was popular among tourists, we were yearning for solitude and wilderness. There was even an "uncharted" place marked on our maps of the Teslin River. In the end, beauty won over a chance to see a fictional derelict.

We thought long and hard about food. We planned on eight of us going, and there was only one place to restock along the river, a small town called Carmacks, where the road crossed the river. We didn't know exactly how long it would take us, so we decided to pack the basics, not individual meals. Daniel oversaw writing a cookbook so we could make pancakes, soups, bannock, oatmeal, and even pasta. There was plenty of safe drinking water in the Yukon, so bringing dehydrated, lightweight basics seemed logical.

One concern was meat. We planned on catching fish but thought that we should have a backup plan. Daniel and I read up on jerky. The Anishinabek jerked bear, deer, fish, and moose. Why couldn't we do it? We bought forty pounds of roast beef and cut it into fine strips. To dry it, we hung it on Daniel's mother's clothesline in the backyard. We built a smoky fire in his grill to keep the flies at bay. Later that day, threatening rain made us bring the meat into the garage, but it was already dry. When we weighed it, we found the forty pounds of meat had reduced to ten pounds of jerky. We were proud of our result.

We didn't know about spicing the meat like commercial jerky. Ours was unspiced, like we understood the Native American variety must have been. I have subsequently learned that the Anishinabek did use wild onions and garlic to spice their jerky. Pemmican is made by pulverizing jerky and adding fruit such as blueberries and rendered bear grease. We didn't do that either.

That night at supper, Mother said she had the strangest call-in to the county welfare department. It seemed someone had been hanging meat out on a clothesline. The caller even gave the address, which was in the Woodland District of Duluth. They suggested that the county investigate. My mother thought it was so odd that she related it over supper. I confessed, "Mother, Daniel and I were making jerky." She laughed and let it pass. No county investigation ensued.

We started packing. The basics we packed were flour, sugar, baking powder, pasta, and some dehydrated vegetables that we bought. With Daniel's recipe book, we expected to have plenty to survive. There was one glitch. How were we going to get there? Paul, one of the eight, had a pickup truck and was willing to haul gear and take some of us in it, but he was unwilling to drive on the notorious Alaskan–Canadian (Al-Can) gravel roads from Whitehorse to Dawson City. He said it would ruin his truck. The paved highway stopped at Whitehorse. We needed to drive the

Al-Can Highway to the border of Alaska at Dawson City, where we expected to end our trip. That was five hundred miles of gravel road.

We prayed about it. No one had a car they were willing to let us use and possibly destroy on the Al-Can Highway. One Sunday in church, one of my mother's clients complained to her that the welfare department wouldn't help her because of her car. Their conversation caught my attention. "How much do you want for the car?" I asked.

"Give me $25 and it is yours. I can't make too much money on this deal, or they will deduct it from my welfare check."

I gave her $25, and she gave me the transfer papers. We had a car. It was a big car, more than ten years old—a blue and white Chevrolet with a huge back seat and a trailer hitch. The next week, Priscilla's brother-in-law, Ron Anderson, gave us a trailer he didn't want. God had provided.

Mother didn't want us to go. She invited Auntie Ellen for dinner with the hidden agenda to talk me out of going. It backfired. After I explained our plans, Ellen thought that it was a great idea, much to the chagrin of my mother.

College classes completed for our junior year, we headed northwest in Paul's pickup truck and my $25 car with four canoes, food supplies, tents, and gear. We brought four extra tires in case of flats on the car and trailer, which happened to have the same kind of tires; we ended up using every one. Someone who had been on the Al-Can Highway suggested that we cut an inner tube in half and put it over the gas tank for protection. We did that too. Some of the seven of us rode in Paul's luxury vehicle, the rest in my $25 car. When we crossed the border into Canada, we picked up Steve, who was living in Toronto. It was a tight fit, but no one complained.

The trip to Johnson's Crossing, a truck stop at the headwaters of the Teslin River, was mostly uneventful. Saskatchewan is flat as a pancake, at least the southern part. When we stopped for a break, we thought we saw a tree on the horizon. As we drove along, the so-called tree turned out to be Saskatoon. The topography became more interesting as we traveled to Edmonton and approached the mountains in British Columbia. There, we stopped at a hot spring and relaxed in the bathwater-temperature water. Heading north, we crossed over into the Yukon Territory.

The road along Teslin Lake was spectacular, with snowcapped mountains on both sides. It was quite a drive, as we just kept changing drivers, driving twenty-four hours a day. There was a great restaurant at Johnson's Crossing, where the lake empties into the Teslin River. The steaks were large and juicy, served with great coffee, and delicious desserts.

After unloading the canoes, we needed to get our $25 car to Dawson so that we had transportation at the end of the trip. Tom and I were elected to drive to Dawson and planned to hitchhike back to Johnson's Crossing.

The drive to Dawson was uneventful. The old car tolerated the gravel road without any problems. We parked at the Royal Canadian Mounted Police lot and registered our trip, speculating how long the trip would take. I think they gave us a week's margin based on their experience with other canoe trips.

But then a problem erupted. Hitchhiking back to Johnson's Crossing was dependent on traffic. The problem was, there was no traffic. Tom and I waited at the edge of town for a day, and there was not a single car. We broke into a fistfight just to stay warm. No one was hurt.

There was a ferryboat crossing the Yukon River to the road leading to Alaska on the other side. To stay warm, we invited ourselves onto the boat, which had a heated interior, and entertained the ferryboat captain. He didn't charge us, as he got lonely at night and enjoyed the company. We crossed the river a dozen or more times that night. Trucks were crossing it going north, but no traffic was going south. So Tom and I decided that we should start walking. We thanked the captain and headed south.

I knew it was absurd. How long would it take to walk five hundred miles? But we could think of no other choice.

I think we walked more than ten miles before a truck stopped. The driver offered us a ride but told us truckers were not allowed to pick up hitchhikers. That meant he had to drop us off five miles outside of Carmacks because there were inspectors in town to check compliance with the rule. We were so thankful.

Five miles north of Carmacks, we got out. The trucker told us, "I'm stopping for lunch at the restaurant there. If you are at least five miles south of town when I leave, I will pick you up again."

It was a quick-paced ten-mile hike; we jogged part of the way. As we walked through Carmacks, we saw his truck was still parked at the restaurant. We couldn't afford the time to stop to eat; we quickened our pace to make sure we were out of town before the trucker finished his lunch. Sure enough, about five miles outside of town, he picked us up. We were so tired, but the driver was quite a conversationalist, so Tom and I took turns sleeping while the other kept himself awake to carry the conversation.

The next city was Whitehorse. He had warned us he would have to ditch us five miles before the city. So we thanked him, got out of the truck, and walked toward Whitehorse, not expecting another ride.

But another trucker stopped. He was from a different company that had no hitchhiker rule. This driver was Dutch and spoke very little English but made it clear he would pick us up if we paid for his dessert and coffee at a restaurant in Whitehorse. We got into the truck and pooled our money.

At the restaurant, he ordered coffee and pie. We had enough cash to buy his coffee and pie but only enough for coffee for ourselves. Refills were free. I emptied the sugar bowl and the cream pitcher into my three cups of coffee. I think Tom did the same. We hadn't had anything to eat for almost four days. Then we climbed into his truck, and true to his word, he dropped us off at Johnson's Crossing.

Our six friends were waiting. When they saw us, they started putting the canoes in the river. Tom said, "Can we have something to eat first?" There were some leftovers from their bountiful breakfast of fried eggs and potatoes, which we scarfed down. And then we left.

My diary documents that it was June 17. Years later, Daniel confessed he and the others had been planning to leave without Tom and me the next morning. They would graciously have left us a canoe to catch up. I'm thankful we arrived when we did. The others expressed no compassion for our trials, as they were irritated that we had taken so long.

We did take a picture with all of us before we left: Steve and I were partners, as were Mark and Tom; the others were Paul and Phil, Dave and Daniel. We decided it was safer to keep the same partners throughout the trip so that during rapids, we would know how our partner would respond. All packed up, we headed down the Teslin River. The wind was against us but the current compensated.

I won't bother with the daily details except to mention some highlights. The current was so strong that a powerful eddy current along the shore went upstream. With careful observation, we were able to discern the sudden change in the current. Crossing to the shore, the eddy jerked the canoe upstream. Anticipating it made the sudden shift less scary. "Don't fight it" was our rule. We saw more than thirty moose snacking on the reeds in the eddy currents along the Teslin River, grizzly bears scrounging for berries, eagles swooping for fish and various ducks squawking as we disturbed them. Each morning, we were greeted with sunshine glistening on the snowcapped peaks.

One problem with camping in the Yukon Territory is that in the summer, the proximity to the Arctic Circle results in almost constant daylight; it never gets dark. We stopped for lunch one day; dug Paul's watch, our only one, out of his pack; and discovered that it was 7:00 p.m. Discerning morning and evening, even what day it was, seemed quite arbitrary.

We were allowed to camp anywhere along the river, but often, we would pick an appealing spot only to discover others had camped there as well. We all have fond memories of one campsite. We camped at the confluence of the Teslin River with the Indian River for two reasons. First, there was a nice flat area, probably a floodplain from spring runoff. Second, there was an area marked as "uncharted" upstream. We were curious to hike to an uncharted area, just to see what was there. The campsite ended up being a great choice. The fishing was great, but only between 4:00 and 6:00 p.m. We caught an Arctic grayling in almost every cast. But we were puzzled as to how the fish knew the time. We fished in the same area with the same lures at other times and didn't catch a thing. But that helped us judge when we should have supper.

Our hike into uncharted territory was invigorating, as there was no trail. We hacked through brush and bounded over fallen trees. We scared up a moose who, by Paul's watch, completed the climb up the ridge in thirty seconds, which had taken us a half hour to climb. We crossed the crest of a hill and came upon a wolverine. We crossed the river on a fallen tree and were pelted with rain in the mountains. The uncharted area held a lake between two peaks with no apparent entrance or exit. Maybe it was spring fed or spring snow melted.

After our three-day hike in an uncharted area, we returned to camp along the Teslin River, needing a bath. We filled one of the canoes with water, adding clean, hot rocks, and all had a warm tub bath. Later, we made a frame of twigs, covered it with all our rain ponchos, and made a steam bath. Then we ran to the river and jumped in. Despite heating up in our steam bath, we were shocked by the chill of the water.

We had time to make some tasty pancakes for breakfast. Lunch on the river was usually trail mix that we passed around from canoe to canoe. For evening meals, we soaked our jerky, sliced it up, and added it to our pasta. It tasted great. Through the course of the trip, we kept our jerky dry. As a result, it never showed signs of spoilage. (Inform the county welfare department about that.)

The Teslin River flows into the Yukon River at a place marked on the map as Hootalinqua. We found the site a great place to camp and fish. I caught one northern pike that was so big I couldn't haul it in. We called for our partners fishing on shore to help us. I played the fish for what seemed like an hour. I finally pulled the tired monster alongside our canoe. Three in the other canoe came parallel to ours. While the bow and stern persons held the two canoes together, the person in the middle reached under the belly of the tired fish and flipped it into our canoe. We tried to weigh it, but our scale bottomed out at thirty-five pounds. All I can say is that from the tip of its nose to the gills was the same distance as across my shoulders. We stuffed it with rice. It fed eight of us for four days. Remember that the water temperature was so cold we could store things in containers and bury them along the riverbank without spoilage. Fortunately, no grizzly bears discovered our cache.

My diary notes we met two canoers, Tom and Stirling, at Hootalinqua and shared some meals together. They had come across Lake Laberge from Whitehorse. They were very disappointed at trying to reconcile the Robert Service poem with their observations on Lake Laberge. There was no derelict. We smiled at our decision to start on the Teslin River.

We met no other people canoeing the river the entire monthlong trip. A kayaker swept by, but he didn't stop.

Steve caught a pike and released it since we had plenty of fish to eat from my gigantic pike. He caught another, and it looked familiar to him. He threw it back. Caught another, and this time, he was sure that it was the same fish. He scratched a small X on its belly with a rusty nail. He caught the same fish ten times that day—or was it evening? Who knows, with no darkness.

Leaving Hootalinqua, we were now on the Yukon River. Some of those campsites were inspiring, especially with the abandoned cabins. Some cabins were still used by trappers; these were locked and in good repair. But others were clearly abandoned. When the Al-Can Highway was done being built in 1942, the riverboat made one last trip. Since there were mountains between the river and the highway, people had a choice: take the riverboat or be abandoned in the wilderness. It appeared from the state of the cabins we investigated that lots of people left in a rush. We found clothes and supplies left abandoned in many.

Another surprise was that the woodstoves in the abandoned cabins were quite functional. With Daniel's recipe book, flour, powdered eggs, and lard, we baked cakes and bread, plenty of tasty treats, including chocolate cake, bannock, and luscious pancakes.

We discovered rhubarb still growing luxuriously in abandoned gardens. We made rhubarb cake, rhubarb pie, and rhubarb sauce. The smell of baking pie was glorious. Of all our supplies, sugar was the only commodity we ran out of, primarily because we had not anticipated the delicacies made from rhubarb.

We tired of the constant daylight and discovered that the bedrooms in most of the abandoned cabins had no windows. We took turns sleeping in the bedrooms just to get away from the daylight to have more restful sleep.

Abandoned towns along the river—Big Salmon, Little Salmon, and Stewart—were always places to visit. They stimulated our curiosity. What must it have been like for the people who lived in these towns? I felt sad pondering what emotions prompted them to leave. Some of the towns had schools with the books still in the desks. Two- and three-room cabins often had dinner plates on the kitchen tables. All had left when the ferryboat arrived to take people out of the Yukon.

When we arrived at Carmacks, it was a breath of civilization. Each person planned to buy something because Tom and I had spoken of the grocery store and restaurant from when we walked by on our hitchhiking trip. My diary notes we indulged in blueberry pie and ice cream at the restaurant. Milk and candy were on the list of things to buy at the grocery store. The milk was a disappointment. There was a bottle, and we brought it to the counter to pay for it, at which the cashier frowned and said, "You don't look pregnant to me."

"What?" we murmured in unison.

"I only sell milk to pregnant women." He made us put it back in the cooler.

Steve was disappointed when the restaurant did not have any pecan pie on their menu, as he and I had planned to share a whole pie. We decided to swap it for ice cream back at the grocery store. As we searched the freezer for the ice cream, we discovered a frozen pecan pie. It was long outdated, so the cashier gave it to us at a discount. We thawed it out and ate the filling, which was tasty, although the crust tasted stale.

The main commodity we required was sugar, anticipating more rhubarb along the trip. The grocer was willing to sell it to us. We needed to make our purchases here because there were no more towns on the river, and as mentioned, the road diverted to the other side of a mountain range. The next civilization was Dawson, at the end of our trip.

Fort Selkirk was a surprise. The town was well cared for because Danny Roberts and his wife lived there. He was the only person we discovered still living along the river. We camped there for several days, enjoying the abandoned cabins, church buildings, and school that were well cared for. We discovered the graveyard of miniature houses over each grave.

Danny was quite hospitable and shared his life with us. He was Athabascan and had married a woman from his own clan, which was taboo. As a result, he was ostracized from his tribal band. The government paid him as caretaker of Fort Selkirk, which is why every building was intact, but he said that the payments had ceased. He and his wife lived off their garden, harvested berries, and hunted moose, and he caught salmon to feed their sled dogs. He explained the salmon that reached this part of the river were too decimated for human consumption, but the dogs loved them.

He seemed quite content with his lifestyle. He knew the benefits of native plants. For example, his wife harvested wild rose hips for vitamin C to prevent scurvy, a deficiency to which many gold miners succumbed. Too bad they didn't ask the Athabascans how to prevent the disease.

He took a trip to Dawson twice a year, once in the summer by boat and once in the winter by dogsled. I asked him while hunting if he ever got lost. He responded, "Lost from what?" He considered the wilderness his backyard.

One curiosity was a library book in the priest's study. I found it while milling through the books on the shelf in the back room of the Catholic chapel. It was thirty years overdue from the Dawson library. I took it with me and placed it in the library drop box in Dawson when we arrived at the end of our trip. I didn't want to take it into the library, as I was afraid that the librarian might ask me to pay the fine. I would have loved to have seen the librarian's face, though.

We enjoyed Danny's hospitality and camped in Fort Selkirk for several days. We took many pictures, including dressing Paul up in the Catholic priest's smock, "Father Fink." Afterward, we carefully hung it back up in the closet where we found it.

Eventually, we had to continue our voyage. We discovered more abandoned villages. One made me sad. We saw a well-made house amid a large grassy field from the river. Now grass is unusual in the Yukon, as it is an invasive species and must be imported. That made us curious enough to stop and check it out.

There was a large, empty barn next to the house. Entering the house, we found cotton dresses, plaid shirts, and coveralls and work pants neatly hung in the closet; canned goods on the shelves, thirty or forty years outdated; a bed complete with bedspread; and a bookshelf filled with books. Included on the shelf was a leather-bound diary. I read it out of curiosity. A family had moved here, cleared the land, planted grass and alfalfa, and then ordered a herd of cows. It seemed the cows did well that summer and the family was content. But the following winter was disastrous. Milk cows couldn't tolerate −60°F temperatures, and all their cattle died.

91

The last notation in the diary described the family, discouraged, having lost hope. The diary documented their decision to leave everything when the riverboat arrived. Investigating the condition of the farmhouse, shop, and barn, they did leave everything. Even though it had been forty years since the family left, I felt their tragedy.

We did not need to portage during the trip. We did run some rapids where the mile-wide river narrowed. They were fun and not particularly dangerous. The famous Five Finger Rapids were easy, mostly because the government had blown up one of the fingers, allowing a much smoother passage. The current was strong.

One afternoon, we were tired of paddling, tied the canoes together, and played cards. We traveled about fourteen miles without paddling a single stroke, so the current in that stretch of river must have been about seven miles per hour. The biggest problem was canoeing just outside the riverbank eddy current, so if we saw a nice camping area, we could get to it safely. If we saw something across the river, it was impossible to get there. We had to review our topographical maps and choose on which side of the river to paddle to find likely campsites.

Less than a day's paddle from Dawson, we found a large, flat, dry camping area. We were sorting, drying, and organizing our stuff from the previous day's heavy rain when a helicopter loomed over us and landed on the riverbank beside us. A forest ranger climbed out and asked if we had seen any fires. He explained that the Canadian government has the right to conscript campers to help fight forest fires, but we had seen no such thing. We described how careful we were to put out our campfires. He thanked us and flew off.

Unfortunately, our parchment topographical maps, laid out to dry, got sucked up into the rotors of the helicopter and shredded.

So, we now have no maps of our trip except my small-scale map that I had in my pack. It's displayed on my wall today. The loss of our maps caused no navigation problems since we were almost to Dawson.

On arriving in Dawson, Tom and I went to the ferry to tell Brian and Norman, the ferryboat captains, that we had made it. We enchanted them with some of our adventures. They were glad to see us and laughed at the miseries of the hitchhiking trip to Johnson's Crossing.

We visited the local museum, toured Robert Service's cabin, and used the local Laundromat. That evening, we ate at the Flora Dora smorgasbord. What a delight. With the car packed and ready to go to Whitehorse, we again met Tom and Stirling, who had pitched camp on Bonanza Creek. They invited us to join them for a few days. There, we met Mr. Fry, a prospector, who was sluicing the tailings left by the massive gold machines. He claimed to have made a living on the gold he recovered. In addition, he had put his daughter through college on the gold. He invited us to pan for gold, and sure enough, we each found gold flecks in every pan.

That evening, Mr. Fry invited us to join him, his wife, and his college-educated daughter, who was home visiting. We played cards, although I can't remember who won. We had a great time sharing stories, drinking tea and adult beverages, as well as arguing politics (he had communist leanings). We played until midnight, but of course, it wasn't dark.

The next morning, we invited Tom and Stirling to join us for breakfast. That year, Canadian Club did an advertising adventure hiding a case of Canadian Club in the Yukon. The clue was a birch tree. Since there is only one birch tree in the Yukon because it's a pine forest, and Mr. Fry knew where the lone birch tree was, Tom and Stirling found the case. The problem was, since they were from Boston, they could only cross the border back to the United States with two bottles each. What to do with the rest? They gave some to Mr. Fry and brought several bottles for breakfast. So, instead of adding only water to our pancake mix, we used Canadian Club, and we made Tang with Canadian Club, and we made maple syrup by adding maple extract to boiled Canadian Club. It was a breakfast that I will never forget.

After saying goodbye to the Frys and spending a few moments with Tom and Stirling, we all piled into the $25 car—three in the front, five in the back—and left for Whitehorse. Fifteen miles outside of town, we got a flat tire, but we had those four spares. When we got to Carmacks, we enjoyed blueberry pie and ice cream again.

Along the highway, we met a Volkswagen Beetle with a single man sitting in the driver's seat in tears. We stopped to see if he needed help. There was a big rock in the passenger's seat. He explained that an asbestos truck had passed him and flipped the rock through his windshield. When asked what it was like driving without a windshield, he replied, "Not a problem if you keep your mouth shut." Then we noticed that his beard was full of insects. There was nothing much we could do to help him, so we waved a tearful goodbye.

The crowded group was glad to drop off Dave and me at Whitehorse. Then there was more room in the car for the trip to Johnson's Crossing, where Paul had parked his truck. On to Duluth they drove with the accumulated wealth of our group to pay for gasoline. That was somewhat of a mistake for me on arriving in Seattle.

Dave and I had tickets to take the train through the mountains to Skagway along the trail of the 49ers. However, the train workers were on strike, so we were offered plane tickets to fly to Skagway at no additional cost. It was a bit of a disappointment because I wanted to see the historical pathway the miners traversed through the mountains.

## Return of the $25 Car

I wasn't involved in driving the car back to Duluth, so this narrative is according to Daniel's description of the events. The Al-Can Highway is hard on cars, so by the time they arrived at Johnson's Crossing, where Paul had parked his truck, the gravel had eroded through the floor behind the driver's seat. But at a stop along the road for a flat tire, they found a fine piece of plywood that just fit in place to block dust and rocks from hitting the passenger in the back seat.

Things went smoother on the pavement. I understand there weren't any remarkable incidents until they stopped at a stoplight in Saskatoon. There, the car's engine quit and wouldn't restart. By grace, there was a garage–gas station across the street. When the light turned green, with one person steering, the others were able to push the car and trailer with canoes and gear through the intersection and into the garage. Saskatoon is very flat.

They had no choice but to ask the mechanics to fix whatever was wrong so they could drive the rest of the way to Duluth. The mechanics said they would look the car over and told the crew to come back in four hours or so. I understand that they walked to a restaurant, had a good lunch, and wandered around town before heading back. When they approached the garage, they heard uproarious laughter. The car was still in the garage, and both mechanics were in the pit under the car, giggling. Daniel was concerned that the car still wasn't fixed and wondered how much it was going to cost and how long they would be stranded in Saskatoon. When the mechanics came out of the pit, and one of them said, "It will run. You might make it to Duluth," Daniel noted that the emphasis was on *might*.

After profuse thanks, Daniel asked the cost. "Oh, nothing," the mechanic said. "We took parts off junk cars in the scrapyard. Besides, the boss is gone today. We haven't had so much fun fixing a car in a long time."

The car started, and without further incident, they drove it until they reached the driveway at Daniel's house. But then, flames and smoke burst out from under the hood, melting all the electrical wires; the driver's seat fell into the hole behind it despite the plywood; and all the tires went flat. Daniel called a junk dealer, who hauled it away and gave him $25. The car was free.

## Dave and I Return to the United States

It turned out that our flight to Skagway followed the mountain pass of the 49ers' trail, so we got to see it from the air. But the train trip would have been more interesting. Disembarking from the plane, we had to go through customs as we entered the United States from Canada. The customs agents met us on the tarmac. I suppose we looked like a couple of criminals, having been in the wilderness for a month. They went through our packs, and the wind flew our clothes across the runway. Skagway, in Athabascan, means the "home of the wind." We ran after our clothes as the officials returned to the airport. No "welcome home" as they maintained a rude demeanor.

We met our ferryboat down the Inside Passage. Unlike a cruiseliner, a ferryboat does not feed you. Dave and I had only pocket change because we had given most of our money to Daniel for gasoline to drive the car home. There was a free water fountain on the ship, so we at least stayed hydrated.

There were no rooms available, but we were allowed to roll out our sleeping bags in the observation room when the customers with rooms left the lounge every evening. The scenery was magnificent. Observing the beauty as the ferryboat, the *Matanuska*, went down the Inside Passage quelled our hungry stomachs. When our stomachs gnawed at us, we went on deck to see the islands and waterfalls; whales, porpoises, and jellyfish following the ship; the magnificent forests drenched in daily rain; and fishing villages, home to First Nation peoples. As the lyrics from the music playing over the intercom said, "I got love in my tummy," we rubbed our hungry stomachs and laughed.

In a few days, we arrived in Prince Rupert at 6:00 a.m., after stops to let cars on and off in Juneau, Ketchikan, Wrangell, and other towns I don't remember. Our tickets said the ferry left Prince Rupert at noon. One small mistake in our understanding was that the ferry left at noon the next day. We asked if they would let us stay on the ship, but they wouldn't. Forced to leave, we had to decide what to do. It was five miles from the dock to town. We sat in a ditch along the road to decide.

### Time to Pray

We were very hungry after almost four days of no food. We decided to pray about our situation. Dave asked me, "What are you going to pray for?"

"I think we should camp along the road," I told him. "We can sleep under our raincoats. We should be all right if it doesn't rain. I'm praying that it doesn't rain." I finished my prayer and looked at Dave. "What are you going to pray for?"

Without the least hesitation, he said, "I'm going to pray for two suppers, a hot shower, and … two mattresses for our beds tonight."

"That is ridiculous, Dave! We'll see whose prayer is answered."

We got up out of the ditch. With more than a day before the ferry left, we decided to walk to town. Once in town, we visited the Tlingit museum. They had coppers from before European or Russian contact. I loved that museum. It was inspiring.

We walked around town until Dave spotted a Salvation Army store. He belonged to the Salvation Army in Duluth, so he wanted to visit the store. Clothes, household goods, and even tools were for sale, a typical Salvation Army store. Dave lit into a long conversation with the proprietor, an attractive young woman. She suggested that we tour the Salvation Army girls' school and gave us directions.

With nothing else to do, we walked to the girls' school and met the lieutenant, a delightful young woman, who gave us a nice tour. It turned out the girls were on summer break, so the school was empty of students. After the tour, she asked if we would like to stay for the night, to which we immediately agreed. But then she said we would have to be approved by the commander. She picked up the telephone and called him.

My heart sank. Bearded and disheveled in camping gear, what chance did we have of being approved?

"While you're waiting for him to come, would you like some supper?" she asked after hanging up the telephone. We blurted out an affirmative, trying to control our rumbling stomachs after four days with no food.

She fixed a nice supper for us while we took showers—our first since washing in the Yukon River. Clean and neat, we met some of her friends: Mr. and Mrs. Harvey, their ten-year-old son

David, and six-month-old Allen. The lieutenant was a cousin of Mr. Harvey's. They had taken their vacation to visit her.

After some formal discussion, we discovered that the Harveys just so happened to also be leaving on a ferryboat at noon the next day. Our hearts fell as they explained that the ferryboat would land on the north side of Vancouver Island. Our tickets to Seattle were for a ferry that left on the island's south end. We had no plans on how to cross the island. I understood the ferry went all the way to Vancouver. Our dilemma was solved when Mr. Harvey offered to take us to the southern landing since they planned to stay in Vancouver. Their car was booked on the ferry.

They then went out to explore the town for a while. Dave and I checked out the library. When the lieutenant returned, we still hadn't been approved by the commander. I was concerned, but not Dave.

The commander arrived about 9:00 p.m. and met with us. He was a massive man. He quizzed us on our theology and then was interested in Dave's involvement with the Duluth Salvation Army. I mostly kept quiet. After our interview, he requested that the lieutenant make him some supper. We joined him, still hungry. He approved of us, ate supper, and left.

The lieutenant apologized that the students' bedrooms were being remodeled. So, the mattresses from the rooms in process were piled on the beds yet to be remodeled. That meant we had two mattresses on our beds.

The next morning, we had pancakes and cornflakes for breakfast. As the Harveys did some last-minute packing, Dave and I did the dishes and cleaned up the kitchen. Then we went in the Harveys' car to the ferry. From Prince Rupert to Vancouver Island, Dave and I watched baby Allen. The Harveys were so grateful that they shared their food with us: fried chicken and cheese sandwiches.

Oh, and it rained that night. I am still chagrined that every part of Dave's prayer was answered and none of my prayers were.

The rest of the tale is benign. We rode with them to the dock for our ferry to Seattle. We thanked the Harvey family with hugs and tears in our eyes. The ferryboat ride to Seattle that evening displayed a vibrant autumn moon. People stepped away from us as we crooned, enjoying the developed darkness we hadn't experienced in the Yukon.

## Lost in Seattle

Arriving in Seattle, Dave found his family wired him some money, so he was set. We hugged, and he was off. I had about a dollar in change and felt lost in Seattle. Not to lose heart, I had a friend from high school, a Vietnam veteran named Neil, who was stationed on a military base in Tacoma. I had no idea how far Tacoma was from Seattle. I had only enough money to call him. So I did.

He said, "Seattle is a big place. Where should I meet you?"

I told him, "I've never been to Seattle before. I have no idea."

"Let's meet at the Greyhound bus depot, Stewart and Eighth Street, at midnight."

"All right. See you there."

I had no idea where I was, or how to get to the bus depot. I asked some people on the street and received some nonspecific directions. At 11:00 p.m., I still hadn't found it. The streets were empty of people except for an intoxicated fellow staggering down the street. I asked him.

He said, "If you help me get home, I will show you."

I held him up and half carried him as we wandered through the bowery. About a half hour later, we arrived at his door.

He said, "Down that alley, and you will see it."

He slipped inside his apartment, and I was left alone on the street. I followed his directions through the alley, and sure enough, turning to the left, and then right at the corner, there was the Greyhound bus depot. Praise God for a wonderful, intoxicated guide.

The bus depot was a safe place, and Neil arrived on time. I hugged him as tears streamed down my face. We had a great time together. We toured the military base and had delightful conversations about his military experience. We are still best friends.

Before he had to return to duty, he drove me to my grandparents' house in Salem, Oregon. My grandmother and I sat at the kitchen table munching on cookies while she advised me on marrying Priscilla. Grandfather took me on a tour of the rugged Oregon coastline as we traveled south to San Francisco to my Aunt Dorothy's house.

I enjoyed all the sights, sounds, and smells of San Francisco. I toured Golden Gate Park, my eyes delighting in the flower gardens. I ate at the Japanese Tea House. I smelled the fragrance of the fresh catch at Fisherman's Wharf. My uncle took me to a hole-in-the-wall Chinese restaurant where the exotic incense delighted me, and ginger flavored my supper.

Totally out of money, I called Priscilla to ask for money to fly home to Duluth. She sent me $300, which paid for my flight home. The Yukon trip was an adventure that solidified a sense of independence. I could survive four days with no food. I could canoe nine hundred miles and sleep under a canoe. I would always remember how prayer could be answered.

# 10

## CAMP VERMILION

As we finished our senior year at UMD, Tom, my hitchhiking partner from the Yukon trip, had applied for a job with Camp Vermilion as a canoe guide. Just before his interview with the director, Melvin Bakke, he accepted a full-time job as a counselor at the juvenile center. Since there were no jobs for chemists that spring, and since I was now married, I needed a job. Tom suggested that I take his interview slot.

There I was at the interview, without even applying for the job. Melvin was interested in my canoeing experience as well as my relationship with Jesus, since Camp Vermilion is a Bible-based camp. I threw in my father-in-law, Charles Fillmore. Melvin knew him since he lived in Cook, Minnesota, where the camp is located. I found out later that my relationship with Charlie was no advantage to my interview because Melvin and Charlie had some theological differences. Despite that, I got the job and Tom was delighted for my opportunity.

My canoeing skills matched the other guides', but I was humbled by their talents to sing, play the guitar, and show physical strength and athletic agility. Our orientation involved one week in camp to go over rules and policies. John Andreasen, the program director, reviewed the in-camp Bible study program. We were to enlist the same programming in the canoe-guiding trips.

Toward the end of the week, Melvin invited his friend Ira Ishim to tell Anishinabek stories. He was a fourth-degree Midewiwin, a member of the Nett Lake tribe,[4] and a federal marshal. He introduced himself and said that stories were supposed to be told from the first snowfall until maple syrup time in the spring, but since none of us were First Nation, he would give us special permission to tell stories to our campers during the summer. He claimed his stories preceded European contact. I researched his stories in subsequent years in the Boston library, the Minnesota Historical Society, and the National Museum of the American Indian and found them to be authentic and pre-European. I conglomerated them in my first novel, *Saving Skunk*. His stories were important to me because even though I couldn't sing, I could tell stories.

The other guides commented on my singing ability: "Don't sing. It ruins the campfires." We are still best friends despite their assessment.

The second week of orientation, we went on a canoe trip with Melvin. He took us over the Wicksteed Portage, as it is the worst portage in the BWCA and Quetico Provincial Park. You must climb up a steep bank with the canoe tilted upward. Arriving on the peak of the hill, you discover massive trees fallen over the trail followed by a walk through a mucky, mosquito-infested swamp. At the end of the mile-long trail, there is a thirty-foot cliff over which the canoes need to be lined. After the Wicksteed Portage, all other portages seem mild.

---

[4] He knew and respected Wahlberg Johnson.

Melvin reviewed policies on the trail, showed us a few good fishing spots, and did some demonstrations. He taught us to pack so that we went over the portage only once, almost a rule. At lunch one day, he told me and my canoeing partner (I forget who my partner was) to purposely flip our canoe to see how the other guides responded in an emergency. They responded well, according to Melvin's instructions, and we were quickly rescued. Back on shore, we reviewed the event and practiced lifesaving skills, including first aid applications.

Melvin observed and confirmed that each guide knew how to cook and care for the food packs. Priscilla was one of the food packers, so each meal was labeled to name the meal and the day of the trip. There was an extra pack, but only the guides knew that the bag labeled "fish breading" was pancake batter in case the group did not catch any fish. Also, we learned how Melvin wanted the food packs set up so that bears didn't ruin things.

What humbled me was that some of the guides could double-pack or could carry a pack and a canoe, including some of the women guides, and then they would run over the portages. I sometimes felt like the weakest link in the canoe guide chain. Melvin told me I chopped wood "like an old woman." But I could tell stories, and the other guides loved them and claimed they couldn't tell stories like I did. So that became my strength, and vindicated my group participation. That week on the trail, we bonded as a group.

Much of our orientation was taking care of the canoes. We were not allowed to drag the canoes up the beach or hit the shore, unless it was sand. Ira had told us that with birchbark canoes, the Anishinabek would get out in waist-deep water to avoid damaging them. Melvin didn't make us go to that extreme. We had Grumman aluminum canoes, seventy-five pounds, which were lighter than Alumacraft, which weighed ninety-five pounds because of the additional bulk of aluminum on the bow and stern to counter abuse. One absolute rule was invaluable: while loading a canoe, someone had to sit on the bow or the stern to stabilize it. If I had known that, my father would never have flipped our canoe and ruined the motor.

Not only did the orientation teach us what Melvin wanted us to do, but it prepared us to instruct each group of campers. We had to be teachers as well as learners. Back in camp, we reviewed the rules with each other, taking turns being obstreperous campers and instructive guides. By the end of the two-week orientation, we were ready.

I didn't anticipate the most difficult part of camper orientation: explaining what campers should not bring. We were instructed to go through each camper's personal pack and remove things that were either dangerous or unneeded. For example, no food treats were allowed in the tents at night. If a camper brought treats, they had to put them in the food pack. This was a critical safety issue. Candy bars in a tent invite bears. Bears are after food, but campers can become mauled in the search.

Going through personal packs, I removed hair dryers (I have no idea where they thought they could plug them in). Some campers brought too many clothes. Switchblades, saws, and additional axes, usually brought by boy scouts, were not needed. The camp supplied knives and hatchets. In terms of what they should bring, everyone needed a raincoat; guides were required to make sure each camper had one. BWCA and Quetico are classified as rainforests, so storms are expected. I always checked that each brought an adequate sleeping bag. Camp Vermilion provided tents.

It was a year of legends and miracles. I can't relate too many details of the trips of other guides, as those are their stories, but two episodes I will relate.

On one trip, a bear ruined the food pack the first night of a group's trip. The guide related that the group had to decide whether to continue or return to the landing and call Melvin[5] since they were only one day into their trip. They prayed, asked God to provide, and decided to continue. The next lake they portaged into provided a surplus of fish every day, and they never went hungry. Upon their return, they told the other guides about the fishing experience. Several of the guides took their groups through the same lake, but all summer, no one ever caught a fish in that lake again.

On another trip, a guide reported that their campers lost all their lures on snags. They met a fisherman angling at Curtain Falls and asked if they could buy some of his, as they had money but no lures. He refused. When he learned that they were from a Bible camp, he scoffed at them and said, "Pray for a fish." They knelt around him and prayed for a fish. He was still laughing at them as they continued down the portage.

At the end of the portage, one of the boys saw a fish swimming in the shallow water. He yelled, "There is the fish the Lord sent us!" and then jumped in the water and scooped out the fish with his bare hands. It was a huge northern pike. There was more than enough meat for the entire group, plus fish to share. When the nasty fisherman smelled the fish frying, his curiosity caused him to paddle over to their camp. He hadn't caught a single fish all day. He was quite humbled as he feasted on their leftovers.

---

[5] This would have required the guide to hitchhike to town. There were no cell phones in those days.

## The Unlikely Leader

One of my trips included a quarterback from his school's football team. He was quite a domineering young man. He was resistant to following camp rules and decided that he needed to be the self-appointed leader. The quarterback, with much bravado, showed everyone how great he was at portaging a canoe and paddled ahead of the group. In the BWCA, it is a very important policy for a group to stay together. I told him several times to wait up for the rest of us. Several times, he was off in the wrong bay, and if someone needed help, he was unavailable.

Another camper on the trip was a petite young woman, Julie. She barely weighed a hundred pounds and had a gentle, servile spirit. The group assigned her the lightest pack. She would race across the portages and then return along the trail to help the others with fishing poles and paddles, as well as encourage the rest of the group. Once in camp, Julie initiated setting up the tents, helped with meals, and cleaned up even when she wasn't assigned to those tasks. By the end of the first day, Julie was the new leader.

Several of the girls and some of the guys said to the quarterback, "You never help us with anything. Why should we do what you say?" The rest of the trip, when decisions needed to be made, they would ask, "What does Julie want to do?" In time, the demoted quarterback started helping; I even heard him ask Julie how he could help.

Months later, I learned that back in school and at her neighborhood church, Julie had become the group Bible study leader because of her humble and encouraging attitude. The quarterback even joined the group and started attending Julie's church, which he had never done before.

107

## *The Ungrateful Sponsor*

Each group was supposed to have an adult sponsor, who was usually a pastor or an assistant pastor from the sponsoring church. Most were very helpful because they knew the campers and could head off problems before they became serious. The guides relied on them for group cohesiveness and participation in the evening discussion around the campfire. Several played the guitar, which compensated for my inadequacies.

There were rare exceptions. If the adult sponsor considered the trip their personal vacation, then they tended to be a hindrance rather than a help. One adult sponsor, the assistant pastor of a large church, was constantly complaining even though I heard no complaints from the campers. He didn't like the campsite, the fish weren't biting, there were too many mosquitoes, and the food was tasteless. I took him aside and tried to talk to him, but there was no improvement. He related that he resented the church council's decision to dock him vacation time to go on this trip.

One night, it rained hard. Water got into the tents. The next morning, the potty box built on the highest point of our campsite was surrounded by water, a literal island, so the campers portaged the canoe inland to pole over to the toilet. Because the morning was bright and sunny, we spent it laying wet things on the rocks to dry out.

The assistant pastor started complaining to me, "You sure picked a lousy campsite."

One of the teenage girls overheard him and confronted him. "Don't you know how to be thankful? Have you read Philippians lately? Don't you see how this whole trip has been planned by God to teach us? We have all matured so much from this experience. What about you?"

He was dumb before her.

I later learned that he apologized to the whole group and started reading his Bible afterward. Imagine a pastor who had not read his Bible in years. The young lady who confronted him that day told me later that his sermons improved a lot as well. I was thankful for her intervention because I had no idea how to deal with him.

## The Four Nurses

So many other wonderful things happened while guiding trips for Camp Vermilion. Lives were changed, leadership developed, and self-esteem renewed. One group was unusual. Melvin knew that I had worked as a hospital orderly for years before, so when he received a request of four nurses, he assigned this group to me. The four nurses had just graduated from the University of Minnesota School of Nursing. They were best friends and wanted to do something together before they parted for employment. One had a job in Seattle, one in Arizona, and I forget where the other two had job offers, but only one stayed in Minneapolis.

When they arrived at camp, I was surprised to meet a young man whom they brought with them. From a guide's perspective, he made the trip easier because now there were six of us. With two canoes, someone could duff in each canoe, or in three canoes, each person would be paddling. They decided two canoes was enough.

He was not a nurse, so I was curious why he was invited to join them. The nurses laughed at me when I asked. They introduced him. He was a young homeless fellow from Minneapolis. They had cared for him as a patient and asked if he would like to join them on a canoe trip. Now, what young fellow could refuse camping in the wilderness for a week with four attractive nurses offering to pay all his expenses when he had no place to live?

The nurses later confessed that they had ulterior motives. They brought him along because they did not want to portage a canoe. If I portaged one canoe and he portaged the other, the nurses wouldn't have to. He had no wilderness experience. He had never traveled outside the confines of Minneapolis. But he was enthusiastic to learn new things; he even asked me to teach him camping skills. He was most excited about portaging the canoe. It didn't matter how long or gruesome the trail was. Once he developed the technique of flipping the canoe and balancing it on his shoulders, he was off. Then he would run back to see if any of his sponsoring nurses needed his help. He set up the tents, assisted with meal preparations, and loved the Bible study each morning. He had never been inside a church.

It was a fun trip, even relaxing for me. However, every evening, we had a "sick call." I was amazed how the nurses skinned themselves, bruised themselves, and cut themselves. My orderly skills working in the emergency department certainly came in handy. I had never cared for so many minor injuries on any other trip.

The following year, the nurse who moved to Seattle invited Priscilla and me to visit her on our vacation out west. We stayed at her apartment for a night. She told stories that enriched my understanding of her compassion as she described some of the patients for whom she cared. We even met one of her patients to whom she provided home visits.

The Arizona nurse invited us for a traditional Navajo Christmas meal: mutton stew! She laughed at our reaction as she explained, "This is what Navajo always eat for Christmas." She worked on reservations for most of her career.

The Minneapolis nurse related that their homeless friend had found a job and an apartment. He even attended church with her. But most remarkable was that he discovered a canoe rental on Lake Nokomis in Minneapolis. He rented a canoe and portaged it all around the lake and then returned it. He never put it in the water. The trip clearly changed his life.

## Miss Teenage Kansas

I never guided any famous celebrities that I know of, although Melvin sent me out with a photographer to take some advertising pictures for Camp Vermilion. Since his focus was capturing great pictures, he was up at first light and took off in the evenings to capture the light of dusk. Of course, I was obligated to accompany him wherever he wanted to go.

His intensity climaxed when we found a lady's slipper, Minnesota's state flower, in a swamp beside a portage. He lay down in the mud beside the flower to get the right angle. I think it took him about a half hour to get just the right view. He seemed oblivious to the mosquitoes, which took him for an opportunity, despite repellent.

That evening, I gave him some Benadryl to take down the swelling in his face. His eyes were so swollen he couldn't focus his camera. By morning, the swelling was down. The medication had provoked a good night's sleep, but he was upset that he missed the early morning light.

My only other celebrity was Miss Teenage Kansas, who came with a group from Overland Park Lutheran Church. She was a very attractive, sweet young woman, but she was aware of her beauty. When we set out on a nice, sunny day, she chose to wear a tiny bikini, which was fine while paddling, but as we approached Bottle

Portage, I warned everyone that every mosquito in Minnesota had a relative living in this portage. Even the French voyageurs in the seventeenth century documented the misery of the mosquitoes on Bottle Portage. I warned the campers, "Please, wear long pants and long-sleeve shirts on this portage. Douse up with mosquito repellent." I shouldered a canoe and ran down the portage as the campers dug out their protective outfits and mosquito repellent.

After depositing the canoe at the end of the portage, I ran back to see who needed help. Miss Teenage Kansas had chosen to ignore my advice. There was a cloud of mosquitoes hovering around her. She was screaming with bites. I rushed her to the end of the portage and sent her swimming in the cold water to alleviate the itching.

Much to the boys' disappointment, she swelled up with massive histamine reactions over her exposed skin. Despite maximum-dose Benadryl, she remained swollen and unattractive the remainder of the week. The cold water was soothing, but she even swam fully clothed the rest of the trip.

Two full years Priscilla and I worked for Camp Vermilion. Priscilla worked in the food shack, packing the food for the trips while I guided. We saw lives changed and confidence won among the campers who saw God's hand at work in their wilderness experience. It was an experience that we still treasure.

## My Most Miserable Trip

I guided one miserable canoe trip. The group was supposed to be from a church in Appleton, Wisconsin. Many of the church members invited their friends. That was good. However, all the church youth canceled, including the adult sponsor. All their friends showed up at camp, but not a single church member who had invited them. None of the group had ever entered a church.

I knew there was trouble from the start. They refused to let me go through their packs and were inattentive to the orientation. The guys demonstrated a lot of bravado, and the girls were fawning over them like bees to honey, rather than listening to my instructions.

Melvin brought us to the landing and remarked that he heard more profanity coming from the back of their van than he heard from loggers. We unloaded the canoes and gear. Melvin left me with a warning: "This group is trouble."

At the end of the first portage, a case of beer erupted from one of the guys' packs. The whole underage group cheered. Somehow, by God's grace, I convinced them that we should save the beer for Friday night. They agreed. The beer was in a small, pressurized aluminum tank.

The portage took forever amid cries of "I'm tired," "This is too hard," and "When will we get to the campsite?" We did find a nice campsite. But no one wanted to help set up camp, complaining, "That's what we pay you for."

I countered that comment, saying, "This trip is supposed to teach you camping skills."

With much griping, they finally got the tents up and started supper. If they hadn't put up the tents, I was going to sleep under one of the canoes, which I had done the entire month on the Yukon. One of the boys caught a nice walleye. I skinned it and prepared the filets. One of the girls offered to fry it. It got a bit overdone on one side, so she exclaimed, "It's burnt! It's ruined!" and threw the whole fish in the lake.

My blood surged with wild anger. I took a deep breath and counted to ten before I spoke. "With that attitude, you will never catch another fish." I turned my back to the group, walked into the woods, and prayed. "God, are You going to honor my prophecy? I know it was rash, but that fish was a gift from You."

All week, they caught fish but could never land one. By God's grace, He honored my rash statement.

All of that happened on the first day. That night, I wanted to make sure none of the boys decided to cavort with the girls in the woods, so I stayed up until everyone was asleep. I decided to read Exodus for personal strength, since Moses had gone through the wilderness with a rebellious bunch. It calmed me and kept me from losing my temper. I gained tremendous insight into Moses's struggles.

The next morning, the campers took an inordinate amount of time to pack up camp. Nobody wanted to help make breakfast or pack up the tents or the packs. Conditioned from the Yukon trip, I could tolerate going hungry for four days, no problem. I decided to instruct them but not do it for them. The only problem was we had to be at the landing by Saturday morning for Melvin to pick us up. I recall it was almost noon before we were ready to go. They wanted to eat lunch before we left camp, but I said they would have to wait until we crossed the first portage. I made sure the food pack was in my canoe. It was amazing how well they paddled and portaged, anticipating the lunch Priscilla had packed: Snickers bars, hardtack, and peanut butter and jelly.

At the beginning of the first portage that day, they left the beer. I always circle back to make sure nothing essential is left, like paddles. The keg sat there on a rock, so with no one around, I sampled it. It was beer, all right, and to this day, I do not like U.S. beer. I left it on the rock, good riddance. But off in the woods, I heard one of the boys yell, "We forgot the beer!" To my dismay, he came back for it.

My new rule of eating lunch on the other side of the portage had excellent results, but there was still rebellious chaos setting up the tents, making meals, and doing dishes. I presumed that they were learning some skills, but it was a constant challenge.

I was exhausted, staying up each night to guard the girls and getting up early to pray for patience and wisdom. Somehow, we made it to Lower Basswood Falls on Wednesday night. It's a nice waterfall next to a white sand beach, but the campsite beside the falls is in Canada, and we did not have a Canadian camping permit. The falls is the border between the United States and Canada, so there are several nice campsites twenty yards away on U.S. islands. Besides, the BWCA sites have potty boxes; the Canadian sites do not. I shoved off with my canoe partner to find a U.S. campsite.

As I shoved off, the others gathered on the shore, protesting, "We aren't leaving! This site is perfect."

"This campsite is in Canada. We could be fined if the Canadian ranger finds us here. Besides, there is no potty box," I said, all to no avail, and I was too exhausted to argue any more.

Thursday morning, I explained that Upper Basswood Falls was even more beautiful. "We should pack up to go see it."

Rebellion broke out! Two girls and one guy wanted to see the falls. The rest refused. "We're too tired." Despite arguing, the stay-at-camp group was adamant, refusing to leave, and the go-see-the-waterfall group was just as adamant.

In the chaos, I made a bad decision. I took the three to see the waterfall against my better judgment and camp policy. I called it a "day trip." I corralled the stay-at-camp group and told them, "You can stay on one condition."

"Which is?" There was a snarl of sarcasm in their response.

"If it gets dark before we return, build a fire on this beach." They agreed, and we set off. I was secretly hoping that the Canadian ranger might come, fine them, and force the stay-at-camp group off the campsite.

Without packs and short portages, we arrived at the waterfall in record time. It is a lovely waterfall with multiple cascades. The waterfall group members were not impressed.

Leaving the falls, there is a horseshoe in the river. It has violent rapids and even a waterfall. A sign hangs over the river: "Dangerous Waters." The portage is where the horseshoe comes together, avoiding all the dangerous waters. However, the current is strong. I was paddling with the guy while the two girls went ahead in the other canoe. Before I could catch up with them, they got caught in the current. I needed to stay with them, so I headed into the dangerous waters.

I convinced them to head for the shore on the left, which they did. But the current was too strong to get back to the portage. I took a deep breath and told them to get out of the canoe and walk it along the cliff until they were past the dangerous rapids. Amazingly, they did it just like I told them until they were in the calm water below the rapids.

It was our turn. The guy and I got out of the canoe and began walking it along as the girls had done. I held the stern, and the young lad held the bow. We walked along the cliff, but he lost his footing. I held the canoe so he could regain his balance, but he panicked and jumped into the canoe. I lost my grip on the cliff wall, and we were off down the rapids. He lay flat in the bottom of the canoe, panic stricken. I had to decide whether to trail along in the water beside the canoe or jump in as well.

I jumped in and knelt in the stern, lowering the center of gravity but still trying to direct the canoe with my paddle. We headed straight for the massive rock in the middle of the rapids. I could envision a bent, shattered canoe and a search for my lost camper.

Just as we were to hit the boulder, the canoe turned sideways and skirted the rock. We never touched it. Soon, we found ourselves in the calm at the base of the rapids. I congratulated the girls on following my instructions and calmed the fears of my companion.

That was the right-hand side of the horseshoe as one faces north. The rest of the rapids were not nearly so dangerous; in fact, I can't even remember what they were like. I probably have post-traumatic amnesia. The problem remained that when we finished the horseshoe, there were still several portages back to camp, and the horseshoe rapids had taken so much time that it was getting dark. By God's grace, I found the last portage in complete darkness, noting the dip in the tree horizon by the light of stars, no moon.

To my joy, the stay-at-camp group had built a large fire on the beach. We paddled straight toward the fire and did not get into the current over the falls. The stay-at-camp group was all excited about the girls' adventures. I overheard them say, "The waterfall was nothing, but the rapids were so exciting!"

I gathered the group together. We were supposed to have a devotional Bible study every night. I was too exhausted to give my planned talk, so I settled them down and said, "Knowing Jesus Christ is more exciting than shooting rapids." Done, end of devotions, and I sent them all to their tents.

That next morning, the group reminded me it was Friday and I had promised them they could drink the beer on Friday night to celebrate. When no one was looking, I took a sip. Yes, it was beer. "Lord," I prayed, "what am I going to do?"

We headed south toward Horse Lake for our final campsite. It is a beautiful site with plenty of flat areas for tents and a white sand beach. In fact, it is so popular that last time I was in Horse Lake, the U.S. Forest Service had closed it due to overuse. A small,

117

meandering stream leads to it, so it would be a pleasant day despite getting off late, as no one wanted to leave the Canadian campsite. I promised that the next campsite was even better. That and the beer motivated them.

I should have packed the beer in my canoe—another mistake. As soon as we entered the northern part of the lake, they saw the campsite on the south side. With yells of "Beer party!" they took off. As hard as I paddled, I could not keep up. They landed and pulled out the aluminum keg. They grabbed cups from the food pack and started pouring. One of the most obnoxious guys yelled, "It's nothing but water!" as my canoe hit the beach.

I shook the keg. It was still full. And I had sampled it twice; it had been beer, and there is no way to fill a pressurized aluminum keg. They were dumbfounded. I told them the story of Jesus turning water to wine and said, "Jesus can turn beer into water too." So much for Bible study that night.

They did enjoy the camp, enjoyed swimming, and we had a good supper of pancakes (recall no fish landed, but the fish batter was pancake batter). The next morning, they were in a hurry to get back home, so they were efficient in packing and paddling. We had about a two-hour paddle to the landing. Sitting in my canoe was one of the more attractive young ladies, who turned to me and said, "All week, we have been trying to make you mad, but we never did. Everyone is impressed."

We landed about thirty minutes later, and Melvin was there to pick us up. Listening to the profane conversation in the back of the van, Melvin turned to me and said, "I don't see any change in them at all. Meet me for supper."

Eating supper with Melvin in his private dining room was a disciplinary measure, not a privilege. I don't think I ate much. I described the whole trip and confessed all my sins. I think he was ready to fire me except he knew the complexion of the group and I had brought everyone home safely despite breaking camp rules. Also, he was mystified by the beer turning to water.

That was the end of my second year of guiding. It sure ended on a sour note.

That fall, I was accepted into medical school. I expected to never guide another canoe trip. But we had a school break the next spring that coincided with orientation for the new guides, and Melvin asked me to come one morning at the end of orientation to tell some of Ira's stories and discuss first aid. After I finished, Melvin thanked me, said that I did a good job, and offered lunch in the camp cafeteria as payment. I was going to decline, but Priscilla thought that we should stay, so we did.

We had just finished our food and stood to leave when a canoe group crashed into the cafeteria. A young, attractive girl ran up to me and started hugging and kissing me. Behind the girl's back, Priscilla mouthed, "Who is this?" I mouthed back, "I don't know."

The young girl grabbed my shoulders and said, "You don't recognize me, do you?"

"No," I admitted.

"Do you remember the girl who told you that we were trying to make you mad?"

My jaw dropped. I was speechless as I recognized her. We sat back down at the table. The whole group joined us there as she related her story. "We went home after the trip and things were bad at home for me and bad at school. I started drinking and popping pills. My parents were so ashamed of me that they went on a Christmas holiday and refused to take me with them.

"One of the other girls from the trip," she said as she pointed at the other girl from across the table, whom I didn't recognize either, "is my best friend. We partied together, but it was all worthless, so we decided to commit suicide together. We gathered all my parents' pills from the medicine cabinet, grabbed a bottle of whiskey, and headed for the attic."

Priscilla and I sat there dumb as she described everything they had tried. "Nothing was satisfying. Then I noticed a big white book sitting on the floor in the attic. It was the Bible from my parents' wedding ceremony. I didn't remember ever seeing it before. I grabbed it and told my friend, 'Remember on the canoe trip our guide said that knowing Jesus was more exciting than going down rapids? Let's check this out before we say that we tried everything.'"

They started at Matthew and read all the way through the gospel of John. They both decided to commit their lives to Jesus. "After that," she said, "my life was totally changed. My parents noted the difference right away, as I was respectful and obedient." She laughed. "I had never been like that before."

Back in school, her friends who had gone with her on the canoe trip noticed a difference. After she told them about that night in the attic, one after another became Christians. All their lives were changed. Even the teachers and the school principal noticed a difference.

She gave me another hug. "So I suppose you are wondering what we are doing here." I nodded, speechless. "We want to go on another canoe trip as Christians since we now have a relationship with the Creator." Everyone from that previous group was there. They all said that the change in her had made them curious about what it was like to know Jesus. It was thrilling to meet them again. It was worth the trauma!

## *Winter Reunion*

As canoe guides, we had become quite a close group. We decided one Christmas break to have a canoe guide reunion. We met at Camp Vermilion and decided that we should snowshoe into the BWCA on a winter campout. Permits are not needed and group size is not limited in the winter. We were quite a group, canoe guides plus a few other Camp Vermilion employees. We packed our gear on toboggans, and everyone had cross-country skis. The snow was deep, so two or three lead people used snowshoes to pat down the trail. Then it was easy to ski on the packed snow. We took turns snowshoeing because it was exhausting.

Finding a campsite in winter is the exact opposite of summer. In the summer, camping on a windy point is ideal because it ensures mosquitoes are blown away. But in winter, hiding the camp among a deep tree grove is warmer. We brought an old canvas tent, which we set up in an area after sweeping away the snow and covering the ground with pine boughs. Then we packed snow halfway up the sides of the tent for insulation. The Anishinabek did that. Inside the canvas tent, we set up another tent so there was airspace between the two tents. Foam mats under our sleeping bags made for a comfortable bed. I would guess that it was about 50 degrees at night inside the second tent with body heat and all that insulation.

Cooking was easy, as we had packed our meals in boil-in-a-bag containers. All we needed was a pot of boiling water, and each person selected the labeled meal they wanted. We had everything from spaghetti to meatloaf. Then, when everyone retrieved their supper bag, we made hot drinks from the boiling water: coffee, tea, or hot chocolate. Breakfast was equally easy: oatmeal. For snacks, we made an interesting discovery: frozen oranges are easy to peel and taste great. Don't thaw them out first, though; then they become bitter.

We went for day hikes and learned an important lesson: don't let your feet get warm enough to sweat, because then they will freeze when you stop. Pace yourself so that your feet are just slightly cool. Then no problem.

On one of our hikes, we came upon a frozen waterfall, which we were able to climb. What a sensation to feel the vibration of the water coursing under the ice. I know now that climbing frozen waterfalls is dangerous, but I didn't know that then.

Winter camping involves two things: staying warm and eating. These two things consume most of your day. It wasn't until we returned from our trip that we discovered the temperature had dropped to 35 degrees below zero while we were camping. Even so, it was comfortable in our tent.

We had one problem. One of the girls stopped drinking any fluids because she didn't want to bare her butt to the cold to urinate. Bad decision. One morning, we found her feverish and complaining of severe belly pain. Since I was an orderly in the ED, I was asked to examine her. She had suprapubic tenderness. I suspected an infected bladder. We forced her to drink gallons of Tang, as Tang is acetic and acidifies one's urine, besides the volume of fluids. One of the other women in the group escorted her on urination trips. By evening, she was feeling much better. When we returned from the trip, she went to her physician and found that she had almost resolved her urinary tract infection.

We learned a lot about winter camping and developed new survival skills. The boys had a pee-man-ship contest to see who could write their name in the snow while urinating. Yes, in cursive. Those with shorter names won.

It snowed while we were camping, which was disappointing

because we expected to cross-country ski on our snowshoe-packed trail back to our vehicles. With the added snow, we had to use snowshoes again to blaze a trail, although it was easier this time. The trip was an exhilarating experience none of us forgot.

We did have one other canoe guide reunion. One of the couples was expecting a baby, so we all got together for a baby shower. It was great fun. Not many baby showers have a mixed group of men and women, but this one had about an equal batch. It was winter, of course, and the home where we had the party had a sauna. We had a great time in the sauna and then scooted out the door to roll in the snow, then quickly returned to the sauna. Then we all joined in the living room to play the games associated with baby showers. The men won all the games, so the women said we would never be invited to a baby shower, ever again. It is true, none of us guys have ever been invited to another baby shower in fifty years.

Recently, we have had two more reunions. We are all older, in our seventies, but still great friends. I did my last canoe trip in 2015. Many of my guide friends continue to take trips. We feel at home in the wilderness.

## Other Canoe Trips

I thought that season of my life was over after leaving Camp Vermilion, but it wasn't. After medical school and residency in Michigan, I joined a medical group in Berrien Springs, Michigan. There, I had the privilege of working with Five Pines Christian Family Center, who wanted to expand their program to include canoe trips. Priscilla showed the Five Pines personnel how to pack the food, and I guided several trips to orient the counselors who would be guides. I always laughed when returning to the BWCA. After nearly a decade, the rocks and portages hadn't moved. I explored some Michigan rivers as well: Dowagiac Creek, Manistee River, and Pine River. They seemed tame compared to BWCA and Quetico Provincial Park, but they were fun.

## Dave's Trips

I developed a close relationship with Dave Flagler, MD, during residency in Kalamazoo, Michigan, as he had trained in Minnesota. When I moved to Duluth to do occupational medicine for St. Luke's Hospital, he asked me to guide several canoe trips for him. I guided him and some of his friends on several trips.

One trip, Dave took his family. I helped set up their route, but I didn't have the time off to accompany them. They decided to pack their own food because they didn't want to bother Priscilla. Unfortunately, each member of the trip wanted to pack their own food. The result was chaos, as the many packs of individual food required multiple trips over the portage trails.

At the end of the trip, they stopped at our house to tell Priscilla and me about their adventures. They repacked for the drive home to Michigan and left all their extra food. Priscilla and I fed for a whole month on what they left behind, which was great for our food budget, but carrying all that unnecessary food across portages had been awfully hard on their shoulders. After that experience, Dave always asked Priscilla to pack the food and told the rest of their crew that they were not allowed to bring anything extra. He also arranged it so that their trip matched my schedule and I could guide them.

I met some interesting characters guiding trips with Dave and his friends. Two were nuclear engineers with PhDs in physics; that made for interesting conversations around the campfire. They explained how atoms were put together as we watched the sparks of the burning logs fly upward. All the physical chemistry and physics that I struggled with in college seemed so easy to them. They even answered the question that I remembered from my physics class's final exam: "Describe the wave motion of a train." I don't think I completely understood the answer, but I learned that trains have wave motion.

Another canoeing companion of Dave's was an engineer with a PhD who emigrated from Turkey and designed the fins on semi tractors that laminate airflow and decrease wind resistance, or something like that. He had a great personality and was a fun companion.

One person who Dave invited on one of his canoe trips was a thorn in his flesh. Bob was an investment counselor who was sure he knew everything. Right from the start of the trip, he decided that he was going to teach Dave how to fish. He demonstrated his fine collection of expensive lures and fishing rods before we even set out on the water. He belittled Dave's equipment and skills and wouldn't let up.

I've never been impressed with fancy lures because my brother Bill won the Island Lake Fishing Contest with fifty-cent jigs, and I've caught plenty of fish in the Yukon with rusty Dardevles.

The first day, I did not plan on fishing, as I wanted to get to our chosen campsite. I was not surprised that we caught nothing dragging a few lines behind the canoes. But the second day, I planned a more casual route so the group could spend time fishing. We stopped early in the afternoon on a small lake with a delightful island campsite. Bob was quick to take advantage of the fishing opportunity. He told Dave, "I have all the best equipment, so I'll go catch some fish for supper. You don't know what you're doing with a fishing rod, so you set up camp and fix the rest of supper."

With that, he picked a partner, and off he went to fish in the lake. The remaining two engineers laughed as Bob left, but since all were Dave's guests, he humbly agreed to set up camp and prepare supper. The two engineers set off fishing in the second canoe.

Dave and I finished setting up camp, rolled out everyone's sleeping bags in their tents, and started a smoldering fire for supper. He made instant pudding for dessert and set it in the lake with a stone on top to cool. We worked together to cook macaroni and cheese, as no one seemed to care if it was hot or cold. It was still early as we sat down on a log to mull over the day. Dave was disheartened by the way Bob had treated him.

I looked out over the lake. Now, most lakes in the BWCA are just wide spots in river flow. This lake was no exception. It had a significant current flowing past our island, and I noticed a small pencil-shaped rock island just off our camp. There were eddy currents that swirled around it.

"Dave, do you want to go fishing?" I asked him. "We won't eat supper until they return." He agreed as he picked up his minimal, inexpensive gear. I chose a small, rusted Dardevles from his assortment of lures, and off we went.

Dave was in the bow to fish, and I was in the stern to control the canoe. Canoeing over to the small adjacent island, which was maybe twenty yards from our camp, I instructed Dave to drop his lure till it hit the bottom. Then I paddled the canoe into the current. His lure dragged on the bottom until it fell off a drop. A walleye grabbed his lure. We repeated the procedure, and every time his lure hit the drop-off, he had a fish. He was laughing so hard I thought he would flip the canoe. When we had enough fish for the six of us to eat for supper, we released the others. I think we quit because his arm was tired.

Back at camp, we cleaned the fish and started frying them.

The smell was intoxicating. In the light of early dusk, we saw the two canoes heading back. A few yards from shore, Bob yelled, "I don't think this lake has any fish. I didn't even get a bite." But beaching the canoe, he smelled the fish cooking. "Where did you get those fish?"

"Dave caught them," I said.

"Where?"

Dave said, "I'm such a poor fisherman that I just fished from camp." That wasn't quite the truth but close enough. The others congratulated Dave on his success, and everyone ate fish until they were full. The rest of the trip, we heard no more bragging from Bob.

## Dave's Grandsons

I had the delightful opportunity to take Dave's grandsons on a canoe trip. Three grandsons and a school friend of the youngest, all teenagers from the Detroit area, went on a trip with their father, Dave, and me. They were quite urban in lifestyle but had done some paddling with their father in lakes near Detroit. They were very receptive to my orientation, and since this was a unique wilderness experience, they were strict about following my guidelines. They were strong youths and paddled well. They pitched right in, setting up camp and fixing meals. I was delighted with their attitudes. We had great conversations about their future aspirations around the campfire. I believe all four were straight A students.

We paddled to the Canadian border from Fall Lake, as they wanted to see Canada. They were awed by Upper Basswood Falls. But I was apprehensive when I saw a yearling bear cub wandering around the falls. There were lots of other groups there, and everyone steered clear of the bear. In fact, we met one group that was moving their camp because of bear problems they encountered the previous night. There was no sign of mother bear, but that didn't mean she wasn't nearby. I explored and found bear scat on the rocks downstream from the waterfalls. There are some lovely campsites around the falls, but I wasn't even tempted to stay there.

After a refreshing lunch, we climbed in our canoes and found a BWCA campsite on an island several hours' paddle from the falls, as I did not have a Canadian permit. I checked the site and found no bear scat on the several trails that led away from the camp, including the trail to the potty box.

That night was lovely. We had a nice breeze to fend off mosquitoes, no rain, plenty of dead wood for our fire, and wonderful camaraderie with the boys. The next morning, as we were planning what to do, I went down to the shore to get a bucket of water and slipped and hyperflexed my right leg, tearing my quadriceps. Dave is a physician, but a neurologist. Yet he was helpful. I could stand on my leg, locking my knee, but had very weak extension. Dave's neurologic exam revealed no nerve damage.

We decided to stay at our campsite. Dave wanted to whisk me off to the Ely hospital emergency department, but I was determined not to affect the boys' camping experience. Besides, if I kept my leg straight, it didn't hurt that much. I went and stood in the ice-cold water for a half hour. I think that prevented a lot of swelling.

We had a relaxing day, but after supper, a huge bear appeared. I scared it off banging pots but told the troop that we had to leave immediately. Our camp was on a shelf, and the canoes were down a steep trail to the water's edge. As we filled the packs, we brought them down and put them in the canoes. I sent the oldest grandson up the slope to make sure we had everything.

By the time we were packed into the canoes, it was pitch dark. We canoed in the dark to another campsite marked on the map. To my dismay, the forest service had closed it. I guess it was too nice and overused. For safety, I didn't care that it was closed. If the ranger came, I was sure he would understand why we had to move our camp. Setting up camp in a closed campsite in the dark was a bit sloppy, but we did it, burning our flashlight batteries.

The next morning, we set out to make breakfast. "Where's the food pack?" I questioned. We counted the packs. One was missing—the food pack.

The oldest said, "I checked. I know we didn't leave anything."

I reviewed our escape. It had been dark. And bears are quiet and sneaky. Bears are after food. "Let's go back to that campsite," I suggested.

We paddled back, and I told the boys, "Bears are lazy, so go down each trail from our camp about forty steps." Each grandson picked one trail, and sure enough, forty steps down the potty box trail, they found our pack. The bear had quietly stolen it while we were packing the canoes, and as a result, the straps had not been tightened. The good news was the bear had not ripped the pack, so no loss to our outfitter. The bad news: The candy bars were eaten, as were any other succulents, like cheese and summer sausage. But bears don't quite know what to do with oatmeal, so we cooked up a hearty breakfast while we decided what to do.

Our pickup was scheduled for the next morning, but we decided to head back early on the strength of oatmeal. I couldn't portage a canoe with my torn quadriceps muscle, but I could shoulder a small pack and use the canoe paddle as a crutch. We made it back without further incident.

When we told our story, the outfitter understood why we had come back early. Afterward, I paid for a hearty meal at the finest burger place in Ely, the Chocolate Moose, before heading home. All the way home, the teens related how exciting the trip had been, so I guess coming back a night early was not a negative. Nor did my clumsiness impair their experience.

I did see an orthopedic surgeon back in Kalamazoo. She said that no surgery was needed since only half my quadriceps was torn, but added, "If you had come right away, I might have done surgery." She emphasized *might* and put me in a most uncomfortable brace. Then she ordered physical therapy.

My physical therapist was a tall, muscular, attractive young woman. She was so sweet when she introduced herself. She asked me to demonstrate what I could do that first day of therapy. At the end of that session, she got mean. "I will never again ask you what you can do. You will do what I tell you to do from now on." She was effective, as I gained 90 percent of my function and I never missed a day of work.

As an aside, I had taught the physical therapists at Andrews University for four years while working at Southwestern Medical Clinic (SWMC). I had some knowledge of how they were trained. It is a principle of physical therapy that they are quite insistent on patients' following their instructions to obtain maximum results. In other words, they are trained to be mean.

A year later, when I returned for another canoe trip, the outfitter informed me the rangers killed a four-hundred-pound male bear in that area where we had camped because it was marauding through campsites. I suspect that was our bear. I have seen many bears in Quetico-BWCA, and that was the biggest bear I had ever seen.

## *Former Partners' Canoe Trip*

I did have the opportunity to guide a trip with my partners from Southwestern Medical Clinic. Ron, Tom, and Ken asked me to guide them on a trip. We went to Canada and discovered some lakes just west of Quetico Provincial Park. Ron and Ken brought their sons. It was a great experience full of memories of our time together at SWMC. We had a nice campsite on an island but hadn't caught any fish.

On the way home, we stopped for lunch on a peninsula. To the east was a shallow bay. We four physicians were enjoying our camaraderie, and I suppose Ken's young sons were a bit bored. They asked their father if they could paddle out in the bay by themselves, to which he agreed. They took their fishing rods and set out in an empty canoe, even though the adults told them it was unlikely that there were any fish in the shallow bay.

A shower of screams caught the adults' attention. The boys had a fish on the line and couldn't seem to land it. The fish pulled the canoe around the bay in comical circles. Ken and I responded by getting into one of the other canoes to rescue the boys. They managed to keep the fish hooked until we got there to stabilize the canoe, and Ken helped the boys land the huge northern pike.

Pictures were taken, as the fish was almost as long as the youngest son was tall. But we were on our way home, so we released the monster. Ken told me later that his sons were subsequently hooked on fishing. They told the story to their relatives, and the fish grew bigger with each telling.

## *Priest Trip*

My partner Ross came to my office one day. He described his uncle who was a priest in Washington State. He had spent his entire career ministering to First Nation people in tribal areas on the eastern side of the state and Western Idaho. He was a student of the culture of the people he served. He was intrigued to compare their culture with Anishinabek culture. Ross had told him that I knew lots of Anishinabek stories, so Ross arranged for his uncle to canoe the BWCA with me. When I met him, I was impressed with his gentle, humble demeanor.

We needed one more person to accompany us so that we had two canoes for safety. I asked Tirzah's husband, Silvui, if he would be willing to come. He was willing and stronger than me, so I was delighted that he agreed.

The priest was enthralled with the lakes and waterfalls. I had seldom canoed with such an enthusiastic camper. He endured the hardships of the trip without a single complaint. Every evening, I told him stories that my Anishinabek friend, Ira Ishim, had shared with me. He related some of the principles of the stories to cultural aspects of the tribes he worked with. He was fascinated with the cultural environment of the lakes and portages and how that related to Anishinabek cultural values. I will never forget the two of us sitting on a massive rock, sharing stories in late afternoon, while Ross and Silvui set up camp. The priest was a profound theologian, curious about my years of teaching the Old Testament. Our fireside conversation lasted late into the night. What an amazing man.

Silvui wanted to climb a cliff opposite our campsite, so we canoed over to the opposite shore and established the safest way up the cliff. We scrambled up the granite face with some slipping and retreating to find better footing. We were all grateful when we arrived at the top, which was loaded with blueberries. It wasn't blueberry season yet, but because the rockface was to the south, it retained the heat of the day. The result was that the blueberries ripened ahead of season. We ate our fill and collected enough for our pancakes the next morning.

After we arrived the next morning at the outfitters, there were hugs, tears, and blessings of a grateful priest as we parted.

Canoeing is the only athletic activity that I was ever good at. I have canoed Lake Michigan (in a kayak), the traveled English Channel between England and Ireland, as well as canoed in a dugout canoe in Sierra Leone. All totaled, I quit counting mileage at three thousand miles of canoeing. Last year, at seventy-four years old, I canoed the St. Croix River with my grandsons. Canoeing is a part of my life. It has taught me endurance, confidence, and a spiritual communion with nature.

# 11

## FINDING PRISCILLA

I had very specific requirements for a spouse. She had to be intellectual, spiritually profound, curious about the world, adventuresome, able to make independent decisions, and most important, tenacious. Without tenacity, a woman (or a man for readers looking for a male spouse) cannot be trusted in difficult times. I preferred dark or black hair, physical strength, brown eyes, and a height of at least five foot ten. Smokers (I can't stand the smell) and women with long, elaborate fingernails; elaborate makeup or clothing requirements (high maintenance!); or a preference for high heels (a stupid invention of Louis XIV) would not be considered. I also wanted someone who could balance a canoe.

### Girlfriend Fiascos

My dating experiences were disastrous. A very attractive young lady who sat next to me in high school art class modeled for clothing advertisements. I had seen her in a JCPenney ad. But alas, she left school the day before I planned to ask her for a date because she was pregnant.

I enjoyed the company of my Jewish friend Marcia, but her father nixed our relationship. Nonetheless, we still enjoyed each other's companionship cheering during the Seven-Day War.

Jenny (not her real name, because her name was so distinctive) was beautiful with long, streaming dark hair and brown eyes. I met her in church and really liked her. But her best friend, Kitty, told me that I wasn't high class enough for her, so Jenny shunned me at church after that chat with Kitty. I met her again during my years as an occupational medicine physician.

So much for finding a spouse among high school sweethearts.

During my university days, there were many young women to whom I was attracted. Recall that I ruined my chances with my chemistry lab partner. I wasn't interested in the women fawning over me because I was a chemistry major and might be able to manufacture LSD. No women who were chemistry majors were of interest either. The few of them didn't consider me worthy of any attention, as they all received better test grades than I did.

I joined InterVarsity Christian Fellowship (IVCF) at the recommendation of Dan (from German class and the Yukon trip). There, I met many lovely, intellectual, spiritually sensitive women. One night, I arrived somewhat late for an IVCF meeting. All the seats were taken, so I had to sit on the floor. To my back was a young woman who said, "I like having a man at my feet." After the meeting, we talked. I thought she was the most obnoxious girl I had ever met. She told me that I was a stick in the mud. Her name was Priscilla, and she was strong and five foot ten with dark brown, almost black, hair, but blue eyes. When we had an IVCF arm-wrestling contest that year, she won, including beating all the men. During the summer, she stacked birch lumber at a box factory, two tons per shift.

## Sue

I fell head over heels in love with Sue, whom I met in one of my non-science classes. She had dark hair and brown eyes and was quite attractive, but wasn't aware that she was. When I would see her in the hall, my heart would sing. She loved Simon and Garfunkel, especially their song "The Sound of Silence."

We had a few dates. I learned she had a fresh perspective on Christianity and she was from a very poor family from Grand Portage. Her parents were alcoholics who had never been to any church. She came to UMD to get away from them. Her roommate at the dorm was a strong Christian who explained her relationship with God like this: "I had a run-in with Jesus and fell in love."

Our dates were fun, as we always had something to talk about. I even paid her tuition one quarter. However, when tuition was due the next quarter, she refused to accept my charity. She said, "I've moved in with a guy." I was heartbroken and shocked. She avoided me after that. We didn't even maintain a friendship.

## Carol

I had tests to study for, and I was working weekends as an orderly at St. Luke's Hospital. That helped me get over my grief. But then a lovely young woman charmed me. Carol (not her real name) was a petite blond gal, very attractive, from my birth town of Virginia, Minnesota. We had a couple of dates, and I enjoyed her company. She was majoring in elementary education. She was intellectual and had a spiritual backbone.

After several weekday dates, I asked Carol out on a Sunday night. I worked Friday and Saturday nights in the emergency department but had Sunday nights free. She said, "I will have to ask my mother." So much for independent decision making, but she had other nice qualities, so I continued to court her. We never did have a weekend date, as she spent weekends with her parents.

We had a date in the Bull Pub University Restaurant that I will never forget. When I arrived, she was already at a table eating a hamburger. I ordered, and as I sat down next to her, she started crying. "What's wrong, Carol?" I asked in my most compassionate voice.

"I'm flunking pottery class," she whimpered.

I wondered how anyone could flunk pottery. All one had to do was make some clay pots and turn them in to the professor for grading. Granted, he was quite famous nationally, having written the textbook used across the United States for university pottery classes. But he was a nice person. I had gotten an A in the class.

We finished our burgers despite Carol's cascading teardrops, and I offered to go to her pottery class to see what the problem was. The art department building was open until 9:00 p.m. so budding artists could work on their projects.

The pottery room was open, but no one else was inside. I sat at a table where a huge glob of clay was being dried on a marble slab. Carol brought over her pot, setting it on the marble table in front of me. She broke into more tears. "He said that he would give me an F for this. I worked so hard on it."

The pot wasn't too bad, but ordinary in design. Carol had decorated it with little inscribed triangles around the border. I knew the professor expected creativity.

"Carol," I said with a laugh, "your decorations, these triangles, were used by the Anasazi to decorate their pots over a thousand years ago. You've got to do something more creative."

She cringed with clenched fists, a blank expression on her face. I don't think she understood creativity. I grabbed a pinch of clay from the vat and stuck it on her pot. "You're ruining my pot!" she screamed.

I thought, *How could I ruin a pot that would be graded with an F?* I stuck another pinch of clay on her pot. "Carol, even that makes your pot better." There was more crying and screaming as I added more pinches of clay.

"It's ruined, it's ruined!" she screamed as she ran out the door. By then, my pinches of clay had covered all the Anasazi-like triangles.

I shook my head and murmured, "No creativity."

I thought that I would probably never see Carol again. But to my chagrin, she joined me at the table in the Bull Pub the next day while I was eating supper. She was all smiles. "The professor gave me an A on my pot. He was impressed with the texture of all those little dabs of clay." All right, she was sweet and attractive, just not very independent or creative. So, I was willing to date her a couple more times.

That spring, IVCF sponsored a canoe trip into the BWCA. Carol and Priscilla both signed up, as did I and others. It was a Friday night to Sunday night trip because the university was still in session; I managed to get the weekend off from the hospital. Friday was calm, and we canoed only about two hours, almost straight north to a delightful campsite. There were no portages. There were thirty of us with fifteen canoes, and group size limits had not yet been legislated, so we all camped together on an island. Saturday was fun and relaxing with singing and dancing around the campfire.

Sunday morning, however, a furious south wind developed. Whitecaps blew right in our faces as we arranged to return to the landing. A canoe trip leader's prerogative in bad weather is to choose who should paddle with whom. I was not in charge. The leader teamed Carol with a UMD football lineman, and me with Priscilla, and suggested we assemble at an island just north of the landing and wait there to make sure everyone made it safely.

Priscilla and I headed straight into the wind. Waves crashed over our bow, spraying both of us. I struggled to keep the canoe perpendicular to the oncoming whitecaps. And Priscilla started singing. She sang the whole time, with waves splashing her in the face as she paddled. She never rested a stroke. I don't recall that she even sang the same song twice. She was adventurous and had strength and tenacity! It took four hours of hard paddling straight into the wind to get to the island. Of fifteen canoes, Priscilla's and mine made it to the island third. The two canoes that beat ours to the island were paddled by strong guys in bow and stern.

As our leader suggested, we waited on the island for the others to arrive. Fourteen canoes eventually landed. One was still missing.

We waited another hour. The leader was suggesting that we paddle back to see what happened to the last canoe when, suddenly, we heard a motorboat. It was towing the canoe with the football player and Carol. As they landed, the football player told the leader, "She refused to paddle. I think I could have made it if she had just been willing to paddle a little bit."

I shook my head—no independence, no creativity, no tenacity. I walked over to her and said, "Carol, we're done." Then I walked over to Priscilla and said, "Would you be willing to be my girlfriend?"

Priscilla laughed. "Yes, you stick in the mud."

139

## *Priscilla*

It was not a smooth courtship, but the more Priscilla and I got to know each other, the more we admired each other. She was spiritually profound. She was majoring in English but switched to sociology. We always had things to discuss, and she understood things that I didn't even know about. She taught me how to change the oil in my car and could change a flat tire in no time.

One problem in our relationship and later in our marriage was that I couldn't tell Priscilla what to do; I could make humble suggestions to which she might or might not agree. Even after fifty years of marriage, I avoid telling her what to do. If I make a request that doesn't sound like a suggestion, she will respond, "You're not telling me what to do, are you?"

Priscilla had a stronger sense of propriety than I did. We had a fight because I was walking in the street toward the university, while she insisted that we walk on the sidewalk. She did not allow *Kleenex* to be a generic term for tissues unless we bought that brand. And we couldn't walk fast anywhere unless there was a specific reason. I preferred to arrive early to things; however, she didn't consider that a priority.

## *Priscilla's Family*

Another problem was her father, Charles Fillmore, who did not believe in physicians. He thought they were unnecessary. God would heal if He so chose. Would he accept me with my plan to go to medical school?

I remember meeting him when Priscilla invited me home to meet her parents at Thanksgiving. Charlie had built their house, or at least added on to the original. Every room was at a different floor and ceiling level. The pump for drinking water was about ten yards from the house. Charlie had put in the plumbing from the well to the house so the family could have indoor water. Priscilla did not have the luxury of indoor plumbing until she attended Cook High School. I believe her initial showers were with cold water before the water heater was added to the system. That Thanksgiving, I took a shower in the shower room, which was shared with the washing machine and a clothesline. A pipe with a nozzle went up the concrete wall. No curtain, no privacy.

The house did have a basement, where Priscilla's mother, Ruth, kept canned goods. The sump pump was always going, as the house was built in a swamp. In fact, that weekend of Thanksgiving, the electricity went out during the night. The result was eight feet of water in the basement in the morning. Priscilla's response that morning was "Look, we have an indoor swimming pool."

Charlie didn't panic, because he had insulated the pump in case of flooding. As soon as the electricity came on, the sump pumped the water out. The canned goods experienced no ill effects; one just had to rinse off the mud before opening them. But I investigated and found the joists under the kitchen to be so soggy that I could poke a hole in the wood with my finger. Ruth had two sets of bricks under the back of the stove to level it for baking because the kitchen floor was sinking into the basement.

After Priscilla introduced me to her father, he said, "We need milk. Come with me," and we drove to get milk. Along the way, Charlie questioned me about everything: my theology, my relationship to his daughter, my parents, and my future expectations. This lasted almost two hours before we arrived at a farm where we went into the milk house to fill our containers. I thought that was a long journey just to get milk, as I knew the grocery store in Cook was only five miles away. But maybe fresh milk was important.

We then drove back home. It took fifteen minutes.

Priscilla told me later that I had passed her father's interrogation. After that, Charlie and I had a good relationship, as I was willing to help him in the blacksmith shop with welding and fixing cars. He taught me a lot.

Ruth was very pleasant but quiet. I just wasn't sure what she thought of me. She had her own business, the Dairy Bar in Cook, which served hamburgers, fries, and ice cream. One afternoon, I volunteered to mop the floor in the Dairy Bar's back room. I was almost finished when Priscilla tracked across my just-mopped floor. I took the mop and whacked her in the hind end. She yelped. Ruth was standing right there. I panicked, wondering about her reaction. Ruth said, "She's needed that for a long time." After that, Ruth and I got along quite well.

After that Thanksgiving experience, I contemplated marrying Priscilla. She met my criteria, except the blue eyes. Maybe I could overlook that. She was certainly strong, had tenacity, and was spiritually profound and creative. Besides, she was quite pleasant (36-26-38).

## Grandparents' Approval

Recall that after the canoe trip to the Yukon, when Neil rescued me in Seattle, he drove me to my grandparents' house in Salem, Oregon. Grandpa and Grandma Bell were excited to see me.

My grandmother graduated from nursing school in 1918. At that time, the hospitals were desperate for nurses because they were filled with influenza victims, and all graduates were immediately hired. She told me her hospital painted arrows on the floor so patients being admitted didn't run into the gurneys of patients being transported to the morgue. Mustard plasters were the customary treatment then, but my grandmother didn't think they had any benefit. What a horrifying way to start a nursing career. It's amazing she never got the flu herself. She worked as an RN till retirement.

On that visit, we spent a long time talking about whether I should marry Priscilla. Grandma Bell wanted to know everything about her. She interrogated me about Priscilla' personality, her spiritual depth, and why I wanted to marry her. I recall that tenacity came up in our conversation several times. It was a great premarital counseling session. She told me that Priscilla seemed like the right person for me to marry.[6]

Grandpa wanted to show me the Oregon and California coast. Grandpa and Grandma drove me down the coast, stopping at San Francisco, where my Aunt Dorothy and Uncle George lived. After a delightful visit and tour of San Francisco, I decided to return home to Duluth. But I didn't have any money left, so I called Priscilla and she "loaned" me enough to fly home. With a dozen roses, I proposed marriage to her on her birthday, August 19, 1970. By the time we married, I still had not paid her back. Once we were married, she claimed the money we had was "our" money, so she says I still owe her $300.

---

[6] Later, after we married and had two children, Priscilla and I went to visit Grandpa and Grandma Bell. They had moved to Escondido, California. Grandpa chose a house within walking distance of the Wild Animal Park, part of the San Diego Zoo. Both my grandparents were delighted to meet Priscilla.

## *Prenuptial Requirements*

I did have some requirements for Priscilla before I was willing to marry her. First, she had never received her childhood immunizations because her father did not believe in physicians. So, I insisted that she complete her vaccinations. I sent her to an internal medicine specialist, whom I knew from my work as an orderly, to get her "baby shots." Her visit was uneventful except for swelling where she received all her immunizations.

Second, she was willing to drop out of UMD to marry me, but I said, "No, you must finish your degree and graduate first." So, she graduated with a degree in sociology and a minor in English at the end of the winter quarter in March. We married on April 2 because she refused to marry on April Fool's Day.

## *The Wedding*

One of the ushers warned me just before the wedding ceremony, "Do you think you are strong enough to handle her?"

I said, "Yes," but his question made me apprehensive. I was already nervous. I knew if I arm-wrestled with her, I would lose.

It was a nice service, lasting nineteen minutes. We invited about five hundred people to the reception. We were blessed with a blizzard, so only about half the people could come.

We made the mistake of having truck drivers' wives cut the cake. We had an open reception so there would be no lines, and as people came to congratulate us off in one corner, I kept hearing, "This is the first wedding I've been to where I got a decent-sized piece of cake." By the time Priscilla and I were ready for some cake, it was all gone. The ladies in the kitchen had saved the tiny top for our one-year anniversary, but a week later, we ate it, still wondering what our cake tasted like.

April 2 was my brother William's birthday. I knew he was upset because he thought we had forgotten, but at the end of the reception line was a cake labeled "Happy Birthday, William." Subsequently, he has been pleased that I never forget his birthday since I must remember my anniversary.

Our wedding cost $300 because we had very little money, and we received $300 in monetary gifts—just enough to pay for the wedding, for which we rejoiced. We then spent the weekend at Cascade Lodge. Priscilla and I were the only guests because of the blizzard conditions the previous day. The owners explained how to check in people, but nobody came; then they left for a much-needed break. The next morning, they had put a pile of hay outside the window of our room. When we opened our drapes, there were deer feasting on it.

For recreation, we went snowshoeing. My goal was to snowshoe to an abandoned cabin that was back in the woods about a mile. As we were hiking, we came across some tracks in the snow. I recognized bear tracks, but I tried to convince Priscilla that they were dog tracks and that we should keep going.

She said, "I know bear tracks, and I know you know, so you are lying to me. I got along just fine before I met you, so I can get along without you now. So don't ever lie to me again." As we snowshoed back to the lodge, Priscilla sang to me a popular song containing similar words. And I've never lied to her since.

Another requirement we agreed on was never to say, "I love you, but …" since *but* in English is a powerful word that negates everything before it. I did, however, make a mistake once and said, "I love you, but—"

She stopped me midsentence and said, "I love your butt too."

## *First Year of Marriage: No Job, No Medical School*

I had one quarter left to graduate. So, Monday morning, I was back at UMD, and I would continue working weekends at the hospital. Meanwhile, Priscilla went job hunting and got a job at a department store in two hours. Our food budget was $25 a month, so we ate lots of oatmeal during my last quarter at UMD.

When I graduated, I had a job at Camp Vermilion. With no rent, and no food budget, I made $75 a week guiding, and Priscilla made $50 a week packing food for the trips.

That summer, we anticipated starting medical school. I had applied to ten medical schools; however, sad to say, I was rejected by nine of them, and I was an alternate at the University of Minnesota. Most years, alternates were accepted before school started. But that year, no alternates were needed to fill the school roster, so I was not accepted anywhere.

Fortunately, Priscilla and I had saved our salaries from Camp Vermilion, as there was no place to spend the money. At the end of the summer, we moved back to Duluth, and I started looking for a chemistry job. The employment office counselor laughed at me. "There are no chemistry jobs in Duluth." But he took my application, anyway.

"What should we do?" I asked Priscilla.

"Let's go on vacation," she suggested.

I thought that was ridiculous, with no income, and no jobs, but she insisted. At that time, in September, the national parks were "closed"; that meant we could camp without paying a fee, which was good for people who had no income.

The climax came when we arrived at Hoover Dam. I was so upset about not getting into medical school that after we set up our tent at the campground and had supper, I told Priscilla that

I was going to take a hike and talk to God. She crawled into her sleeping bag and let me go. I think she was praying for me.

## Yelling at God

I climbed the nearest hill, and at the top, I started my rampage, yelling at God. "You gave me the desire to go to medical school. I applied to ten schools and didn't get in. This isn't fair!" I yelled at God until I was hoarse. Then I collapsed on a rock.

In response, a still, small voice said, "I have it all in control."

It was dark. The stars were blocked by clouds as I headed back down the hill. I have great night vision, so I didn't trip.

I crawled into the tent, trying not to disturb Priscilla. As soon as I was comfortable, she whispered, "What did God say?"

"He said that He has it all in control."

"I could have told you that," she said and went back to sleep.

## Quality Control Supervisor

Back in Duluth, Priscilla got a job as a fry cook. She encouraged me to try again to get a job. I eventually got a job working for R. J. Reynolds's food division as a chemist. Ten applicants had already interviewed for the job before me, so the employment office said that I had very little chance of getting the job. But my interview went like this: "What shift do you want to work?"

"Any shift you have available."

"What equipment can you operate?"

"I can operate a nuclear magnetic resonator and paper and gel chromatograph."

With a blank look on his face, my future manager said, "Can you work a can opener?"

147

"Yes," I said.

I got the job as quality control supervisor for the afternoon shifts because all the other ten applicants had insisted on day shift. In this position, I was required to check the pH of the sweet-and-sour sauce, count the bean sprout hulls in the product off each line every two hours, and make sure the fortune cookie folders were putting fortunes in the cookies. The benefit was I could eat any Chun King product that I tested at work, including the fortune cookies. Priscilla also received a meal at her fry cook job. That really helped our food budget.

I had several painful experiences at the bean sprout factory. I met a fascinating man who planted the bean sprouts in the large tanks on the upper floor. He was paid well because planting bean sprouts requires precise attention to the temperature of the water and the chemicals required to inhibit rootlet growth. He was quite the philosopher, an atheist whose hero was the German author Nietzsche. We had great discussions over meal break. The young fellow was clearly a genius. He said that he loved his job because no one bothered him.

When my boss found out that the two of us were eating together, I was reprimanded, "You can't socialize with the workers! You are management." We still talked when I went upstairs to inspect the bean sprout tanks, but we were not allowed to meet in the dining room. How stupid.

Other painful experiences related to bullying among the workers. One of the line bosses planned to have sex with every girl on his line. Those who refused him were assigned the dirty jobs and were constantly teased and humiliated.

The maintenance workers resented a worker who was hired after months of sobriety from alcoholism. They wanted to get rid of him, so one of the line bosses offered him a bottle of whiskey for his birthday. The worker became intoxicated before the shift was over and was fired.

It was a difficult year because of those experiences. I was discouraged about being rejected from ten medical schools. Priscilla was a huge psychological lift.

Toward the end of the year, several things happened at once. Chun King decided to move the factory to Albany, New York. And, since I was part of management, I was offered quite a substantial raise in salary and my boss's position in the new plant, since he refused to move to New York. The offer came on a Monday. I was told to give my answer by Friday.

## Finally Admitted to Medical School

Priscilla had made me apply to one more medical school, UMD. In fact, she filled out the application except for my signature. I was too discouraged to fill it out.

It was to be the first medical school class of UMD. I remember the interview so well because after a review of my credentials, the rest of the interview was about fishing and canoeing. The interviewer was interested in the best fishing lakes in the BWCA and Quetico Provincial Park. I assumed that since he took very little interest in my credentials or why I proposed to be a physician, I would not be accepted. But I was.

I received my acceptance letter on Thursday afternoon, so on Friday morning, I turned down the advancement to Albany. I was surprised when the other management people congratulated me and cheered. I was expecting a cold shoulder.

The plant closed that spring. Medical school didn't start until fall, so I told Melvin that I could guide canoe trips again. I was offered the assistant program director position, and I accepted.

John Andreasen, the program director, and I put the program together based on the biblical book of Galatians. It was a great year of guiding, and it was exciting to have such spiritually sensitive guides to work with, many of whom are still close friends fifty years later.

At the end of the guiding season, Priscilla and I returned to Duluth to start medical school. I include Priscilla because without her application, I would probably have been a bean sprout supervisor in Albany, New York, instead of a physician.

# 12

## MEDICAL SCHOOL

The first week of medical school was inspiring because I felt that I had finally achieved my dream. Several of the physicians who had sponsored the establishment of the school were well known to me because of my years working as an orderly. Dr. Boyer gave the initial address, explaining to us that our choice required us to be students for the rest of our lives. We could never know everything about medicine. The second point he made was not to become arrogant, because although we would care for and treat patients as physicians, only God heals. The reason he gave that first medical school address was because he made a huge contribution to start the school, promoting it among the other physicians in the community and raising their support.

I knew Dr. Boyer from my time as an orderly at St. Luke's Hospital. He was a cardiologist and a widower; I never heard how his wife died. He always made rounds at the hospital in the evening. I think he saw patients in the office during the day. Since I worked 3:00 to 11:30 p.m., we often met in the emergency department when he admitted patients.

One day, he came to the emergency department and asked me where there was an empty room. He entered, lay down on the gurney, and ordered an EKG on himself. A technician arrived and attached the leads, printing out an EKG. I was standing there to assist him, as neither the emergency physician nor the ED nurse had checked him into the department.

Dr. Boyer looked at his tracing and in a quiet, calm voice said, "It looks like I'm having a heart attack." He turned to me, asking, "Can you wheel me upstairs to critical care?" I did. He admitted himself, wrote and signed his own orders. It was a good decision. He coded twice that night but made a full recovery.

Dr. Boyer had an interesting habit. I had dated the hostess of the Pickwick Restaurant, Kathy, who was quite elegant and interested in fancy clothes—in other words, she was high maintenance—but we remained close friends. She told me that every night, Dr. Boyer came to the restaurant; sat at the same table, which she always reserved for him; and ordered the same meal. So Kathy worried when he didn't show up for his evening meal. I explained the situation to her. She was heartbroken. As soon as he recovered, he returned for his evening meal to a welcoming hostess and joyful waitresses.

Because of my respect for Dr. Boyer and my work with him in the ED, his address inspired me to be a student forever and remember that only God heals.

Ours was an unusual class. We had two First Nation students, one Iroquois and the other Anishinabek. One student was a nun who got permission from her order to go to medical school; Sister Sue was already a registered nurse. The class also included identical twin women with long black hair; I never could distinguish who was who. One of the men was an Irish redhead; another young man was the state of Minnesota's mushroom expert; Burton, from

International Falls, was an outboard motor mechanic; and we had a couple of hippies.

All twenty-five of us became close friends. We tutored each other, especially those who struggled with certain material, so that we would all get good scores. There was only one fellow who tried to be the best in the class. His problem was he was not the smartest. (He became a surgeon.)

Because we were the first class, our professors were subjected to scrutiny. The state representatives made a visit emphasizing their skepticism that UMD should even have a medical school, which pressured the faculty even more. This attitude resulted in our professors responding positively to any suggestions we had to improve.

Our classes were held in the old teachers' college building, which had to be updated for our anatomy and physiology labs. Despite old rooms and old desks, the advantage of a tennis court just outside the door made for pleasant breaks. Lee was quite the tennis player. In fact, no one wanted to play against him because he was so good. I had never played tennis in my life, so he chose me. He told me where to stand, and to hold my racket just so and to swing when he told me. Then he went to the other side of the court and hit the ball so it would bounce off my racket, which allowed him some practice.

Despite the encouragement of my classmates, school was hard. Research has shown that from the first day of medical school until graduation, a student's vocabulary doubles. Each day was a barrage of new words and concepts. I felt overwhelmed, but Priscilla was a constant encouragement. John, Rod, and Gus studied with me and quizzed me through the courses so that we all passed the tests. Sometimes, they would come to my house and Priscilla would make treats for them.

Temujin was born that year, so Priscilla was busy with a new baby as well as a new student—me. She wasn't working, so the question was what we would live on. I applied for a student loan. We waited and received no notification. I decided to join the U.S. Air Force because they would pay for school and give us living expenses. But I had misgivings about serving in the military. Fortunately, two days before I signed up, our loan was approved.[7]

Pharmacology was the worst, despite my degree in chemistry, because the professor wanted us to memorize things instead of understanding how drugs worked. I have never been good at memorizing anything. I subsequently retaught myself pharmacology conceptually and now enjoy it. As a professor emeritus, I still challenge residents considering the differential diagnosis of a patient with odd complaints to first think of drugs, as the medication the patient is taking may be the cause of their unusual symptoms.

Anatomy was another struggle because every bone, blood vessel, muscle, and organ has a name to memorize. My team's cadaver had died of peritonitis, so her abdominal organs were all stuck together. We had to work with another team on abdominal anatomy. Anatomy quizzes consisted of the professor putting little tags on wee structures, so our quiz sheet was blank except for numbers that correlated with the numbers on the little tags. I knew and understood the structures, but sometimes, my mind went blank and I couldn't remember their names. I would stand there going through the alphabet in my mind, trying to think of the names of the tiny structures.

Physiology was delightful because it just seemed like storytelling. Two aspects of physiology, about which I had no

---

[7] That was important later because when we first went to Madagascar, it was a communist country. If I had been in the military, I would not have gotten a visa.

previous understanding, were platelet function (I didn't even know platelets existed) and the coagulation cascade (this is why blood clots). How complicated. How amazing! I sat in awe as the professor explained them.

We had a dog lab with a veterinarian present who anesthetized the dogs. We were studying cardiology and observed how various drugs affected heart function. During the lab, we had to cannulate veins and arteries, which was an important skill for my future critical care rotations. The cardiology professor, Lois Jane, knew of my interest in photography and asked me to make a tutorial for future students. At our twenty-fifth class reunion, she said that she still used the pictures.

I found endocrinology fascinating. I think it was the only class in which I received an outstanding grade. I was thrilled to learn the feedback loops and the functions of the various hormones. About that time, the negative effects of excess cholesterol were being discovered. *Ladies' Home Journal* recommended a low-cholesterol diet, but without cholesterol, there is no sex! Sex hormones—estrogen, testosterone, progesterone—are all made from cholesterol. So, eat your eggs. (Years later, the discovery of LDL and HDL refined the mysteries of cholesterol metabolism. The secrets of cholesterol are based on liver metabolism and genetic predisposition; diet has minimal effect. So, eat eggs.)

I became awed by everything the liver does. Our professor claimed that the liver does more chemical reactions in one day than all the chemists in the world could do in a year. The liver became my favorite organ. I almost chose a hepatology fellowship as a career.

I remember two questions from the physiology tests. "Trace the route of the sperm from the testes to ejaculation" was one. What a route that is. The other question was "Can you vomit and defecate at the same time?" I didn't understand the point of the question. The correct answer was yes, because they are both parasympathetic autonomic phenomena. I just answered, "Yes, because I have done it." The professor gave me half credit.

Basic science was not my strength, but I managed to make it through with my fellow students' help. Part I of the National Board exam is all basic science with little practical patient care correlation. When I passed, I was excited that passing opened the door to meeting and caring for patients.

## Clinical Years 3 and 4

Working as an orderly for four years did provide an advantage for classes on patient care. In the first two years, these classes were mostly introductory. However, we had to learn the process of history and physical exam (H&P).[8] My mentor was a British pulmonologist who required that I learn an organized, concise format, which helped organize my history taking and physical exam. Not one extra word was allowed, and no redundancy. This format has helped me during my entire career. I am so thankful to him.

Some of my classmates felt shy about asking personal questions of patients. I had resolved that years before as an orderly, and I understood how to make patients comfortable answering me.

An interesting opportunity became available: the Rural Physician Associate Program (RPAP), which is still available under the auspices of the University of Minnesota Medical School. It involved working with a rural physician for either six or nine months as part of the second half of medical school. I signed up

---

[8] Read the chapters in *Physician's Muse* related to the first years of medical school, as they are autobiographical.

and was accepted. In addition, there was a stipend, which helped support my budding family.

I was sent to Cloquet, Minnesota, to work with Drs. Byron, Lloyd, Orville, and Monsreud. Byron was an internist, Lloyd was a surgeon, Orville focused on family medicine and obstetrics, and Monsreud was an orthopedic surgeon. As a result of working with them, I had a very well-rounded clinical experience. They were encouraging and excellent teachers. I chose to stay for nine months. I learned so much. Every day was a thrilling experience to work with physicians who were so willing to teach and involve me in their patients' care.

## Obstetrics

I learned to listen to and have compassion for my pregnant patients' stories because Priscilla's experiences with pregnancy were so disastrous. Temujin was born during the first year of medical school. He was a big baby, and Priscilla developed preeclampsia. The physician hospitalized her early because of high blood pressure and spilling protein in her urine. The delivery was difficult. Our OB-GYN professor had to do a special maneuver to extract this ten-pound, four-ounce baby. And if that wasn't enough of a scare, Temujin coded while Priscilla was breastfeeding. The nurse grabbed him and left the room while she resuscitated him. She returned later to tell us that he had survived.

Tirzah was born while we were in Cloquet. Gus was also in Cloquet, in RPAP with the other physician group, so he and his wife, Marsha, cared for Temujin while I attended the delivery. We had been told not to worry although Priscilla had preeclampsia with Temujin, as it was unlikely to reoccur with the next pregnancy. That was wrong. Priscilla had a seizure, full toxemia with Tirzah.

As she lay unconscious in a postictal state, I watched with horror as my daughter was delivered limp, blue, and not breathing, Apgar = 1. It was the scariest moment of my life. It took over ten minutes of resuscitation before Tirzah took her first breath. Priscilla did not regain consciousness until later in the morning. I immediately scheduled a vasectomy with Lloyd.

Back home in Cloquet, while Priscilla was recovering, it was decided that the old school next to our rental house would be torn down. The crew came with heavy equipment and cranes. Temujin would sit in the window and watch them for hours, allowing Priscilla to pay attention to the new baby and get some rest. Later, Priscilla recalled, "Those heavy-equipment crews were the best babysitters."

Because of our experience, I became very aware of my pregnant patients' blood pressure and potential obstetric problems. Orville taught me how to assess pregnant women, do Pap smears and pelvic exams, and deliver babies. He had an excellent rapport with his patients and taught me how to make women comfortable with pelvic exams.

My first delivery was a shoulder dystocia. I silently gasped when Orville broke the baby's clavicle to deliver the child. Most of the thirty-plus deliveries after that were normal, with a couple of C-sections. Neither Priscilla's experience nor deliveries with Orville endeared me to obstetrics. I decided then to pursue internal medicine instead of family practice so that I didn't have to do deliveries.

Orville's practice included a fair number of children, so I became familiar with outpatient pediatrics, snotty-nosed kids with upper respiratory infections and ear infections. I don't recall many in-patient pediatric cases, which is why the university required me to take hospital pediatrics in Minneapolis.

## Surgery

Surgery with Lloyd was so helpful. He had me assist in hernia repairs, appendectomies, and gallbladder surgeries. As a general surgeon, he taught me how to assess the acute abdomen and when not to attempt surgery. My surgical knot-tying techniques and abdominal anatomy reached new levels of understanding. I recorded dozens of surgeries, so many that when I returned to the Minneapolis campus, the registrar said I had enough surgical experience.

## Orthopedics

Monsreud was almost ready to retire when I worked in Cloquet. He was quite an orthopedic surgeon and taught me so much about assessing fractures, paying attention to compartment syndromes, and focusing on potential nerve injuries. I learned to cast fractures and when not to cast. It was creative, like pottery. He taught me how to reduce radial head subluxations and shoulder dislocations, which was important when I later worked in the emergency department. He told me, "Never trust an orthopedic surgeon who doesn't do woodworking as a hobby." I have found that to be a common hobby among orthopedists. But I have found exceptions to his rule. Orthopedics does require significant forearm and shoulder strength, so those muscles have been very well developed on every orthopedist I have met, even women orthopedic surgeons.

## First Nation Patient

I had many Anishinabek patients in Cloquet, which gave me further insight into their culture. UMD now has a rotation for medical students who wish to learn about Anishinabek healers.

Several times, I saw one First Nation man in his twenties who complained of low back pain. His pain was an inflammatory ligament strain. I explained it to him, but he just could not accept the diagnosis. I decided he must have a low pain tolerance, although I was aware that studies done on Navajo patients have demonstrated First Nation peoples have the highest pain tolerance of any cultural group studied.

One morning, he was on my schedule again. I was unsure what to do. "I still got pain in my back, Doc," he said.

As I went to examine him, I noticed that his right hand was swollen. "What happened to your hand?" I asked.

"Oh, nothing. I got mad and hit a guy," he replied.

I examined his hand and felt the crunch of broken bones. I ordered an X-ray and showed him that his hand had two broken bones in it.

"Yeah, I thought so. But what are you going to do for my back pain?" he asked me.

I realized that his problem was he couldn't understand why he had back pain, but he could understand why his hand hurt. He did not have a low pain threshold. I was learning that patients have to understand why they are hurting.

## Return to Main Campus

After nine months of RPAP, I was forced to transfer to Minneapolis, as UMD did not have a four-year program yet. RPAP had required that I keep a log of every patient I saw, and this log was reviewed to determine which rotations in the Twin Cities I needed to complete my training. It was decided—I don't recall that I had any choice—that I needed to take dermatology, in-patient pediatrics, pathology, neurology, and cardiology.

Priscilla and I, with our two children, found an apartment in the Twin Cities area to complete my medical school requirements. We lived in Richfield, which, despite its name, is a low-rent area because it is at the end of the Minneapolis–Saint Paul airport runway. We rented an apartment facing the airport, for which we received an additional discount. It was a boon for us. The children spent endless hours watching the airplanes land and take off. Priscilla was grateful for the free entertainment. We had no television.

Tirzah was born with a club foot. Priscilla took her to an orthopedist who had recently trained in Iowa with a specialist in non-surgical casting. The casting was very effective, but Priscilla had to take Tirzah to the orthopedist's office every two weeks to replace the cast. The surprise was that they never charged us anything because I was a medical student, despite medical school health insurance.

## Dermatology

Dermatology was at the Veterans Hospital. They had lots of curious cases because veterans from all over the four-state area came to the Minneapolis VA hospital for follow-up. They had a registry of patients with various rare diseases and paid their way, providing them room and board to present their skin problems to medical students. We saw tremendous pathology, weird and wonderful cases, some of which allowed me to make important diagnoses later in my career because I recognized rare and uncommon problems from those VA patients.

## In-Patient Pediatrics

I did in-patient pediatrics at the University Hospital because the registrar said my experience in Cloquet did not include unusual inpatient pediatric cases. And unusual it was. At the University Hospital, I personally assessed fifteen children for growth hormone deficiency and cared for many children with terminal cancer.

I cared for a young boy with rhabdomyosarcoma, a rare cancer of the masseter muscle. I was intrigued to see the lineup included the young boy the morning after I had admitted him. So I asked one of the pediatric residents, "Why the lineup? Did you all want to see the rhabdo?"

"No," he said, "we have seen many of those cases, but in your H&P, you mentioned that he had otitis media. We haven't seen much of that."

I was chagrined. Otitis media is so common. I had seen dozens of cases with Orville. But the residents at the university had not had much outpatient experience at that stage of their careers.

I was exposed to much pediatric tragedy at the University Hospital. At the inborn errors of metabolism clinic, I cared for a child who wasn't functional, brought in by a couple from North Dakota. They discovered after they were married that they were consanguineous back seven generations. I was instructed by the physician attending to take the baby into the total darkness of the bathroom and use a bright flashlight on the child's head. There was total translucence, no brain. A nub of the brain stem kept the heart functioning and the lungs breathing. I felt the emotional tragedy to the parents. I almost cried as the pediatric attending physician explained the result to the parents: no prognosis that the child would develop.

Another day, I helped the team resuscitate a twelve-year-old boy with a lymphoma who subsequently died. I did code a one-year-old burn victim. His five-year-old sister had decided to help her mother give her brother a bath. She used only hot water and scalded her brother. Eighty percent second-degree burns required admission to the burn unit. On the fourth day, he coded.

The reason burn patients are at risk on the fourth day after a severe burn is that the body mobilizes the fluid in the blisters, and the fluid ends up in the lungs. The patient was in congestive heart failure, a problem with which I had experience in adults but not children. I was the first one on the scene, started CPR, and when he responded, I treated him with Lasix. He recovered rapidly. The pediatric resident who subsequently arrived asked what I did. I told him and he said, "Good job. That's what I would have done." But he wasn't there.

My scariest episode occurred in OB. The pediatric resident was supposed to attend deliveries to care for the neonates. This pregnant woman went into delivery unexpectedly. The obstetrician and the pediatric resident were called STAT to the delivery room. I was the first to arrive.

The nurse looked at me and said, "Do you know how to deliver a baby?"

I said, "Yes." Orville had taught me well.

She said, "Then do it." The baby was delivered before the obstetric or pediatric resident arrived.

The baby was blue. I gave oxygen and did a quick exam. The heart sounds were peculiar, and the abdominal exam was odd as well, so I ordered an X-ray. By the time the pediatric resident arrived, I had the X-ray back. "Scimitar sign," she said, "and the liver goes straight across." I didn't know the scimitar sign, but I knew the baby had unusual malformations. The mother was a professor's wife, which made it more tragic. The baby died two days later of multiple malformations.

## Pathology

I found pathology to be fascinating. Of course, I was most interested in the liver, my favorite organ.

I had the same pathology preceptor the entire rotation. He had an interest in tropical diseases, so he had me review malaria, schistosomiasis, and brucellosis slides, which he had in his teaching file. I spent hours reviewing normal tissue and comparing it to malignant tissue. The mitotic figures in cancer cells reminded me of my physiology slides. I must have impressed him because at the end of the rotation, he offered to write me a letter of recommendation to any pathology fellowship program I desired. I was very tempted, but I still wanted to work with patients, so I declined. I still considered a hepatology fellowship, though.

## Neurology

I appreciated the intellectual aspects of neurology. Based on a physical exam, we were supposed to determine the site of a brain or spinal cord lesion. It was stimulating, like a good mystery novel.

Our orientation was by the famous A. B. Baker, MD, who at that time had written the main textbook of neurology. He was dogmatic, inspiring, and a great speaker. The other students teased behind his back that he had a connection with the Mafia because he insisted we get Italian reflex hammers. His enthusiasm impacted my interest in a complete neurologic exam, which I later insisted that my residents perform when I became faculty in Kalamazoo. I did not tolerate the comment, "The patient was comatose, so I didn't do a neurologic exam."

"No," I would counter, "that is when you must do the most careful exam."

At that time, Minnesota reported the highest incidence of multiple sclerosis of any U.S. state, so we had many young patients with curious exam findings. But the focus of our attending was on neurologic emergencies: drug intoxication, seizures, brain hemorrhage, and meningitis. We learned how to assess the patients and make quick decisions regarding treatment.

Other than A. B. Baker's clinical text, we were required to read *Stupor and Coma*, which is still the premier text for assessing the comatose patient. There are now additions on CTs and MRIs, neither of which was present in the original text. But the evaluation principles have not changed.

Seizure treatment in Minnesota was avant garde. Most clinicians were using phenobarbital for seizures, but Minnesota had researched using IV Dilantin, which did not cause as much sedation and was not a habit-forming barbiturate. The problem was that it was a vasodilator and could drop the patient's blood pressure. We were taught to monitor their blood pressure and accompany the treatment with plenty of fluids but drip the Dilantin slowly. Then the problem with dropping blood pressure was abated.

One patient I will never forget. He presented intoxicated to the emergency department, where he was briefly examined by the ED physician. I was assigned his case since he had withdrawal seizures, which we treated with benzodiazepines. He sobered up quickly.

I was instructed to discharge him. But the morning of discharge, he had erased the blackboard at the nurses' station and was sitting there laughing. The nurses were furious because the blackboard had all their patient assignments on it. The charge nurse told me, "Get that drunk discharged."

I went to him and politely asked him why he had erased the blackboard. He said, "To watch the cartoons." I asked him to explain. "If I keep my left eye covered and look at a blank screen, I can see cartoons. They're so funny."

Curious, I performed a cranial nerve exam right in the hall and discovered he had a right Marcus Gunn pupillary response, meaning the right eye's optic nerve was not transmitting nerve impulses properly.

I called the attending and reported my findings suggesting a tumor on the patient's optic nerve was causing irritation that presented cartoons to his brain. Sure enough, subsequent imaging showed a tumor. He had surgery to remove it. He was disappointed with the result because he could no longer be entertained looking at a blank screen. However, he did not erase the nursing assignments anymore. The nurses were much nicer to him when they understood that he had a brain tumor.

## Cardiology

Cardiology at Northwestern was exhausting but dynamic and fun. I suppose for medical students today, it would be a duty-hour violation because of the long hours. I was to report at 7:00 a.m. to read EKGs done during the night and early morning. By 8:00, my first admission arrived. There were six admissions every day, and I was to have them completed by noon. I met my attending in the physicians' lounge to go over the H&Ps.

The food that the hospital provided free to medical students was great. Often, we had shrimp, scallops, roast beef, and sometimes lobster. I had to finish my six patient admission presentations to my attending during lunch because by 1:00, he took me to the cine lab to review the heart catheterizations of the previous day's patients. My attending spent time going over all the details, so for example, if I had heard a heart murmur during a patient's exam the day before, I got to correlate it with the valve pathology on the cine. If I had taken a history suggesting severe coronary artery disease, then the next day, I saw the coronary angiogram. After reviewing the cines, or the videos of the catheterizations, I made rounds to check on all my patients. This format gave me an excellent correlation of physical exam with cardiac pathology.

One patient I will never forget. He had open-heart surgery for bypass and valvular surgery. One day post-op, he coded. I started the code, but the surgeon soon arrived on the scene. No progress was made, so he split the patient's stitches and performed an open-heart massage. The patient did not respond. He had to be sewn back up for the undertaker.

I don't recall ever leaving the hospital before 7:00 p.m. I had anticipated the long hours. Since it was summer, Priscilla and the children left to live with her sister in Wisconsin. We set up a tent next to the strawberry field, and the children thought they were camping. They were having so much fun that summer they didn't miss me. Besides, I had every weekend free to join them.

## Internal Medicine Rotation

My experience at Hennepin County Hospital was exhausting as well as intellectually stimulating. The old hospital was right in the middle of the red-light district. When you looked out the upper-floor windows in the evening, you could see the prostitutes' doorways beautifully lit up.

As medical students, we had to draw our own labs at night

since the phlebotomists all went home at 3:30 p.m. The nurses refused to turn on the lights in the hospital's huge fifty-bed wards, which would have awakened all the patients, so we had to draw blood with a nurse holding a flashlight. But sometimes, the nurse was called away. The result was that one had to draw blood by feeling the vein, poking in the needle, and knowing one got blood when the sample tube got warm and the vibration stopped when the sample tube was full.

In the morning, we would see the patients we were assigned, as the attending would come at 10:00 to round. We had better have memorized all the patients' histories, exams performed, laboratory values, and X-ray findings and reviewed the differential diagnoses. We couldn't use notes, as the attending required eye contact. We were severely chided if we forgot one detail. Much of the morning was spent trying to find the X-rays, which often were not in the X-ray department, since someone else had them to review. This required scurrying around the hospital to round them up before the attending appeared. That attending experience disciplined me to be succinct but comprehensive in my presentations.

Medical students were assigned to teams. My senior resident, besides being a brilliant clinician, was a pool shark. He would ask students to play with him on the pool table in the residents' lounge when we were free. It didn't matter if I broke or he did; he would put all his balls in the pockets. I would never get another chance. It entertained him that I broke differently every time.

On the internal medicine rotation, we were restricted to six H&Ps per week. I suppose it was against school policy, but my senior resident would give the H&Ps to the interns all week and wait until the night our team was on call. Then he would tell me, "Do the first six admissions. Wake me up when you're done." He would then go to a call room and sleep. That experience taught me to be efficient. We always had at least six admissions, so I was busy. I would then wake him up and report my findings. "Good job," he would say and then go see the patients I had admitted. The interns did the rest of the admissions, as our team often had as many as fourteen per night call.

Then I would go to the cafeteria to get some supper. The night chef was quite comical. He was a huge black man, at least six foot four with massive muscles and a great sense of humor. He explained that his job was to get rid of the day cook's leftovers. He would pile your plate with some concoction he had conglomerated from the day's food. It was always delicious, but I had no idea what I was eating. Then I would go to one of the call rooms to rest.

One morning, I awoke to a young, attractive medical student who had crawled in bed next to me. We were in scrubs, but I was embarrassed. "All the other beds were full," she said, "and I saw your wedding ring, so I knew you were married. Since you were already asleep, I didn't think you'd mind." I did call Priscilla and explain what happened. She laughed.

Some patients made quite an impact on me. We had a patient admitted in delirium tremens. When an alcoholic was admitted, benzodiazepine (Valium) was used to prevent delirium tremens because it's very effective. But this patient presented seizing. Valium didn't help, and his blood pressure initially went high and then dropped precipitously. Catecholamine and massive fluids didn't help, and he died despite a frantic code. That patient helped me understand how serious alcohol withdrawal is, and the pathophysiology involved. Delirium tremens overloads the catecholamine receptors. Once the blood pressure drops, the receptors do not respond to appropriate drugs.

A pimp was admitted for pneumonia. He requested a private room despite the added expense. The men's ward had only two private rooms in between the two fifty-bed wards. During his hospital stay, his women attended him, providing meals, silk sheets, curtains for his window, and a Persian carpet beside his bed, all of which disappeared at discharge.

The new hospital was under construction. It wasn't completed until the end of my rotation. The patients were transferred in truck trailers. My last day of the rotation, I stayed with the patients in the hospital. Some of the medical students went in the truck trailers to monitor the transit to the new hospital.

That was the last rotation of my medical school training. I was done. I had graduated from medical school. After the last rotation, I visited the registrar, as she required. She silently reviewed my attendings' evaluations, looked up at me, and said, "You've graduated." Then I went home and told Priscilla. She found a babysitter and took me to a steakhouse to celebrate.

# 13

## MADAGASCAR

There were still three months before I would start residency, and I was interested in using my skills in a developing country environment. Jan, one of my canoe guide partners at Camp Vermilion who graduated from college with a BA in secondary education, went to Madagascar to teach at the expatriate school in Fort-Dauphin. During the time that I was in medical school, she had written several letters to Priscilla and me suggesting we go to Madagascar when I graduated.

A close classmate of mine had gone to Bangladesh as an away rotation. His expenses were largely paid for by Medical Assistance Program (MAP).[9] After discussing his experience, he encouraged me to apply to MAP. He added that I was more likely to receive a stipend if I had already chosen a place to go. It just so happened that the administrator for the hospital in Manambaro, Madagascar, was home in Minneapolis on furlough and agreed to interview me. He approved of me and suggested that I speak with Mark and

---

[9] This was funded by *Reader's Digest*.

Sherilynn, who had been missionaries to Madagascar. Mark was a semiprofessional photographer, so he had great pictures.

In any case, by the time of my interview with MAP, I requested Madagascar. Mrs. Yancey, Phillip Yancey[10]'s wife, interviewed Priscilla and me. We were quickly approved. MAP paid 75 percent of our travel expenses, so off we went with a three-year-old son and a one-year-old daughter to Manambaro Lutheran Hospital at the southern tip of Madagascar, just north of where Jan was teaching.

Madagascar was a communist country in those days, so it was important that I had not signed up for the Air Force, nor gone to Vietnam. That would have hampered our visa application.

The trip had some glitches. The airport in Antananarivo was chaotic. When we were to have our luggage checked by immigration, Tirzah started screaming. The official covered his ears and told us to go. Our luggage was never checked. We did have some equipment on which they could have charged duty, but it was never discovered.

A missionary couple picked us up at the airport, fed us, and gave us a nice place to sleep in Antananarivo. The couple suggested that we avoid much time in the capital city, so we boarded an Air Madagascar flight to Fort-Dauphin the next morning. My seat was next to a tied-up goat in the aisle. The plane stopped at several coastal towns.

At one town, we had to leave the plane while it refueled. Temujin had to urinate, so we went to the airport building. It was a one-brick façade, no bathroom, so I took him to the edge of the dense jungle surrounding the airstrip to do his business.

When we landed at Fort-Dauphin, Jan was supposed to meet us. She was not there. All the other passengers left, and still

[10] Theological author

172

no Jan. One taxi remained, the driver smiling at us. I spoke no Malagasy or French, so we felt hopeless. But Mark had taught me one Malagasy word: *tranovatu*. So, I went to the taxi driver and said, "Tranovatu." He smiled, loaded us up, and drove us toward the expatriate school, the only stone building in town, which is what *tranovatu* means. Jan appeared on her moped when we were halfway to town and followed us. Since I had no Malagasy money, the taxi driver waited patiently while Jan negotiated to pay him.

We stayed the night with Jan, and the next morning, we went to the bank to obtain Malagasy currency. There was no ATM in 1976. I recall that I also had to present myself to the health inspector since we had flown through Nairobi, Kenya. Although we had received yellow fever immunizations in the United States, at the airport we were told, "U.S. physicians didn't know how to give them properly." Finally, we were transported to Manambaro Lutheran Hospital, which took about an hour with two river crossings north of town.[11]

We were given a nice place to live, a palm tree bark–sided house with a tin roof, complete with a nice kitchen, dining room, and bedroom. It even had indoor plumbing with a nice bathroom, shower, and toilet. Palm tree bark cracks a bit when flattened out into a wall panel, so while sitting on the bathroom toilet, you could see through the cracks in the walls, which was somewhat bothersome for modesty. The kitchen had a nice gas stove and a small refrigerator. We were set. It was a five-minute walk to the hospital, up a short hill.

What about food? The hospital physicians said, "Pray for it, and it will come." So, we prayed. Priscilla was impressed. People

---

[11] In 2018, it took thirty minutes, as there were then two bridges. The following year, the bridges washed out and had to be rebuilt. In the interval, the hospital was isolated from supplies.

came with rice, fruit, and seafood for sale at the door. In the market, one must negotiate prices, but someone must have told them that we were hospital workers who didn't know how to negotiate. Priscilla would give them money and they would give her the proper change for a fair price.

Since we had a bathroom and were returning to the United States in a few months, I wanted Temujin to use the toilet and not urinate in the bushes where his newfound Malagasy friends urinated. He agreed. However, when I went home for lunch one day, which I did because there was always a two-hour rest when the hospital electricity was turned off and nothing could be accomplished, I found Temujin urinating in the bushes. I scolded him.

He responded, "But there are monsters in the bathroom." I thought that was a creative excuse, so I took his hand and dragged him to the bathroom to show him that there were no monsters in there. On entering, he pointed at the bathtub and said, "See, monsters."

It turned out a salesman had come by with fresh lobsters. Priscilla bought them but was unsure where to put them, so she had the merchant put them in the bathtub. I had to apologize to Temujin. There were monsters in the bathroom.

The only bothersome thing about the house was that when it rained, the sound on the tin roof was so loud Priscilla and I could not hear each other talk, even lying right next to each other in bed. When it rained, we spent the time in silent prayer.

Dr. Noel, an amazing Malagasy physician, was head of the hospital. He spoke English and French as well as Merina Malagasy, the dialect of television and radio, and at least two other dialects, Tanosy and Tandroy. I was impressed with his clinical acumen and patient care in an environment of technological limitations, *en voie de development* in French. I worked directly with him until he was confident with my expertise.

It wasn't long before Dr. Noel had me doing surgeries with a surgical assistant and deliveries with the obstetric nurse. He stayed busy with emergency surgeries, with which he often invited me to assist. During the time I was at that hospital, I recorded eighty-plus major procedures in the log I had to keep for MAP. I developed a fair amount of expertise with so many deliveries, including breech deliveries with the application of Piper forceps.

## Neonatal Tetanus

Neonatal tetanus was a major problem in 1976. The first tetanus baby taught me a lot. I gave the baby IV Valium as I observed the baby's respirations. They increased. I paid attention. When the respiratory rate plateaued, I checked on the dose. I had given the four-kilogram baby 25 mg/kg (100 mg). I also noticed when I tried to suction the baby, the heart rate dropped. I improvised two treatments: I did a tracheotomy on the child and used atropine to prevent bradycardia. Tetanus toxin causes not only muscle spasm but also increased parasympathetic tone. Valium IV is very caustic to veins, so additional doses needed to be given orally, but the baby couldn't swallow, so a nasogastric tube was inserted for medications, as well as nutrition. Atropine was required, as the tube placement caused bradycardia.

A social problem was that the nurses ignored these patients because they assumed the children would die anyway, so why bother. After three weeks, the first child went home with her mother, breastfeeding successfully and breathing well. The child had been weaned off the Valium, and the tracheotomy had been closed.

What that neonate taught me about tetanus toxin was not yet in the medical literature: Patients with tetanus do not become sedated with high doses of Valium because of the neurologic stimulation of the toxin. The parasympathetic nerves are stimulated, causing vagus nerve irritability. The human body could metabolize the toxin,[12] but it was a slow process, at least three weeks. As the toxin was metabolized, the baby could be weaned off the Valium. I reduced the dose by half each week. (One can adjust the dose to the respiratory rate.) And a nasogastric tube was essential for medication and nutrition. The nurses learned to help the mother pump her breasts and give her breast milk down the nasogastric tube.

After the first neonate survived, the nurses' attitudes changed. I didn't have to do all the suctioning, and they were willing to administer medication, which I had done with the first case. The nurses no longer felt that it was futile.

We had fifteen cases over six weeks. I set up a protocol for treatment. Of the fifteen, one died of Klebsiella pneumonia despite appropriate antibiotics. And one died on admission before I could get to the hospital. The nurse came to my house and knocked on the bedroom window. I ran up to the hospital, but the baby was already dead and couldn't be resuscitated. The other thirteen babies went home feeding well, off medication.

Subsequently, I have treated twenty-eight cases of tetanus, including a teenage girl and a thirty-year-old man, using the same protocol. They have all survived. But I have always wondered if those babies suffered brain damage in the process. In 1996, I received a letter saying that one of my original tetanus babies had graduated from the University of Madagascar in Antananarivo. At least that one had no brain damage.

---

[12] Some textbooks claimed that the body could not detoxify tetanus toxin.

## *Ectopic Pregnancy*

Another remarkable case was a woman who complained, *"Misy biby ny kibo."* The nurse translated, "She says that an animal has crawled into her belly." The nurse added, "She wants it removed."

The woman's menstrual history was intriguing. She had no menses for six months, then resumed for two months, but now presented with no menses for another two months. In the exam, I could feel a baby's hand and foot through the abdominal wall, but her uterus seemed normal to palpation. X-ray confirmed a fetus outside the uterus.

I consulted Dr. Noel. He told me to do surgery and remove the fetus since there was no heartbeat. The abdominal pregnancy was clearly dead.

I prepared the patient for surgery with my assigned surgical nurse. I removed the abdominal fetus and cut the umbilical cord as instructed. The textbook[13] claimed that the placenta would atrophy, so it could be left in place. The problem was that the left tube attached to the placenta had massively enlarged to five or six centimeters in diameter because of placental stimulation.

I draped a saline cloth over the open abdomen, unscrubbed, and left the patient to the care of the scrub nurse and nurse anesthetist so I could confer with Dr. Noel as to what to do. He was busy, so I went to the library until he was available. There, I found an up-to-date obstetric text on the bookshelf. It was no help. I consulted with another physician, who suggested that I remove the tube and purse-string the uterine opening, like repairing the colon after an appendectomy.

I returned to surgery, cross-clamped the tube, and removed it. I put in a purse-string tie and cut off the clamped tissue. Curious,

---

[13] Very few texts even address this issue.

when I observed decidua coming out of the opening, I pushed it back in with my finger and discovered she had another pregnancy in her uterus! I closed the purse-string and inverted it into the uterus and did another purse-string tie, tying it tight, as I had done with appendectomies. Post-op, she did well, but I assumed that she would miscarry the uterine pregnancy since I had had my finger in the uterus while sewing up the tubal opening.

The next day, she felt fine and asked to go home. I asked her to stay another day, which she did, but she refused to stay any longer. When she was returning home, I asked in which village she lived and asked our chaplain to inform the village elder that she should come back if she started bleeding or started labor.

After returning to the United States, I was informed that she delivered a normal baby vaginally! I have discussed this case with several U.S. obstetricians, who claim that I did the right thing but are unsure what they would have done in the same circumstances.

## Syphilis

A very pale woman presented to the clinic. Her hemoglobin was 2,[14] but her VDRL was 4+. I was amazed that she could still walk without losing consciousness. I treated her syphilis, found the source of her bleeding, and transfused her to a hemoglobin of 6. After that, she felt great, ready to hike home. I laughed at her lab, wondering if the spirochetes were carrying oxygen, since she had so few red blood cells and minimal symptoms.

---

[14] Normal is 14 to 16.

## Jungle Tour

A missionary, Roger, was climbing into the mountains to check on a village that was planning on building a church. He asked if I would like to accompany him. I wanted to see what village life was like for the 80 percent of Malagasy who lived in rural areas, from both anthropological and medical perspectives, so I agreed.

We hitched a ride with a trucker. I was assigned the task of keeping him awake as we drove all day and all night. The road was gravel in some places, but full of potholes.[15] Other places resembled two parallel goat trails. The driver wasn't much of a conversationalist but spoke some English.

Deep in the middle of the night, he asked me, "Are you from America?"

"Yes," I answered. Then there was a long pause.

"Do you know about Ford trucks?"

"Yes." Another long pause of ten to twenty minutes followed.

"This is a Ford truck."

"Yes." I already knew that but waited for the reason he told me.

He pointed at the manual transmission gearshift. "I have a question." Another long pause.

"Yes. What is your question?"

"I have been a truck driver for many years. I use this first gear. What are the other gears for?"

"They are for going faster."

"Oh. I have never been on a road where I could go faster."

In fact, he had never driven faster than fifteen to twenty miles per hour his entire truck-driving career because of the roads.

At sunrise, we arrived where the road ended in a small village

---

[15] The Malagasy have a joke about potholes. The French term for a pothole is *nid d'oiseau,* which means "bird's nest." In Madagascar, a pothole is referred to as a *nid d'autruche,* which means "ostrich nest," but there are no ostriches in Madagascar.

in the mountains of Ranomafana. The village elder greeted us, and Roger introduced me. The elder said that the last time a physician had come to their village was thirty years before. To honor me, the elder arranged a clinic.

Patients came to the elder's house from several neighboring villages for consultation. Most of the problems were minor. I was cautious, although I did write a few prescriptions on scraps of paper that the elder planned to send down the mountain to be filled at the hospital pharmacy. Then the elder decided to be a patient. His symptoms sounded like gastric reflux or an ulcer, so I wrote a prescription for an H2 blocker.

After a fine supper of rice with something on it, we stayed in the elder's home. Roger pulled Raid Yard Guard out of his backpack and sprayed the bed. "I'm always welcome in the villages," he said, "because every home I stay at, they know that I'm going to spray their beds with insecticide." I had to admit that the bed, though uncomfortable, did not have any bugs.

The next morning, we were served breakfast: a mountain of rice with a hardboiled egg on top. I questioned Roger about where we were going. This village already had a church. "Up in the mountains," he said.

"But the road ended," I noted.

"We have to walk the rest of the way."

Our guide appeared as we left the elder's home. He was carrying eighty pounds of oranges on his back. Village gossip had told him that I was a physician, and he claimed he was not allowed to walk in front of me.

"But I don't know where we are going," I replied.

"On the trail," he explained.

It was awkward to have him behind me. I did see the trail, but once in the mountains, there were many cross-trails. I always took the wrong one. He would set down his oranges, come and escort me to the correct trail, and then shoulder his oranges. Then we were off again with our guide walking behind me. Roger followed, amused at the process.

Walking in the jungle has its own code. I had worn tennis shoes, but they soon became soaked, and I was afraid of blisters. So I took them off and walked the remainder of the fifty-five miles barefoot over a ten-day trip. When I had to urinate, I walked a short way off the trail. And once, when I returned, my legs were covered in grass leeches. After that, I learned to stay on the trail, even to urinate.

We visited several villages on the way to the one where Roger was encouraging the villagers to build a church. One day, we stood on the side of a cliff and observed a village below. "See the new hut?" Roger said, pointing at a distinctive hut that hadn't been weathered like the others in the village. He explained, "That means there is either a wedding or a funeral."

As we went closer, we heard singing. Roger said, "It must be a funeral." So we approached the new hut in a solemn procession. Roger knew the village elder, who spoke English, so we entered and sat next to him. An elderly man lay in the center with villagers sitting around the perimeter.

As I watched, I noticed that the man was breathing. I whispered to the elder, "But he's not dead." The elder explained that the man decided he was dying, so the funeral was started. The villagers started with the first song in the Malagasy hymnal and sang every song in order.

I asked permission to examine the dying man. The elder thought it was a good idea, so I pulled my stethoscope from my pack while the elder explained to everyone what I was doing. The dying patient was complaining of severe chest pain. I listened to his heart and lungs and heard a snapping sound as he took a deep breath. I turned to the elder and asked about the history. The elderly man had been climbing a tree to get some ripe bananas and had fallen. My exam demonstrated that although he had several broken ribs on the left, he did not have a pneumothorax.

I returned to my place, next to the village elder, and explained, "I don't think he is dying."

"In that case," said the elder, "we will finish singing all the songs in the hymnal, and if he is not dead, we will stop the funeral."

Roger and I excused ourselves and resumed our jungle trail hike to the village with the proposed church. "Why did they start the funeral before the person died?" I questioned Roger.

"It's a custom. That way, the dying person gets to see who comes to their funeral. It gives them psychological support when they're dying."

*How unique*, I thought. *Maybe we should incorporate that custom into our culture.*

We finally reached the village where the church was to be built. In the village square, I saw the pile of building materials, but no evidence of construction. Roger was annoyed. He had arranged for the building materials to be sent to the village several weeks before and had expected the church to be built by the time he arrived. He had planned on holding a dedication service as the missionary representative of the Evangelical Lutheran Church in America (ELCA).

This resulted in an elder meeting under an orange tree. I didn't understand much because it was all in Malagasy, but it seemed to be a heated discussion. A young boy was summoned to climb the tree as the village elders met. During the meeting, with an elder's nod, the lad would pick an orange and toss it to the one who requested it. Thus, treats were provided during the meeting.

It was a long, drawn-out meeting. When it was over, I asked Roger what the decision was. He seemed frustrated but told me, "The elders said that it wasn't the right day to build the church."

Every day in the Malagasy calendar has a meaning just as we attribute meaning to our holidays. Of the 365 days, some have positive meanings and some negative meanings. Just like Priscilla refused to be married on April 1 (Fool's Day), the elders were waiting for a proper day. The result was that two weeks after we left, the right day came. The whole village assembled and built the church in a couple of days. Unfortunately, Roger was unable to attend to make a dedication speech.

As we hiked back down the mountain trail, and we came near the village of the premature funeral, an elderly man ran up to me and hugged me. Roger explained this was the man whose funeral we had attended. He was excited that he was "resurrected from the dead." I was careful to explain through Roger's interpretation that God had healed him, not me, but he was convinced he had been dying and now he had a new life.

When we arrived back at the village where the road began or ended, depending on one's interpretation, the village elder told me he had received the prescription that I had written and taken the pills. As a result, his reflux symptoms were gone. He gave me a kilo of vanilla beans as payment.

Our Ford truck driver was there to drive Roger and me back to Fort-Dauphin. When we walked into the mission house, we found the floor was covered with a monolayer of grapefruit. I was led to understand that Roger had requested some grapefruit for the expatriate schoolteachers. I don't think Roger ordered a whole truckload, though—just a few, maybe a bagful. We spent the afternoon loading grapefruit into the back of the truck.

A small child climbed on top of the fruit when we finished.

The village elder explained that the child was going with us. I was curious as to why. It was because these grapefruit were a gift. The child was the son of the farmer from whose trees the fruit was harvested. The son was sent along to make sure we did not sell the grapefruit. If we sold them, the farmer would never give a gift to the mission again, as selling a gift is taboo. The irony is Malagasy do not eat grapefruit, as they think that it tastes bad. The French had forced them to grow the crop during the imperialistic days. Even so, we were not allowed to make a profit on a product we had not grown. This is part of the reason that Indian merchants are resented for making money from other peoples' products. There were no middlemen in aboriginal Malagasy culture.

We abided by the rules. When we arrived at Tranovatu, the expatriate school, we distributed the grapefruit among the teachers under the lad's watchful eye and accepted no payment.

One Sunday, one of the pastors asked if I would like to join him at a church in the jungle. He was a circuit preacher with responsibility for several churches, to which he made rounds during the month. When he wasn't at one of the churches, a catechist, usually a village elder, provided the service for the attendees. I readily agreed; I wanted to attend a village church in contrast to the large congregation in Manambaro.

I recall it took about three hours that Sunday morning to hike to the church. In the process, we had to cross a river. I was apprehensive, as it was flowing fast, ice cold and waist-deep in the middle. The pastor turned and told me, "Put your hands on my shoulders and put your feet where I step."

As we headed across the raging stream, I gripped the pastor's shoulders and put my feet where he had stepped. We crossed without incident. As we stood on the far bank, he said, "We follow Jesus. If we stay close to Him, and walk where He walks, no problem."

Up a steep incline, following a narrow trail, we arrived at the church. It was made of palm tree bark with a thatched roof of banana leaves. What surprised me inside the church was a huge tree stump the size of a small car. It appeared that people had cut down the tree to position the church, but the massive stump remained. I asked the pastor, "Why haven't they removed the stump?"

"Two reasons," he said. "First, the children crawl around on it and keep quiet during the sermon; second, if it gets chilly, we can chop off a piece to start a fire in the front of the church to keep warm. It is a very useful stump."

It was a delightful service. The pastor gave me a Malagasy hymnal, and since I had studied the language enough to pronounce it properly, I could sing along, even though I did not understand the words. He told me the hymn numbers in English. I understood nothing of his sermon, but while we hiked back down to Manambaro, he explained it to me.

As we descended the mountain, we saw two men walking on the path below. The pastor said, "Those two men are Christians."

"How can you tell?" I asked him. "They're too far away to even see their faces."

"Notice their hats."

One wore a conical hat and the other a square hat. "Yes," I said, still confused.

"That conical hat is Tandroy, and the square hat is Tanosy. If they were not Christians, they would never walk together."

It was a rich experience to go with the pastor, sing with the village congregation, hike the mountain trails, and ford the rivers.

## *Desert Hospital*

Southwestern Madagascar is in the rain shadow of the central mountains; Manambaro is in a jungle habitat. The hospital director, thinking I also needed to see medical problems associated with the desert, arranged to transport my family to Ejeda, a hospital in the middle of the desert. Ejeda Hospital was part of the Norwegian Lutheran Church ministry, then part of the ELCA, and now part of SALFA, the health organization of the Malagasy Lutheran Church.

There, we met Stan and Kathy Quanbeck. Their history would fill a book. In fact, Lutheran Press is publishing Stan's memoirs. In short, he was born and raised in southwestern Madagascar. His parents and grandparents were missionaries in Madagascar since the late 1800s. He attended the mission school in Fort-Dauphin, where his sister died of malaria and was buried. And he went to the United States for college and medical school, studied tropical medicine in Belgium, and returned to Madagascar with his mission-oriented wife, Kathy.

The diseases in the desert were quite different from the jungle diseases in Manambaro. Malnutrition was a problem because of lack of rain, whereas in Manambaro, people could grow plenty of rice, have gardens for vegetables, and raise a few chickens.

Ejeda is cattle country. Cacti are used for fences, including the familiar Christmas cactus with its red flowers. It is quite a sight to see a coral of cacti all in bloom. In Madagascar, they flower all year round, not waiting for Christmas. Unfortunately for the Malagasy, the spines carry some fearsome organisms, so skin infections[16] are common. The cowhides harbor anthrax, so I saw my first anthrax cases there. Despite the hysteria in the United States regarding

---

[16] The Pasteur Institute grew chromoblastomycosis from the cactus spines.

laboratory-developed resistant anthrax, in Madagascar, it is easily treated with penicillin.

Every Mahafaly man has a spear, which resulted in a theological controversy: Should the men be allowed to bring their spears into church with them? A council meeting was held where it was decided that since the men felt naked without their spears, they could bring them into church but had to take off the blades and hide them in their clothes. As soon as they left the building, they would fit their blades back in place.

Stan and Kathy had twin girls, Vicky and Lily, who were preschool age in 1970. I recall that Temujin had just turned four, so they played well together. However, they got in trouble when Temujin taught the girls how to make mud pies and Vicky and Lily carried them home to show Kathy their prizes in her shopping baskets. But the baskets were made of grass and were easily hosed clean and left in the sun to dry.

Priscilla really enjoyed Kathy, and the feeling was mutual. Kathy enjoyed visiting with someone from the states who was not a missionary, and Priscilla enjoyed the process of homemaking in the desert with minimal facilities, shopping for food at the local market, and caring for the children in this desert environment.

The desert grounds around the hospital fostered a hard clay tennis court. Although I am a pathetic tennis player, it provided some exercise after hospital rounds. But it was hot! Also, it was dry, so there were very few mosquitoes, making malaria less of a problem.

Schistosomiasis mansoni, a parasite carried by snails that migrates through exposed skin, is quite a problem in the jungle area, causing liver problems, and in the desert, Schistosoma haematobium causes bladder problems. The bladder becomes infested with parasites, and the body's inflammatory response calcifies the bladder wall. The result is a solid non-contractile bladder that causes kidney failure. Stan introduced me to a procedure in which a portion of ilium is attached to the dome of the bladder, maintaining the vascular supply of the intestine. This can expand and contract without parasite infiltration because Schistosoma haematobium does not infect the small intestine. More recent modifications include removing the bladder, then attaching the urethra and the ureters to the pouch of ilium. It's very effective but a much more involved surgery than the one Stan invented.

## Canoeing in Madagascar

Stan needed some relaxation and refreshment. When he heard that I had been a canoe guide, he suggested a canoe trip down the Onilahy River. He had a foldboat packed in two suitcases. We unloaded it and followed the directions to put it together. I was impressed. It was stable in the water and easily maneuvered.

We started out at a famous bridge. Why was it famous? It was a bridge intended for military use in Vietnam. It was unloaded by mistake in Madagascar. The Malagasy government informed the United States that they would gladly reload the bridge onto the next ship, but for a substantial price. The United States, in their infinite generosity, told the Malagasy that they could keep the bridge. So, it was set up over the Onilahy River. The only problem was there was no road to or from the bridge.[17]

We drove cross-country, and our driver found the bridge. There, we put together our foldboat, wished our driver farewell, and started down the river to Tulear. It was relaxing and peaceful. We saw very few villages and there were no rapids. Stan did have

---

[17] Now there is a village on each side and a desert trail.

concerns about camping on islands because the river could rise suddenly. He was also concerned because Madagascar has a unique species of crocodile. When we met a woman washing clothes in the river, Stan inquired about the possibility. She said, "No crocodiles here. We ate them."

As we approached the coast of the Mozambique Channel, the river became wider and shallower. We managed to get off the river where there was a road, and our driver found us. It had been a delightful trip and something Stan had wanted to do for a long time. He was thankful that I had been willing to do it with him. Along the way, he had shown me the area where his parents had been as missionaries. They had reached their home by going up the river in rafts loaded with their supplies. He claimed that it was much more pleasant to go downstream in a foldboat. His memories were such a blessing to me.

## Completing the Rotation

Our time in Madagascar was coming to a close, so Priscilla, the children, and I had to head back to Antananarivo to fly home. There is a landing strip in Ejeda, but it takes local farmers several days to knock down the anthill towers so a plane can land. Besides, it is very expensive to ask Mission Aviation Fellowship to fly there. They prefer coming for medical emergencies, and we were not an emergency. So, we drove back to Antananarivo.

What an adventure. Pastor Torvic drove us back. The road ended south at Betroka, which was at least a day's drive from Ejeda, so we drove cross-country. I never saw anything that resembled a road during that journey. Priscilla kept Torvic awake, as he kept falling asleep during the nocturnal drive. Granted, there was no road to drive off, but there were cacti to avoid.

We came to a river and stopped. There, a young boy suddenly appeared. Torvic asked him to try to cross it. Once the child was waist-deep in the water, Torvic said we had to wait. We had a picnic lunch and took naps in the shade of a tree. Even in the desert, trees grow along the rivers. A few hours later, the child walked across the river in knee-high water. Now we could drive across.

When we arrived in Betroka, we discovered the road. It seemed almost magical that Torvic could drive cross-country to arrive at the town, but he had done it many times as a career missionary pastor.

The trip back to Antananarivo seemed uneventful after that, despite potholes and washed-out tarmac in places. We stayed at the ELCA/Norwegian guesthouse until our scheduled flight.

We flew to Amsterdam. We had a reservation at a hotel in the historical district, but we got lost trying to find it. At that time, I did not speak French, and of course, knew no Flemish. I tried to ask directions in English but was ignored. Priscilla suggested German, so to the next person on the street, I asked directions in German. He understood me and gave us the directions we needed to find our hotel.

It was an elegant historical hotel with high ceilings and old-fashioned facilities. I took the responsibility of bathing the children after the ten-hour flight. The reason that I remember it so well is because as we used the shower, which the children enjoyed, the water suddenly became steaming hot. Somehow, the cold water ceased. I jumped in the shower, turning my back to the water to protect the children as they scrambled out of the tub. I scalded my back, but it healed.

Our breakfast was good. The Belgian pastries looked sweet but tasted quite bland. I heard the people at the next table speaking

Flemish. I could understand quite a bit of what they were saying. Maybe the man on the street had understood my German because of the cognates with Flemish, or maybe he did speak German. But the Flemish newspaper was impossible for me to read. There were too many doubled vowels and odd endings.

As required by MAP, I had kept a diary, recording eighty major surgeries, thirty deliveries, as well as the fifteen cases of neonatal tetanus. I had a new sense of medicine without technology. I had seen how Malagasy physicians functioned in such an environment, providing amazing care. I had matured in my skills, and now, I was ready for residency.

# 14

## RESIDENCY

When we arrived in Kalamazoo and went to the Southwestern Michigan Area Health Education Center (SMAHEC) office, we were informed that I had not answered fifteen letters they had sent to my Malagasy address. I explained to them that the mail delivery in Madagascar was unreliable, but here I was, with wife and children. What were the questions in the letters?

The director said, "I presumed that since you were coming from Madagascar, you wanted to stay in resident housing."

"Yes, we do," I said. "I'm so thankful for your presumption." I apologized for not answering his letters as we set off to find our appointed housing. This housing was across the street from Bronson Hospital. It was convenient during residency while I was assigned rotations at Bronson. Also, our apartment had plenty of space and a nice kitchen. Priscilla really liked it.

But Borgess Hospital was across town, across a railroad track that went through the middle of Kalamazoo. I later discovered another way to the hospital by driving north of downtown and then east, bypassing the railroad track. When driving to the hospital, I had to choose that route about six blocks in advance.

Kalamazoo had been the celery capital of the United States around the turn of the century; the celery was picked in the morning and immediately loaded onto the train. Kalamazoo doesn't grow celery anymore, but the train still goes right through the middle of town. When you need to go to Borgess Hospital on the other side of the city and the train is stopped, you just wait. It is the only legitimate excuse for being late for work.

## Hospital Rounds

Orientation went well, and we received our assignments. I was on call the first week of July at Borgess Hospital. After rounds on the hospital's academic medicine patients, our team was on call for emergency admissions. I was called to the emergency department for a patient who was having continuous seizures. I had cared for several patients like this in the neurology service at Minnesota University Medical Center, where I gave Dilantin intravenously until the seizure stopped. I proceeded to give the recommended dose.

Unknown to me, this protocol was not universal. It had never been used in Kalamazoo hospitals. The nurse assisting me panicked and called the neurologist, saying, "I have an intern here in the emergency room who is killing the patient."

The neurologist, Dave Flagler, had trained in Minnesota. He immediately came and asked me, "Did you train at Minnesota Neurology?"

"Yes. How did you know?"

He laughed and calmed the nurse, and we became best friends. When the patient's seizure stopped and he regained consciousness, the nurse was impressed but didn't apologize for her "killing the patient" comment. She trusted me more in the future, though.

The residency program was on call for the whole hospital, so our team was very busy answering the requests for our academic patients and also other physicians' patients. Most of those calls were routine, but sometimes, they were challenging because we didn't know the patient. When I responded, I had to read the chart, find out why the patient was in the hospital, and then answer the question the nurse posed. Most of the time, I had to examine the patient as well. Meanwhile, I was being paged for other patients.

Our team dropped everything if a code was called. The most critical were the unexpected codes—for example, the patient was hospitalized for a benign reason, such as knee surgery or cholecystectomy. Our team was usually successful at resuscitating those patients. The codes I disliked were those that should not have been codes in the first place—for example, a patient was dying of lung cancer. I felt that it was disrespectful to the person to pump on their chest, give them IV medications, and even hit them with joules when the treatments were futile.

One code I will never forget. I was the senior resident with a new intern, and a nurse called a code and yelled, "He's on the toilet!" I happened to know this patient from previous order requests. He was a pathologically obese man with severe heart problems complicated with lung disease. He also had prosthetic eyes.

The intern ran into the bathroom to find the patient sitting on the toilet, blue and cold. He had expired long before the code was called. The enthusiastic intern gave him a precordial thump. When the patient's prosthetic eyeballs consequently fell out and rolled across the floor, the intern fainted. We decided to resuscitate the intern instead of the patient.

## The 1978 Blizzard

One day before work, I awoke to heavy snow. We didn't have a radio in the house or in the car to inform me that the police had closed all the roads in town, so I proceeded to drive. I had learned to drive in Northern Minnesota, so snow was part of my driving experience.

I was on call at Borgess Hospital, and an intern, Dr. White, who lived in resident housing, had asked me for a ride. So I revved up the car to get us out of the parking lot. The wind had blown some of the streets clear, but there were big drifts across some other roads. Minnesota driving skills allowed us to smash through the drifts and slide through the intersections as the stoplights weren't working.

We made it to Borgess without ending up in a ditch. I was so focused on my driving that I hadn't realized Dr. White was curled up on the floor in front of his seat. When I stopped in the Borgess parking lot, he crawled out and said, "I am never riding with you again." Then he stormed into the hospital. We were the only residents to show up for work that day.

With the snowstorm still raging, I was called to see a patient who was confused. I found him delirious. He had been admitted by the rheumatologist for an exacerbation of his rheumatoid arthritis. The rheumatologist had increased the patient's dose of high-dose corticosteroids on admission.

I called the rheumatologist to discuss the patient's change of status. I thought the patient needed a spinal tap; the attending didn't think it necessary. He didn't seem impressed, presuming the increased dose had caused the confusion. After a long discussion on the telephone, I said, "I'm going to do a spinal tap unless you come in and assess the patient." Of course, with the blizzard, I knew he wouldn't come in, so I did the spinal tap and discovered that the patient had cryptococcal meningitis. The rheumatologist was chagrined when I called him about the result, but later, he took credit for the decision to do the spinal tap and make the diagnosis. It upset me that he didn't acknowledge my expertise. Subsequent experiences with this rheumatologist proved him to be quite arrogant and obnoxious.

It took a couple of days to clear the roads, so I ended up working a forty-eight-hour shift. With the residents who couldn't leave, Dr. White and I, the patients received good care. Bronson Hospital was not a problem, because the residents who lived in resident housing across the street were available.

When I did make it home, Priscilla and I took our children snowshoeing. We snowshoed cross-country through parking lots and streets that still had not been plowed. It was an exciting adventure for the family, and the exercise relieved my tension from the hospital call.

## Outpatient Clinic

Internal medicine residents were required to spend one afternoon a week in an outpatient clinic. I found it relaxing because of my experience in medical school with the Backus brothers, who taught me how to empathize with my patients but also be efficient. Several patients I will never forget.

One middle-aged woman needed a Pap smear. She had never had one, so I recommended a pelvic exam and Pap smear. She refused. I was surprised because she didn't seem shy or inhibited about the other parts of her exam. Her blood pressure was under good control with medication, which I renewed on a regular basis. And each follow-up visit, I again recommended a Pap and pelvic exam. After I had been caring for her over a year, she finally trusted me enough to schedule the exam for the next follow-up visit, three months later.

At that visit, the nurse prepared the Pap tray and assisted me in the exam. As I tried to place the speculum in her vagina, there was an obstruction. I pulled out three one-hundred-dollar bills. At this point, the woman said, "And put them back where you found them when you're done, Dr. Roach." I did her Pap, which showed no cancer, and replaced the bills.

An intelligent young woman with cerebral palsy (spina bifida) was always trying to get married. In those days, the patient had to have a pelvic exam and gonorrhea and syphilis evaluations to get a marriage license. She came to the clinic multiple times, but something always caused the proposed marriage to fall through.

One more time, she came with her boyfriend. I first examined him and found him to be severely mentally deficient. After her exam, the young woman asked me, "Do you think I should marry him?" I was hesitant to give her any advice, especially when I found grass in her vagina. She and her boyfriend had had sexual relations in the city park.

I suggested, "Go to your friend's house and give him the directions to find you. If he shows up, marry him." She liked that advice. Later, she told me that he never showed up.

A hostile young man presented with chest pain. On examination, I found a pericardial friction rub, a sign of pericarditis. After I explained the finding, he was unwilling to be hospitalized or have any further investigation, so I offered him Indocin to resolve the problem and reviewed the medication's side effects. I made sure he understood the consequences of his decision and the medication. I reviewed this plan with my attending, who had trained in the Bronx. He agreed with it.

Two hours later, my attending received a telephone call from a lawyer who claimed that he wanted to sue me for giving his client a medicine to make his stomach bleed, which was one of the side effects I had explained to the patient. I was staffing another patient with my attending when he received the call, so I heard the whole conversation. My attending explained the decision for the medication and said to the lawyer, "You obviously have a fool for a client." The lawsuit was dropped.

Most of our patients were more routine, with urinary tract infections, hypertension, and anemia. But a fair number of them also had psychiatric disorders that required adjusting psychotropic medications. Scheduling a psychiatrist evaluation was very difficult, so we had to make the adjustments to their psychiatric medications. The running joke was Kalamazoo Psychiatric Hospital closed in the 1950s and the discharged patients made it as far as the internal medicine clinic.

## Morning Report

Morning report occurred every morning before seeing patients. Usually, a junior or senior resident presented a case, and the residents attending tried to make the diagnosis based on the history and physical exam findings. Then the presenter would give the diagnosis and review the learning aspects of the case.

The best morning reports were given by my colleague Robert Roschmann because he would dress up as the patient and present the case in the first person. I will never forget the morning he dressed up as a bag lady to present her case. He got a standing ovation, but I don't remember what her diagnosis was. He was a great actor and a great teacher. He subsequently fellowshipped in rheumatology and was Priscilla's rheumatologist when we returned to Kalamazoo two decades later.

At graduation, the faculty and residents voted to award the resident who had been the best teacher with a cash prize. Robert and I received equal votes, so we had to split the money. I used mine to buy Sheila Sherlock's hepatology book, *The Liver*.

Years later, I went to a hepatology conference in Georgia where Sheila Sherlock was the speaker. The audience was told that we could have breakfast with Dame Sherlock (the queen had awarded her a damehood by that time). Several attendees signed up, but I was the only one who showed up. I had a private breakfast with her and her surgeon husband. Before leaving, I asked her if she would sign my copy of her book. She laughed because she had published a newer edition and said, "Why do you want me to sign this old thing?" She signed my book for me, anyway.

## Clinical Pathology Conference

As a requirement of graduation, each senior resident has to present a clinical pathology conference, a case prepared by a faculty advisor. The resident reviews the history, physical exam, and laboratory studies presented and then, after about two weeks of mulling over the case, presents the case to community physicians and faculty. Most internal medicine residents never forget their case because the cases are weird and wonderful, requiring much research to make a formal presentation. The anguished hope is that they conclude with the correct diagnosis.

I will never forget my case. It was very confusing. The history, physical, and laboratory data suggested several different types of cancer. But which one was the correct diagnosis? After two weeks, I still wasn't confident I had the diagnosis, so at the end, I suggested three different cancers that I thought the patient might have.

Dr. Krishna, the oncologist, joined me at the podium to discuss the final diagnosis. The patient had five primary cancers; I had discerned three of the five. Dr. Krishna turned to me and said, "Richard, if the patient has one cancer, they are more likely to have a second one, and if they have a second, they are more likely to have a third, and if a third, they are at greater risk for a fourth and a fifth. You should have guessed that."

"Yes, Dr. Krishna, I will remember that."

"Well, you did a pretty good job," he said.

## Favorite Rotations

My favorite rotations in residency were cardiology and infectious disease. They were the two rotations where it seemed that the clinician made a dramatic change in the patient's life.

I really enjoyed working with Dr. Francis, who was a Southern gentleman. He allowed me to do many procedures, including assisting with heart catheterizations and pacemaker placements. He taught me cardiac physiology during lunch while reviewing patient records.

His partner, Dr. Leguizamon, was a radical character. Many of the residents refused to take cardiology at Borgess because he was so crude. When I would present a patient to him and describe the workup, he would criticize me in his Argentinian-accented English, "You are such an ass, Richard." But one day, I finally got his respect. I had admitted a patient with dysrhythmia and ordered a digitalis level. At first, he took me into the stairway and reamed me out. "Why did you order that? You are such an ass, Richard. You know digitalis levels are inaccurate."

When he finished his tirade, I said, "Yes. I know. I ordered it to see if the patient was taking his medicine, not to check the level for toxicity."

He thought about that. There was a long silence. Then he said, "That was very clever." I think that was the only compliment I ever received from him, but he didn't call me an "ass" anymore after that.

Dr. Leguizamon was quite avant garde; he did many things that had just been reported in the literature but were not common practice in Kalamazoo. He was the first physician to give high-dose propranolol to a patient in hyperthyroid storm, which saved her life. He gave beta-blockers to patients in heart failure, which was contraindicated at that time—and now is common practice. The most important thing I learned from him was "If you understand the pathophysiology and the pharmacology, don't be afraid to treat the patient with medications that haven't been approved yet by the FDA."

I considered doing a fellowship in cardiology, but the lifestyle was gruesome because of the long hours and call schedule. If I had been single with no interest in having a family, I think that I would have been a good cardiologist. Because of the procedures and teaching of Dr. Francis and Dr. Leguizamon, I handled several difficult cases in practice. I was always thankful for that.

The infectious disease rotation was my favorite. Dr. Dehaan, who invented clindamycin and did the original testing of the drug, was my attending. I would review a case for which Dr. Dehaan had been consulted and then go to his Upjohn office to present the case to him. He allowed me significant freedom to order tests and think out the diagnoses. When I finished the rotation, Dr. Dehaan gave me an outstanding evaluation. He called Dr. Carter, our program director, suggesting that I consider an infectious disease fellowship at the University of Michigan Hospital in Ann Arbor. He made the contacts and arranged my rotation with Dr. Carol Kauffman.

It was my last rotation of residency, so Priscilla and the children kept up the household as I arranged to live in Ann Arbor for the rotation and come home on weekends. In Ann Arbor, I stayed at the medical student fraternity house. It was walking distance from the hospital, and the rent was very inexpensive. I was told that I had a roommate. I was a bit apprehensive about that, but it meant I would only pay half rent. And I never actually met him. Some of the other students at the frat house told me that he was living with his girlfriend.

My first day of the rotation was memorable. I was directed to Dr. Kauffman's office, but no one was there. I sat and waited, unsure what to do. Quite a while later, she showed up rubbing her hands together. I noticed many scratches and cuts. "What happened?" I asked her.

She smiled and said, "The ferrets don't like to have their blood drawn."

She was doing research on lymphocyte response to fungal infections using ferrets as her model. She was employed by the VA, so we had to cross the street to the University Hospital. There, she introduced me to Dr. Silva, a handsome physician who had done research on giardia. In the corner of the research lab was a short man sweeping with a broom. I thought he was the janitor, but Dr. Kauffman introduced him to me as Dr. Fekety. I had heard about him and wanted to meet him since he had published research on tetanus.

At that time, Dr. Fekety ran the only biologic test for Clostridium difficile by feeding guinea pigs patients' stool samples. If they developed diarrhea, the test was positive. The only treatment, until he and others discovered the bacteria that produced the toxin, was cholestyramine. He laughed as he said, "It's a stupid drug. It absorbs everything, even the toxin."

Back at her office, Dr. Kauffman explained the rotation and my requirements. Then she asked about my interest in infectious disease (ID). I spoke about my experience in Madagascar. She suggested a "small meeting" of the ID fellows to explain my experience. I was apprehensive, as the fellows would all know more about ID than I did. On what basis could I explain anything to them? I questioned. But she insisted.

The meeting took place in an auditorium at the University Hospital. This "small meeting" actually filled the auditorium. Dr. Kauffman specifically wanted me to discuss the protocol I developed in Madagascar for treating neonatal tetanus. As I entered the auditorium and scanned the audience, my legs became like rubber. I shook when Dr. Fekety came down the aisle and sat in the front row.

I stuck to the facts of my protocol and described the fifteen babies whom I had treated with thirteen survivors. When I finished, Dr. Fekety stood and shook my hand. He said, "I learned some new things. I'm very impressed with your results."

After my talk, one of his fellows, Dr. Don Batts, came forward to greet me. He had moved to Kalamazoo when he finished his fellowship. He was a fantastic teacher who led the residents through some confounding cases, and he invented and researched vancomycin. We became longtime friends.

Infectious disease rotation kept me very busy. I learned so much about assessing critically ill patients with sepsis. Dr. Kauffman was the national fungus expert, so I was able to see referred patients with rare and unusual fungal infections. And Drs. Fekety and Silva wrote many chapters in the infectious disease textbooks. At first, I was intimidated presenting cases to these famous people, but I found them to be warm and encouraging of students.

# 15

## LOOKING FOR A JOB

Toward the end of residency, I started looking for a job. I had loans from medical school that would be forgiven if I practiced in rural Minnesota. So, I returned to my home state to find a good place to practice.

I really wanted to return to Cloquet, Minnesota, because I had such a great experience with the Backus brothers there, and Cloquet qualified for loan forgiveness. They were enthusiastic about my possible return, but their clinic had some financial problems since Dr. Monsreud, the orthopedic surgeon, retired that meant they couldn't hire me as a partner. Dr. Byron Backus and I talked to the Cloquet hospital CEO. They wanted to hire me as a hospitalist, but I would have needed to set up an office of my own. I never understood economics, as Priscilla and my brother Bill can tell you, so I had no ability to set up my own office.

The state of Minnesota offered several other choices. Bigfork needed a physician. Again, this position required someone who could set up their own practice. Years later, I discovered that I could have joined the multiple-physician group in International

Falls, Minnesota, as a satellite clinic, but the offer wasn't made then.

Another choice was Olivia, Minnesota. That was intriguing because the family medicine physician there was a friend whom I met in Madagascar. So, I interviewed. I enjoyed the practice, but there was only one surgeon in town, and he was an unethical rascal whom I knew from previous experience. I could not work with him. I needed a practice where I could refer surgical patients with confidence. He left three months later.

## Mississippi

I tried to expand my search outside of Minnesota. A friend, Dr. Peter Boelens, had a practice in Vicksburg, Mississippi. His practice to poor people in Yazoo County was quite a ministry. He invited Priscilla and me to an interview. There were several problems.

It vexed Priscilla's and my souls to see the prejudice still rampant in Mississippi in 1979. The church in town had a sign: "We believe in the separation of the races." Peter had attended that church when he first moved to Vicksburg, but when the church elders discovered he had a clinic for African Americans, they asked him to leave.

When the Supreme Court ruled that segregated schools were illegal, the state of Mississippi complied with the law by closing all the Black people's schools and changing the education requirement to only first grade. After completing first grade, Black children were encouraged to drop out of school. Peter used this idiotic solution to buy the school in Yazoo County that had been closed because it was all Black with Black schoolteachers and a Black school board, who all lost their jobs. Peter made the vacant school into a clinic. He hired some of the teachers for special education

205

classes. And the athletic facilities became a community center. Priscilla and I were impressed with his ministry. I spent time seeing patients and recognizing the need.

The hospitals were segregated as well. A rich Jewish man who despaired over segregation built a hospital for the poor Black patients. Peter took me there to meet the physicians. They were doctors who had not been accepted into residency programs because they had not passed their board exams. I hung my head as they presented misdiagnosed cases. Peter said, "They had poor teaching. But you could teach them."

I was interested in joining Peter. I felt that I could teach the physicians to become more sophisticated in their expertise. I had worked with a Haitian student in Berrien Springs who did not pass his exams, and after a year of working with me, he passed with high scores. I was willing to see the work as a mission.

Peter was sponsored by a Christian organization. However, they were not interested in sponsoring me. Peter suggested that I apply for a National Health Service position, for which his practice qualified. But they only promised that I could work at the Yazoo Clinic for two years, and then they could place me somewhere else. Priscilla and I did not think that plan was viable. I had nightmares for two weeks because of the racial discrimination we observed.

## Working for SWMC

Back in Michigan, I received a phone call from a physician group in Berrien Springs, Michigan: Southwestern Medical Clinic (SWMC). It was a multi-specialty practice with surgeons and pediatricians, but only one internal medicine specialist. The internist, Dr. Patton, really wanted a partner.

Berrien County Hospital had a six-bed intensive care unit and a forty-five-bed hospital ward with a separate obstetric unit. Attached to the hospital was a ninety-bed long-term care unit. SWMC's practice was based on the principle of allowing physicians to go to developing countries for up to three-month stints, which meant that I could periodically return to Madagascar and still get a salary while I was gone. The salary wasn't huge, but it met our needs and provided enough to buy a house and vehicle and still pay back our student loans.

After my orientation to the hospital and clinic, Dr. Patton took a vacation. It was much needed, as he had not had a day off in three years. That week, as the only internist, I had seventeen consults. Our office manager thought that since I didn't have a clinic practice, I could work in the emergency department for a few shifts. I was busy, too busy. When it came time to take my board exams, I mistakenly thought I had been so well trained that I didn't need to study. Wrong! I missed passing by two points.

I was discouraged and tired. Priscilla suggested that I sign up for the next exam, which I did, and take some time off to study. For the next exam, I spent every afternoon two weeks prior to it at the library at the University of Notre Dame, where I could not be reached. I studied the Medical Knowledge Self-Assessment Program sponsored by the American College of Physicians. I also attended a board review course. I passed without any problem. As a result of that experience, I realized I needed to take time off.

Dr. Patton and I were on call every other week. My family medicine partners sent us their most challenging patients. That had good and bad effects. The good thing was that my practice was incredibly intellectually stimulating. The bad thing was that the weekend call was exhausting.

## *Pseudomonas Endocarditis*

Over the course of the thirteen years that I worked for SWMC, I cared for nine cases of pseudomonas endocarditis.[18] These cases are very hard to treat because pseudomonas is resistant to most antibiotics. Even when it is reported by the laboratory as sensitive, the organism can develop resistance during treatment. There have been cases in which the organism is resistant to all known antibiotics. Those patients die. Such a case presented to my family medicine partner. He called me, saying, "Richard, this patient has a heart murmur, and last time you saw her for her blood pressure, you did not hear one. She is sick."

She was admitted on Friday night. I started her on two antibiotics and consulted the cardiac surgeon. He reviewed her echocardiogram, which showed a huge vegetation on her valve, and agreed to do surgery on Monday. Saturday, she was stable and her fever had resolved. The antibiotics were effective. Sunday, part of the clot on her valve migrated to her brain, causing a massive stroke. Tuesday, she died.

Subsequent cases responded to treatment without mortality or were transferred to Ann Arbor.

## *Pheochromocytoma*

I cared for four cases of pheochromocytoma.[19] Pheochromocytomas are very rare tumors. In fact, in medical school, our professor discussed them only briefly and added, "You'll probably never

---

[18] Benton Harbor had pseudomonas as the coliform bacteria in the public water system. The literature states that pseudomonas causes less than 1 percent of cases of infective endocarditis.

[19] A rare endocrine tumor that produces catecholamine hormones

see a case." One of my Berrien Springs cases was the first case of a pheochromocytoma in the right atrium, which the Ann Arbor cardiac surgeon published without acknowledging my diagnosis and referral.

That patient had an interesting presentation. She was a nineteen-year-old African American who presented to Dr. Johnson, her obstetrician, twelve weeks pregnant. Dr. Johnson's nurse always took a patient's blood pressure while they were sitting in the exam room chair. Her blood pressure was 90/60, not unusual for a young pregnant woman. Dr. Johnson then always rechecked the patient's blood pressure while they were lying on the gurney waiting to be examined. This patient's blood pressure was now 200/90. Dr. Johnson had the patient stand, and it was again 90/60.

When the Mayo Clinic did a study of seventy-five consecutive pheochromocytoma patients, all of them had an orthostatic drop of at least 20 mmHg. In fact, the Mayo Clinic endocrinologist claimed that if a patient does not have an orthostatic drop, they need no further evaluation.

Dr. Johnson called me to the OB clinic to assess the patient. I examined the young woman and discussed the case with Dr. Johnson. We agreed that there must be an endocrine problem. I checked the patient's catecholamine level and found it to be ten times what's normal. With alpha-blockers, which are safe with pregnancy, I controlled the patient's BP until delivery. The delivery of a healthy baby was uneventful. Then began the search for the tumor.

Most pheochromocytomas are near the adrenal glands or alongside the abdominal aorta. Her abdominal CT scan was normal. No tumors. Ann Arbor had recently developed a scan that used radioactive cholesterol, so since a pheochromocytoma uses cholesterol to make catecholamine, I requested the scan, explaining the evaluation that had been done. The endocrinologist was skeptical. He said, "We'll do the scan, but I doubt she has pheochromocytoma."

She went for her scan. Her right atrium lit up like a light bulb. The diagnosis was made. The endocrinologist, who didn't believe me, contacted the cardiac surgeon.

After that, the patient had surgery, the tumor was removed, and she was returned to Benton Harbor to care for her newborn. And the Ann Arbor endocrinologist scheduled no follow-up visit, as pheochromocytomas are not only rare, but 95 percent benign.

Four years later, the patient presented to the ED in St. Joseph, Michigan. The Benton Harbor hospital, near where she lived, had been closed as if poor people did not need a hospital. I was on call for patients without physicians or patients whose physicians were from Berrien Springs. I found her to be very short of breath. A chest X-ray revealed metastatic cancer in her lungs. The pheochromocytoma had metastasized into her lungs. I just cried as she died in my arms, knowing she had a four-year-old daughter at home and there was nothing I could do. There probably wasn't any chemotherapy for such metastasis, but I still felt like the endocrinologist had dropped her.

I felt like writing a letter to the editor of the journal that published about her surgery, but I didn't have the expertise or the heart to do it.

## Wilson's Disease

A teenager with Wilson's disease, a copper storage disease (1:100,000), was diagnosed late because only his brain was involved. The patient ended up semicomatose in our nursing facility. I was asked to consult because he would grasp the side rails of his crib, have muscle spasms, and break the crib. The nursing home was tired of replacing it.

When I examined him, I noted the diagnostic Kayser-Fleischer rings in his eyes. He was responsive only to noxious stimuli. However, his mother insisted that he have a television in his room, which she provided. One day on rounds, I noticed that he smiled at the jokes on the television. I concluded that there was a person inside who could respond to humor.

I asked the admitting physician if I could take over the case. He agreed. I studied the literature regarding treatment of Wilson's. I discussed the treatment with the mother because the treatment is quite toxic. She agreed because her son was in no condition to respond to her the way he was. I proceeded despite the drug toxicity.

Over the course of two years, he became alert and responsive. He was able to ambulate with assistive devices and communicate with a special computer. Eventually, the mother was able to care for him at home, where he had a tutor to teach him, as he had dropped out of school at age twelve before he was diagnosed. She continued the toxic treatment as an outpatient treatment.

The other Wilson's disease case I diagnosed because the teenage boy complained of abdominal pain. He had an enlarged liver, so I offered to do a percutaneous liver biopsy. The needle bounced off his liver. I suggested to my surgeon colleague that the patient have an open biopsy, which made the diagnosis. He had no other symptoms; only his liver was involved. This patient was treated and responded, avoiding liver failure.

The two rarest forms of Wilson's disease are brain-only (5 percent) and liver-only (10 percent). I have never seen the most common type (85 percent).

## *Intensive Care Unit Patients*

Our ICU was always full. Since he was tired, Dr. Patton, who had fellowshipped in cardiology, taught me to put in pacemakers. I had assisted with pacemaker placement in many cases with Dr. Francis in residency. Before an interventional cardiologist, Dr. Duge, came to St. Joseph, Michigan, I put in twelve. And then I referred my thirteenth patient to him. I'm glad I did because it was a disastrous case, as the pacemaker tip kept causing dysrhythmia. He managed it, but with great difficulty, and I was thankful. "You sure sent me a difficult case," he told me. "That is the worst pacemaker I have ever placed."

Finally, SWMC hired two more internists. Weekend call was still exhausting but only once a month. It was because of this harrowing practice that Priscilla and I decided to celebrate our children's birthdays for a whole week in case I was called to the hospital on the exact day. I'm delighted that my children have continued this custom with their families.

Other adventures while at SWMC included ED admissions. A young man came with second-degree burns on both hands. He said, "I threw gasoline on a fire." I cared for his burns and admitted him because with both hands badly burnt, he couldn't care for himself.

The next morning, there was a county sheriff with a rifle outside his room. I entered and found him shackled to the bed with cuffs on both legs. While I was changing his dressings, I asked him, "Why is the county sheriff here? Why are you cuffed to the bed?"

"I got a speeding ticket," he said.

Outside the room, I said to the sheriff, "You guys are pretty tough on speeding tickets these days."

The sheriff laughed. "Did he tell you what he was speeding in?"

"No. Should I have asked?"

Further explanation revealed that he had stolen a cattle truck, with the cattle. He drove from Alabama and sold them in Michigan. The police were notified. Speeding in the cattle truck, he could not outrun the police car. So, he ditched the truck and poured gas all over it to burn the evidence. He had come to the ED in a getaway car.

When he was admitted, he said he wanted his valuables placed in the hospital safe. The registrar counted out his $10,000 in front of him, as was required when a patient deposited valuables with the hospital. Since he couldn't sign the receipt because of his burns, a witness to this deposit was required. And because this witness was curious as to why he should have so much money in his pockets, she notified the county sheriff, who was always present, since Berrien County Hospital was a county-owned facility. He called the state police to find out if they were looking for someone with burnt hands and $10,000 in his jeans pocket, which they were.

On that occasion, I learned that what a patient tells his physician is not always the whole story.

One patient whom I cared for in the ED, I later presented for a Clinical Pathology Conference when I returned to Kalamazoo as resident faculty. This elderly lady walked into the ED unregistered and climbed onto a gurney, stating, "I have the flu."

Since the laboratory technician was in the ED to draw blood on another patient for whom I was caring, and since the nurse informed me the woman had a fever, I ordered some preliminary labs.

Moments later, the technician returned to the lab and called me. "Your patient has a hemoglobin of 12 but has no red blood cells. I suspect that she has clostridium sepsis." As I hung up the telephone, the patient coded. She could not be resuscitated.

Two hours later, the technician called. "Her blood cultures just blew up in the incubator. She has clostridium sepsis."

We obtained permission to do an autopsy. No cause was found. I reviewed the literature. About 10 percent of clostridium sepsis cases occur without a discernible source.

That lab technician was incredibly clever, not only in the lab. She was also an opera aficionado. She invited Priscilla and me to accompany her to the *Elijah* oratorio presented in South Bend, Indiana. We enjoyed the famous oratorio in our unsophisticated joy, but I chuckled quietly when the lab technician whispered in my ear, "He missed a note."

Unfortunately for Berrien County Hospital, her astute acumen was noticed by a guest speaker from Johns Hopkins whom I invited to speak for our hospital grand rounds. He requested a tour of the hospital after his talk. When he met the head lab technician, he interviewed her. He later went back to the lab and offered her a job as chief laboratory technician for Johns Hopkins University Hospital. She felt bad about leaving our hospital and sent me a letter, which read, "I couldn't give up the opportunity. I love my job here. Besides, they quadrupled my pay."

## Outpatient Clinics

After a few months, I had accumulated enough patients and consults that I was assigned to three outpatient clinics. I had a clinic at the end of the hospital driveway, another clinic in Berrien Center, and a third clinic in Benton Harbor. I had to see hospital patients before the clinic started, which meant early morning rounds. In addition, the surgeons wanted the required EKGs reported prior to the first surgery at 8:00. I am an early morning person, so most of the time, I finished rounds and completed my consultations before the clinic.

Thursday was the most difficult day for several reasons. The Benton Harbor clinic was twenty miles away from the hospital. Dorothy, my receptionist, had worked in the clinic for another physician until he died. She contacted our business manager, asking SWMC to take over the practice.

The issue with that clinic was the patients were so sick. It was 95 percent African American patients whom my family medicine partners cared for Monday through Wednesday; they referred the patients they struggled to care for to my Thursday clinic. Hypertension was a serious problem among the patients. In thirteen years, I never saw a case of mild hypertension. All the patients had moderate to severe hypertension.

Several examples demonstrate the struggles. One young woman presented with a headache at about 11:30. Her blood pressure was 240/130. I offered to admit her, but she said, "Give me medicine to bring it down. I'm a schoolteacher and must get back to my classes." She promised to follow up later, so I gave her samples of a beta-blocker, a diuretic intramuscular injection, and an angiotensin-converting enzyme inhibitor. She sat in the waiting room for thirty minutes, during which time her headache was resolved and her BP went down to 130/90. Then she thanked me and went back to school. She did later return to the office for medicine prescriptions that I had given her. She was incredibly grateful.

I struggled with a young man with severe hypertension. I arranged prescriptions and then asked him to return in one week. His BP was much better at that time. But when he came for his three-month checkups, his BP was always out of control. I thought he was noncompliant, but on further questioning, I discovered that his medications were always stolen. Dorothy and I discussed how to keep his medicine safe. First, we suggested that he keep his medicine in the refrigerator. But soon, the thief figured that out. Why did the thief want his BP medicine?

"Because they're capsules," he said. "The drug dealers want capsules, which they empty and fill with illicit drugs."

Dorothy thought that the solution was to buy him a lock for his refrigerator. She bought him one at the hardware store and showed him how to install it on his refrigerator door. Success. After that, his BP was always under control.

Another difficult case of severe hypertension involved a delightful young man. It took me years to bring his BP under control with five different medicines. The day he came to the clinic and his BP was perfect, we danced together down the hall.

Weeks later, he presented without an appointment, requesting that his BP be rechecked. It was out of control again. I asked, "Are you taking your medicine?"

"Yes," he answered.

I was reluctant to add a sixth medicine, so I asked him, "Why do you think your blood pressure is out of control?"

"Because I have been going to a lot of funerals."

"Oh," I said, "have a lot of people in your family died?" I was thinking maybe his blood pressure was out of control because of grief.

"Oh no, I didn't even know these people. But, Doc, they serve the best barbecue ribs at funerals. I know that I shouldn't be eating all those ribs, so I came to the clinic so you could give me a Lasix shot to get those ribs out of my blood." He understood the sodium load from the barbecue, and I gave him a shot of Lasix.

He explained to Dorothy when she rechecked his blood pressure, "Tell Doc I peed out a storm from those ribs. Thanks." His blood pressure back under control, he left the office.

The ten cases of hyperaldosteronism, an endocrine abnormality in which the adrenal glands secrete excess aldosterone, that I saw were Benton Harbor patients. I would see these women,[20] give them a diuretic (hydrochlorothiazide) as is recommended for initial treatment, and check their potassium in a week. When it was low, I would stop the diuretic and check their aldosterone level and other labs to make the proper diagnosis. The results were diagnostic. Then I would stop all their medications and substitute aldactone. All ten presented with perfect BP.

Each had been referred to me because my family medicine partners were unable to control their BP with three or four medicines. When they noted the low potassium, they would add another drug, a potassium supplement in massive doses. Frustrated, they would refer the patients to the Thursday clinic. The patients were delighted to get this under control with a single medicine.

Seeing forty-five patients a day in Benton Harbor was overwhelming, so I hired a physician assistant (PA), John Kittredge. He was a Kalamazoo College graduate, so, by definition, he was smarter than me because with my high school GPA, I would not have been accepted to Kalamazoo College. I recall that he was a history major before deciding to go to Western Michigan University's PA school.

John initially worked with physicians in Traverse City, Michigan. He enjoyed the physicians there, but the patients were so snooty that they didn't want a PA caring for them. That wasn't the case in Benton Harbor. In fact, many of my patients preferred him to me. One woman whom John hospitalized said to me when I checked on her, "Don't you order anything for me until you talk to Dr. John first." I complied. I didn't bother to explain that John was not a doctor.

---

[20] I never saw a man with hyperaldosteronism. Curious sampling error?

We saw so many hypertensive patients that one day, I asked John, "What do you think we should do?" He suggested going to the churches. I didn't understand what he meant, but over the course of several months, he went to a different church in Benton Harbor every Sunday. Imagine a tall, young, handsome Caucasian attending African American churches. He managed to meet with the pastors and the elders. He discovered that there were trained nurses (RNs) in each of their congregations who were willing to check BPs and encourage patients to comply with their medications during the coffee hour after the sermons. Within six months, the BPs in our clinic were under much better control. John taught me that sometimes, it takes a community intervention instead of a medical one to solve a medical problem.

## Seizure Disorder

One remarkable patient developed an allergy to Dilantin, the medicine I prescribed for her seizure disorder. I had to stop it, but a week later, she had another seizure. I called the neurologist in Kalamazoo, who suggested Tegretol since it had a different chemical structure. Unfortunately, she was allergic to that as well, so I stopped it (Keppra hadn't been invented yet) and counseled her to not get too tired, drink plenty of fluids, and avoid alcohol—that is, lifestyle therapy.

A week later, her husband brought her to the ED. He was very angry that I had not given his wife any medicine for her seizures. He told the ED physician, Dr. Taylor, to call me down to the ED. I came immediately. When the husband saw me, he ripped the electrical conduit off the wall and tried to spear me. In a flash, Dr. Taylor, who was seventy years old, disarmed him and had him under control.

"How did you do that?" I asked.

"You forget, Richard, that I have spent twenty years working with the Zulu in South Africa. I've disarmed Zulu warriors many times."

I sent the patient to see a neurologist in Ann Arbor, as I clearly had lost rapport with the patient's husband. They gave her an experimental drug to which I had no access.

One elderly lady with whom I had an excellent rapport had developed TB when she was younger. In those days, before the development of isoniazid, the treatment was to collapse the lung and fill the cavity with Ping-Pong balls. (She had a very interesting X-ray of her left chest cavity filled with Ping-Pong balls.) Two years later, INH was invented. She was treated with a full course so that she would not be contagious.

One year, she developed influenza. When I checked her sputum, it was positive for acid-fast bacilli. But when the flu resolved, it was no longer positive. Besides, the organism did not grow in the lab, so the ID specialist suggested no further treatment. It took me a long time to understand this patient's pulmonary function. She refused to see any other physician because she didn't want to explain her medical history or that she did not want to be resuscitated under any circumstances.

After several years of my care, the patient arrived to the ED by ambulance, presenting in full arrest. I informed the ED staff not to resuscitate her. But just then, her son, whom she hadn't seen in years, ran screaming into the ED. He was frantic and said, "I need to talk to my mother." So I intubated her and resuscitated her to full alertness.

Over the next day, mother and son reestablished their relationship with many tears. The next day, I extubated her. After smiling at her son standing at her bedside in the ICU, she looked at me and scowled. "Dr. Roach, I will forgive you once," she said. "Don't let it happen again." Two days later, she died. I did not resuscitate her.

A challenging situation related to the head of a religious sect of personality. The leader presented with an end-stage brain tumor after radiation and maximum tumor debulking in Indiana. His oncologist told him there was nothing more to be done. He did have some lucent moments after massive steroids that decreased the swelling around his tumor mass. During one of these, he told his congregation, "When the doctors pronounce me dead, don't believe them. A few minutes later, I will rise from the dead."

When I admitted him, he was comatose with neurologic evidence of uncal herniation syndrome, which means the swelling was crushing his brain. Because he was in the ICU, he was monitored. Eventually, the swelling crushed his medulla and stopped his heart. I pronounced him dead.

Then the hullabaloo commenced. The ICU filled with thirty to thirty-five people yelling and waiting for him to rise from the dead. It didn't happen. I called the hospital chaplain to help me because the patient had told his congregation not to believe any physician. It took at least a half hour before things settled down. The nurses stayed busy explaining to the other five patients in the ICU what was happening.

## Matriarchal Culture

Another ICU incident taught me a lesson. A young African American man presented with appendicitis but was septic and delirious. He needed emergency surgery. When I asked his wife to give her permission to do the surgery, she said, "I can't do that."

"Why? Aren't you legally married?" I questioned.

"Oh yes, we are, but I cannot make decisions for him. His grandmother must do that." She explained their matriarchal culture; the matriarch had to make the decision. She called the family while I got the surgical team set up.

About twenty minutes later, the matriarch arrived with her entourage. There were twenty-five people in the ICU waiting room. In the corner of the room sat the dignified, white-haired, elderly woman, who did give the wife permission to sign the permit. I knew there were quite a few matriarchal families in Benton Harbor, but this was the first time I had to deal with a matriarch to get a surgical permit signed. I learned that the legally responsible person is not necessarily the culturally responsible person.

## Alcohol and Drug Treatment Program

For twelve years, I was the director of New Horizons, the drug and alcohol recovery program. First, it was in Berrien Center, Michigan, and then our program transferred to Benton Harbor. When Mercy Hospital was closed, our treatment program secured one of the wards. We had treatment counselors who had trained at Hazelden, so our program was fashioned after their approach. While Ford was president, our program received federal funding because Betty Ford had problems with addiction. Our success was better than the reported literature.

After several years, one of our sponsors offered to host a party for the program. Our alcoholics who had maintained three years of sobriety were invited at no cost. They required a letter from their AA sponsor, their significant other, and one other person, usually a minister or priest, in order to receive an invitation. Three hundred qualified for the party. It was an amazing event.

We did accept heroin and cocaine abusers as well. One of our cocaine-addicted patients saw his dealer out the window one day. He broke the window, ran across the roof, and jumped from the second story to the street. After that, we had security windows placed in our unit.

One young woman was brought to the unit by her boyfriend. He explained, "We would take cocaine before sex because it made it so exciting. But my girlfriend discovered that she could get an orgasm by taking cocaine without sex. Now she doesn't need me. Fix her!"

When I went to an addictionology conference in Philadelphia, I heard a speaker discuss using amantadine for cocaine abusers. We tried it on thirty of our admissions, randomly dividing the group in half. I was blind to who received amantadine and who did not. When we unblinded the study, the results were astounding. Half the patients who received the placebo signed out against medical advice. None of the patients on amantadine signed out. We even had patients ask for a prescription at the time of discharge because the medicine prevented craving. I was delighted that the medication worked so well. It became our standard protocol.

Narcotic abuse has a terrible withdrawal, with abdominal pain and muscle spasms. We used clonidine with excellent success, as it blocks the adrenergic barrage of withdrawal. The only problem was that because nurses are taught to check the patient's blood pressure before giving clonidine and to hold it if their blood pressure is low or normal, many of our patients developed withdrawal symptoms when the nurses would hold the dose.

I instituted a new procedure. The nurses were to give a patient their clonidine first, and then check their blood pressure. If it was low, which it often was, they were to give the patient a bag of potato chips. That solved the problem. Patients had no more withdrawal symptoms, the nurses knew what to do if someone's blood pressure was low, and the increased salt load from the potato chips prevented anyone from fainting in the ward. The patients loved the program.

Today, there is more focus on maintenance programs, so few physicians are interested in using clonidine. Back in Kalamazoo, I used it with equal success for narcotic abusers who were hospitalized. It amazed my residents. One patient wanted to discontinue her narcotics use because the medication gave her severe constipation. She agreed to check her BP and eat potato chips if her BP was low, and she called me every day. She successfully stopped narcotics by using clonidine at home.

One day, I returned from a nice vacation to discover that I no longer had a job at the program. While I was away, it was determined that programs such as ours no longer needed a physician supervisor. I was shocked and disappointed. Without a physician, the program could no longer administer medications for our patients other than what the referring physician had prescribed prior to admission. Most admitting physicians were unaware of amantadine and clonidine for addiction problems. I felt this was a federal financial decision that lacked insight into addictionology. The Ford era was over.

## Medicaid Problems

Medicaid decided that an office visit to see a physician was only worth $11. Meanwhile, a haircut in Benton Harbor cost $20. This meant that our Benton Harbor clinic was operating in the red.

Also, Michigan developed a lottery system that "randomly" chose certain in-patient billings that would not need to be paid. We had an elderly woman present with a right leg arterial blood clot. My surgery partner did emergency surgery to restore her circulation, and I spent gruesome hours managing her acidosis, fluid, and electrolyte abnormalities. Her ten days in the ICU saved her life and her leg, and wouldn't you know it, her bill was "randomly" chosen by the lottery not to be paid. The next year, the Michigan Supreme Court declared the lottery illegal. But there was no reimbursement for lost revenue.

I was working eighty hours a week and my income was plummeting. Four quarters in a row, I billed $500,000, and because of poor government reimbursement, I was barely making $70,000 a year. Michigan Medicare and Medicaid were not paying. They even randomly chose to deny admission for one of my patients with pericarditis because he "improved too fast." So we had an efficiency expert review our clinic policies. After two weeks, he said that our clinic was the most efficient clinic he had reviewed. Efficiency wasn't the problem.

## Nursing Home Side Job

I also did some side jobs. I cared for the patients at Bry-Fern Nursing Home. The staff were delightful, and I enjoyed the patients. Several of the patients I still remember. One man didn't seem to relate to other patients or the staff. He seemed like he was in his own world since he was noncommunicative, never saying a word to anyone.

One summer was particularly hot, with temperatures near 100°F. I admitted two patients to the ICU because of dehydration and used that as a stimulus to appeal to the board to air-condition Bry-Fern Nursing Home. The board approved and decided to do some painting and make some other cosmetic changes as well.

Then we had an open house celebration, to which all the

patients' families were invited. For some reason, the administration rented a piano for the open house but had not arranged anyone to play it. My odd, noncommunicative patient sat down at the piano when guests started to arrive and played for four hours, never playing the same song twice. His masterful playing was appreciated by our guests. After that, the administration decided to keep the piano. My patient would play at mealtimes for the other patients, but still did not communicate.

Another patient I will never forget was an elderly black woman who couldn't speak and couldn't walk. Her family was quite distressed, as she just lay in bed and didn't communicate. She required a bedpan for urination and defecation. One day, a new certified nurse assistant who didn't know what the patient couldn't do was caring for her, and she started singing while she cared for the patient. The patient responded by singing back to her. When the certified nurse assistant got her up, the patient ran down the hall. At this point, the certified nurse assistant yelled at a fellow worker to catch the patient since she would run right into a wall because she couldn't stop.

I presented this patient's case to our visiting neurologist, who was quite intrigued by it. My patient could run but not walk; she could sing but not talk. After that, the staff communicated with her by singing their questions, and she would sing back her responses. Our staff demonstrated her behavior to the family when they next came to visit. They thought our staff had performed a miracle.

### Precepting Students

I precepted Western Michigan University PA students. Since I knew the patients at Bry-Fern so well, I would send the students over to do exams. We had quite a garden of pathology, and the students learned a lot from my patients. I enjoyed teaching the students. One student who was almost ready to graduate said that he saw more pathology in the Berrien Springs rotation than in all the rest of his training.

On rare occasions, I had medical students from the University of Chicago rotate with us. One had worked with Jane Goodall researching wild chimpanzees in Gombe Stream National Park in Tanzania. He entertained us with stories of his experiences every lunchtime. He had long hair streaming down his back. I was concerned that he might be offensive to some of my Benton Harbor patients who tended to be quite conservative. One elderly black woman faithfully came in to have her blood pressure checked every quarter. I knew her quite well, and after the long-haired medical student saw her, I privately asked her if she was bothered by his long hair. She laughed and said, "I like it because if he turns around and isn't listening to me, I just pull it."

Another medical student was a young Jewish man from the Bronx in New York. He was clearly well-to-do. We got to talking about his family. "My uncle became a millionaire during the Depression," he said. I was curious as to how that could happen. He explained, "He was a baker and everyone, no matter how poor, wanted bread. He priced his bread so people could afford it. His bakery did a thriving business as a result."

"Did you work in his bakery?" I asked him.

"Yes. I worked with him growing up."

"Did you make bagels?"

"Yes. That was my job in my uncle's bakery."

"Can you teach me to make bagels?"

He laughed. "You couldn't learn to make bagels."

"Why not?"

He stared into my eyes. "It takes thousands of years of suffering to make bagels."

I've always remembered that. When Priscilla and I went to New York, we had bagels at a Jewish delicatessen. I have never had a better bagel. In fact, once bagels became more popular and available, I found most of them disappointing. I guess that I couldn't taste the suffering.

## Teaching Physical Therapy Students

I offered to teach a medicine review course to the physical therapy students at Andrews University in the late 1980s. They were a bright group, as there were strict criteria for admission. Most of my students had straight As all through college. Therefore, they were all smarter than me. I am not sure how I got the job, but I did have several professors from Andrews who were my patients.

I was apprehensive about the gastroenterology sections of my lectures. I questioned how I should approach the class. My focus was on liver metabolism. In some ways, the students knew more about nutrition than I did. Andrews University is a Seventh-day Adventist school, and most Seventh-day Adventists are vegetarians who know a lot about nutrition. I worried that they would be bored, so I needed something to capture their attention. I decided to start the class with an attention grabber.

"All food is poisonous," I said. "The liver has to detoxify everything you eat."

One young woman raised her hand to reply, "Peanut butter isn't poisonous."

Coincidentally, prior to class, I had just finished rounds in the ICU at Lakeland Hospital in St. Joseph, Michigan, where I had admitted a young woman who attempted to get high by injecting peanut butter intravenously. This caused multiple pulmonary peanut butter emboli in her lungs. I paused long enough to explain the patient's experience and then continued, "All food is poisonous. The liver must detoxify everything you eat." I had their attention.

The director of the program insisted that I test the students. I was willing to just give them all an A, as they were a very attentive group. But I was required to give them an exam after each section of my curriculum. I asked the class what kind of exam they wanted. They responded that they wanted to use a class session to go over the exam. "That is fine with me," I said. "But in order to make that class period a learning experience, I need to design a difficult exam." I saw some sad faces, so I continued, "Or I could make an easier exam, in which I am sure you would all do well, and skip the review session."

They were adamant about a review session, so I made a difficult exam but agreed to grade on a curve. I still intended to give everyone an A or B.

The top score was 68 percent. Every student clustered around that score. There was only one outlier, who got 48 percent. She admitted she hadn't studied. I awarded her a B. When we reviewed the exam, everyone felt they learned from the review. It was indeed a teaching session.

One student came up to me after class with tears in her eyes. She wanted credit for a question she had misunderstood. She presented quite a vehement argument, so I offered to accept her answer if it made a difference in her grade. I looked at her test. She already had the highest grade in the class. I asked her, "Why do you want credit for that question when you already have the highest grade in the class?"

Through tears, she said, "All through college, I have never scored less than 95 percent. This is so embarrassing."

I laughed. "Since you already have an A for the exam, I am not going to give you credit for the question you misunderstood." She admitted it was, in fact, a learning experience. She left with a smile.

The next year, I was forced to digitalize the test. The result was that everyone scored 80 to 90 percent. The director of the program graded the exams. That time, I reviewed only the questions that a significant part of the class had gotten wrong. It was a very short session.

## Chief of Staff

In the 1980s, I served as chief of staff of Berrien County Hospital for four years. For the most part, it was fun. I shortened the meetings, which every participant appreciated. I interacted with the CEO, a very thoughtful, encouraging woman who had a heart for the patients we served. But there were a few problems.

I wanted two of the physicians off the staff. We had one physician who had not kept up on CME. He was making errors in patient care, and consultants had to compensate for his poor decisions. I had lunch with him one day and suggested that he resign. Much to my surprise, he said he found in-patient care very stressful and would be glad to resign.

The second physician was more difficult. He was a surgeon who brought a lot of money to the hospital, but he yelled at the surgical nurses and threw instruments at them when something didn't go correctly. Eventually, his obnoxious behavior caused a young woman's death. The parents of the young lady did not sue him because they did not want anyone to know that she was illegitimately pregnant. But her death was my stimulus to have him ejected from the staff.

Months of anguish among the physician staff followed. Then the Michigan Medical Board terminated his license, which made the final decision easier; a physician cannot be on staff without a license. In the interval, he sued the clinic for my decision and had the audacity to send his lawyer's bill to our clinic. The clinic voted to pay the lawyer's bill, but not me. All the physicians that quarter lost their bonuses. I lost $11,000.

The surgeon had an Indiana license, so he left to practice in Indiana. No hospital would accept him, but the Indiana prison accepted him. I always thought it was providential that he spent the rest of his clinical years in prison.

## Lawsuits

I did incur ten lawsuits while working in southwestern Michigan. It was quite a litigious time. Later, when there was required arbitration for medical lawsuits, the suits filed against my partners dissipated to nothing. A couple of my suits are worth reviewing; other than the ones described, the rest were dropped.

The first lawsuit—you always remember the first one—was related to a tragic car accident. The patient's wife had just finalized divorce proceedings. In anger and frustration, he sped his car into a telephone pole. I'm not sure whether he was suicidal or just careless and angry. He presented to our ED with bilateral pneumothoraces. My surgery partner, Dr. Wesche, was in the ED seeing another patient at the time. He immediately put a chest tube in the right chest, and I put one in the left.

The problem was the patient had bilateral bronchopulmonary fistulae, so on the ventilator, half of each breath by volume came out of the chest tubes. Since Dr. Wesche felt that we did not have the required facilities at Berrien County Hospital to do surgery to close the fistulae, I wanted to transfer the patient to a tertiary hospital that might be able to help. I called for the helicopter to take him to Ann Arbor, but they refused, stating the helicopter did not have a ventilator that could reproduce our ventilator settings. I called for an ambulance to transport him, but they refused for the same reason. So we were stuck with him. Dr. Wesche and I spent hours explaining to the patient's mother his poor prognosis and exactly what we were doing. She was very understanding.

After almost a week, we seemed to be making progress. He was stable in a pathologic sense, and Dr. Wesche felt that the chest tubes would keep his lungs up against the pleura and his fistulae would close. We tried again to transfer him but heard the same refusals.

That weekend, Dr. Patton was on call. I reviewed the case with him, explaining the ventilator settings and problems. As a trained cardiologist, he was well prepared to manage the patient.

But Monday morning, I was informed that the patient had developed a fever and died. Dr. Patton had done blood cultures, and we were both chagrined the bacteria that grew from the cultures was sensitive to the antibiotic we had been giving the patient. Dr. Patton spent a lot of time with the mother explaining everything. She felt she understood and was comforted by his communication.

Months later, I was informed that the brother was suing me for malpractice based on failure to transfer. I felt betrayed, as the brother never once came to see the patient in the hospital. He was suing me for $200,000. My partner, Dr. Johnson, who had been sued several times and won almost every case, spent time counseling me. I really appreciated her wisdom. "This is not about right and wrong, Richard; this is about tort law, not criminal law.

This is society's way of financially compensating someone who had an injury."

Next, I met with the lawyer assigned by the insurance company. He was very thoughtful and explained many aspects of the legal world to me. "For a physician," he said, "it is like playing chess when you only know how to play checkers." He calmed me as we met to prepare our case. "You didn't do anything wrong, and you documented your decisions well." That was encouraging.

We answered the interrogatories. Both lawyers proceeded to do depositions. The brother's lawyer deposed a pulmonologist from Indianapolis. When he finished his deposition, reviewing the facts of the case, he added, "I'm amazed that such great care could be given in such a small hospital." That comment was added to his deposition.

At my deposition, after reviewing what I had done, my lawyer suggested that the case be dismissed based on the opposing lawyer's expert witness's testimony. The lawyers then excused me and went into a private session. At the end of it, my lawyer came out and informed me that the other lawyer was willing to settle for $7,500. I agreed to the settlement because it paid the lawyer but gave nothing to the money-grubbing brother.

Another suit was filed by a husband of a patient who presented to the ED at Lakeland. He was a contractor who was used to getting his way. His wife had been sick for a week, and he didn't want to spend a lot of money on her, so he sent her to an inexpensive physician who had lost her hospital privileges because of ineptitude.[21] She gave his wife Bactrim but never assessed the patient further. A week later, she presented semicomatose to the ED.

That Saturday night, I was scheduled to be responsible for

---

[21] This is documented in St. Joseph hospital records.

admissions of patients who didn't have physicians with hospital privileges. I evaluated the patient and found she had been to the Caribbean the week before she got sick. Blood tests, including a malaria smear, were unhelpful, so I explained to the husband that his wife needed a spinal tap because I thought she might have encephalitis or meningitis. The Bactrim given by the outpatient physician only confused the situation. Bactrim could result in partially treated bacterial meningitis. He refused, yelling at me, "She doesn't need that! Just give her some antibiotics."

I ordered antibiotics and consulted the only neurologist on staff. When he came to see the patient on Sunday morning, he agreed that she needed a spinal tap. Initially, the husband again refused, but by midafternoon, he changed his mind and agreed. The neurologist told me he would take over the case. When I examined the patient on Sunday morning, she was more lucid, so I was more than happy to let him take over.

Monday morning, my partner, Dr. O'Neill, took over. The spinal tap results showed mixed lymphocytes and PMNs. That was not diagnostic of anything but possibly a virus, so he added acyclovir since the neurologist had not responded with any new orders and had not managed the case as he said that he would. Then Dr. O'Neill transferred the patient to Ann Arbor.

Weeks later, I received a lawsuit for failure to start acyclovir in a timely fashion. A resident in Ann Arbor told the husband that his wife probably had herpes encephalitis, although the tests for herpes were inconclusive. The resident said, "The acyclovir should have been started in the ED." It was on that basis the husband sued me.

My defense in court was the husband had refused the spinal tap and starting acyclovir without a spinal tap was not the standard of care. The neurologist might have started it after he performed the spinal tap but didn't. To confuse the issue, the patient had been sick for a week and treated with Bactrim, and my exam on Sunday documented that she was improving. My additional defense was the literature reported that acyclovir was only effective if given in the first forty-eight hours of symptoms. She had neurologic symptoms for at least a week.

The husband sued me for $500,000. When the lawyer prepared me for my deposition, he said he thought I had an 80 percent chance of winning. But then, just before my scheduled deposition, he asked to meet with me. He explained that although he was sure I would win my case, the insurance company had previous bad experiences with the neurologist testifying, as he was arrogant and sarcastic in court. Therefore, he wanted me to settle for $200,000 so the case would not go to court. Dr. Johnson advised me that the money would help the husband pay the nursing home, since his wife had continued to improve but still required continuous care. As a contractor, the husband was not able or willing to care for her himself. So, I agreed to the settlement to provide for her care. But I was irritated because my lawyer said that I could have won.

My last lawsuit bordered on comical. Dr. O'Neill had admitted an alcoholic in atrial fibrillation. The patient went through detox, during which Dr. O'Neill controlled the rate, and then the patient converted to normal rhythm. I was on call for the weekend, so on Friday afternoon, Dr. O'Neill signed the patient out to me. When I asked why the patient, who was completely stable, couldn't be discharged, Dr. O'Neill said, "Because it is Friday. That is when he goes out drinking. Just keep him until Saturday and then discharge him."

Because the patient was in normal rhythm, Dr. O'Neill had discontinued the monitor. Friday night, however, the patient coded. Without a monitor, the code had been called by the nurse who noticed the patient's condition when she came to administer medications. I was on the ward for another admission and resuscitated the patient back to normal rhythm and normal respirations. In any case, the patient did have residual anoxic brain damage.

The wife sued me for $200,000. She said that she owned a motel and her husband was the fix-it man. She claimed a loss of income because she had to hire out repairs at the motel. Later, when she presented her claim to the court, it was noted she had saved money because her husband always drank while he was repairing things. He usually messed up, and his mismanagement made fixing things more costly. The person she hired, who did things immediately and correctly, saved her money. That part of the lawsuit was dropped.

### In the Interval

Before my deposition was scheduled, an important situation developed that affected the case. There was a bad apartment fire in Benton Harbor. One of my patients was living in the apartment and developed complications of smoke inhalation. The patient sued the owner because he had disconnected the fire alarms in the apartment complex. It was a clear case of negligence. My patient hired a Jewish lawyer, Attorney Conybear, to represent him.

I was deposed as an expert witness, which required a court appearance, not just a deposition. Before a jury, I explained how smoke inhalation resulted in chronic lung damage. I was on the stand for more than a half hour. Attorney Conybear thanked me as I left the courtroom.

## Returning to My Lawsuit

I was to be deposed at the lawyer's office. I appeared as scheduled and was instructed by the secretary to sit in a nice plush chair. Moments later, Attorney Conybear walked into the office. He recognized me. "Aren't you the physician who won the case of the smoke inhalation for me?"

"Yes," I replied.

At that, he walked out. It was almost noon, and the secretary told me that he was deposing someone else first. I folded my hands and waited. The secretary left the office and returned later with a pastrami sandwich. "Your case has been dropped," she told me. "Attorney Conybear will not require your deposition." It was the best pastrami sandwich I have ever eaten.

I was never sued again. I heard through the grapevine that Attorney Conybear told the other lawyers in town I was very polished in court and not to bother suing me.

## Working at SWMC

My twelve years at SWMC were very fulfilling and intellectually stimulating but exhausting. I was working eighty hours a week but receiving poor compensation, so I could not afford to pay for my children's college education. When we went to Minnesota for Thanksgiving with family, my brother Bill decided that I looked exhausted. He actually applied to a job at St. Luke's Hospital in Duluth for me without asking.

Back in Michigan, he called me one Friday to warn me the vice president of St. Luke's Hospital was going to call on Monday for a telephone interview and I should be ready. The vice president was very impressed and offered me a position, saying I would be seeing patients who had work injuries. (St. Luke's contracted with seven hundred companies.) St. Luke's would double my pay and cut my hours to forty per week maximum.

I accepted.

## Benefits of Leaving

As a result, several things happened that benefited SWMC. My partners did not want to care for all my no-paying and low-paying patients; so, our manager went to Lansing to protest the $11-a-patient payment. In his description, they scowled at him and with a sarcastic grin asked, "How many patients do you take care of?" Back at Berrien Springs, he tallied up the numbers of patients I and my partners cared for and proved to the representative that SWMC cared for 75 percent of the Medicaid patients in three counties. He negotiated an increase of $45 a visit, but the patients had to be seen at a single clinic. That was unfair to the three counties' patients. Many of my Benton Harbor patients had no transportation and walked to my centrally located clinic. Anyway, a clinic was established, and John Kittredge became the manager. Someone else saw my ninety nursing home patients when it was decided that they needed to be seen only once every *other* month and a PA could do it.

I felt bad about leaving my partners, whom I loved, but our house quickly sold, we found a nice home in Duluth, and the benefits to SWMC were long overdue. I have maintained good relationships with my former partners to this day, even recommending some of my residents from WMed to join their practice.

# 16

## OCCUPATIONAL PHYSICIAN

I had kept my Minnesota license from medical school, but to start work at St. Luke's Hospital in Duluth required a Minnesota address to the Minnesota Medical Board. That took a month because the board met only monthly to review applications. Priscilla said it was by the grace of God that I couldn't start work right away because I needed the rest. I slept in late, worked in my woodshop making furniture for our new house, and interacted with my children. It was a much-needed rest from working eighty hours a week in Michigan.

With a valid Minnesota address, the glitches were resolved, and I could start work. At orientation, I met my new partner, Katie Kastamo, MD. She had been working for a couple of years as an occupational physician. She was quite pleasant and taught me some basics of occupational medicine, caring for patients with work injuries and consulting with companies to prevent future injuries. She was interesting because she had worked at an archaeological dig in Caesarea, Israel. We had some great conversations about archaeology.

I usually saw about ten patients a day, quite a contrast from seeing forty-five a day in Benton Harbor. I had time to read the literature, which was necessary because I had never done occupational medicine (OM). In Benton Harbor, I had limited experience as an occupational physician for Whirlpool employees. They were my only Caucasian patients. I did executive physicals for Whirlpool administrators, and I cared for one chemical engineer who developed an allergy to the paint she invented. That was the total of my OM experience.

Many of the patients with work injuries in Duluth presented with back pain. I asked my manager, through St. Luke's librarian, to obtain all the recently published articles on back pain. When I retired, I still had that voluminous folder and still referred to it.

One patient made a huge impact on me. She came because of a repetitive hand injury she had from the factory where she worked. She was disheveled, haggard, and unattractive. Her name was distinctive, so I'll refer to her as Jenny (not her real name; see chapter 11). Jenny's hand problem was routine. After finishing the exam and making recommendations, I asked her about her name, stating that I knew someone thirty years ago by that name from First Presbyterian Church. "That's me," she said. I couldn't believe my eyes. She explained that she had never gone to college because she married right out of high school. She had been divorced multiple times from spousal abuse. She was a chain smoker and a recovering alcoholic. "Back at church, I thought you were nice," she said. "But Kitty didn't like you."

After our long talk, she decided to make dramatic changes in her life. She chose not to marry ever again and decided to return to church. My heart was broken for her.

In addition to seeing patients, my manager arranged for Katie and I to do on-site visits at one of the seven-hundred-plus companies we served. I went on Thursdays; Katie went on Tuesdays. We would review the log of patients we had seen from the company and pay attention to where most of their injuries occurred. Katie had already been to the taco factory and made recommendations related to multiple employees with wrist injuries. These injuries all occurred at one specific station. She briefed me, so when I toured the factory, I paid attention to that station, which required the employee to take the tacos that came out of the fryer and twist them ninety degrees. I suggested they straighten the line so this position would be unnecessary. The manager said, "That's what Dr. Kastamo said."

I said, "Yes, she is a very sharp physician."

"But that will cost about $10,000, to straighten the line."

I turned to my manager, who had accompanied me. "How much has the company paid us to see their injured employees?" She pulled out the statistic sheet describing over $50,000 in payments for injuries. "Straightening the line is insignificant compared to the cost of injuries you're paying for." Managers seem to think in terms of money, not people.

When I returned to the clinic, I told Katie, "We finally convinced them to do what you suggested." She was delighted. During a slow part of the taco season, they knocked down the outside wall, straightened the line, and built a new wall. Their occupational medicine bill plummeted after that.

Occupational medicine diagnosis is not usually intellectually demanding. If a patient cut their finger on a saw, the differential diagnosis is not a challenge. The area of mental stimulation relates to discerning how to prevent the injury, which is why the factory tours are important.

A subtler part of the job was making sure an injury was, in fact, work related. Sometimes, it was difficult to determine. For example, an employee tying the laces on his steel-toed boots herniated his lumbar disc. Was that because he was tying his bootlaces in the company locker room, or was it related to a weekend of snowmobiling on rough terrain? Just because he tied his shoes in the locker room at work, did that mean it was work related? I thought not.

## The Blond Twins

I toured a life-jacket manufacturing company. The manager was so proud of two of his employees. They were twins in their early twenties, blond and quite attractive. "The twins are performing at 150 percent of the other seamstresses, and they don't even take breaks."

I watched the twins. Their ergonomics were poor, and they seemed to be racing through their work. I suggested to the manager that he slow the twins down, force them to take breaks, and I made some ergonomic recommendations.

My recommendations were ignored. That turned out to be a very expensive decision. Both twins developed severe median nerve injuries within six months. After wrist surgery, and extensive rehabilitation, they both quit. The manager was chagrined, and the executive officer subsequently required him to make sure employees took breaks and slowed down if they were working too fast.

## Torn Rotator Cuff

One case that went to court involved a taco employee who claimed she hurt her left shoulder on the taco line. Her job involved putting a paper insert into a stack of six tacos so that they wouldn't break in the box. I understood her job well because on a factory tour, I had performed her job for a short period of time. I wasn't very good at it. I examined her shoulder and found her muscles to be quite tender. I initiated treatment with medication and physical therapy.

She did not improve, so I ordered an MRI of her shoulder, which showed extensive tearing of the rotator cuff. I discussed the situation with the employee and learned that she had fallen off her horse the weekend prior to her reported injury. The reins had tangled in her left arm as she fell and jerked her shoulder. I decided that this injury was not work related. She didn't like my conclusion, so she went to her own physician for treatment. Her primary physician then sent her to an orthopedic specialist who did surgery to repair the extensive tearing, which was even worse than the MRI suggested. She convinced the orthopedic surgeon that her injury was work related. The result was a lawsuit to get her employer to pay for her medical and surgical care.

In court, the orthopedic surgeon's testimony was comical as he tried to describe how sorting tacos could cause the extensive rotator cuff damage. Then it was my turn. I described my history of the patient falling off her horse with the reins tangled in the affected arm. Then I described her factory job in precise detail. The lawyer asked, "How is it that you can describe her job in such detail?"

"Because I have done her job on a factory tour," I responded. That dismissed the case. However, I felt bad that the factory did not provide adequate health insurance for their employees. If they did, the lawsuit would never have happened. She could not afford the treatment or surgery with her minimal income.

In Switzerland, when a company provides insurance, it covers both work-related and non-work-related injuries. Such a system would be more expensive for employers, but would save a lot of questions of work-relatedness and subsequent lawsuits.

## Mercury Poisoning

The most interesting case of my career related to two men who were training to be officers on the Great Lakes Fleet. As part of their training, they were required to spend a month on a ship so they could experience life sailing around the Great Lakes, which was a good idea. The problem was, at their stage of training, they weren't qualified to do anything. The captain didn't know what to have them do, so he sent them to the chief engineer to give them some jobs.

The chief engineer had nothing specific for them, so he told them to go through the storeroom and catalog the inventory. So that is what they did. They discovered a polyethylene bottle, which they grabbed to see what it was. It contained mercury, which is used on ships to fill the gauges that balance the ballast while the ship is loaded with ore. The problem was that mercury is very dense. It weighed a lot more than the men anticipated, so when they picked it up off the shelf, they dropped it. Some of the mercury spilled onto the floor. They decided to go for lunch and clean up the mess after. When they returned, the floor was clean.

Later, they reported to the chief engineer that they had spilled the mercury. He went to the storeroom and, noticing that there was nothing on the floor, locked the storeroom to avoid further exposure and notified me.

The problem, of which he was aware, was that the floor of the storeroom was the ceiling of the engine room. The temperature of the floor was about 90 degrees, sometimes higher. And mercury vaporizes at 80 degrees. The officer trainees thought someone had cleaned up their spill, but in fact, it had evaporated while they were having lunch.

When they arrived in port, I ordered mercury levels for the two men. Both trainees were toxic but didn't quite meet criteria for chelation, which involves injecting a chemical to absorb the heavy metal and remove it through kidney excretion. But it has toxic effects.

I ordered follow-up levels. One trainee's level had plummeted since he had no further exposure. The other was a problem, as his levels had increased. I tried to notify him, but he was out shopping. I told his mother what the problem was. When he came home, she took him to their family physician, who checked the level and found it to be more elevated. He promptly admitted the trainee and consulted a toxicologist. How could his level increase? The answer was provided by the nurse, who found his boots full of mercury. He required chelation and disposal of his favorite boots.

When the ship arrived at the Duluth port, I notified the hazmat personnel and accompanied them onto the ship. Since the chief engineer had locked the airtight steel door, the problem was contained. In our hazmat gear, we measured the mercury levels in the storeroom. They were very toxic, which required extensive hazmat cleanup.

I received permission from the USS *GLF* to publish the case. It's available in the EPA's journal, if you're interested. This incident prompted the fleet to find different ways to balance the holds. It took some engineering, but most ships now have a more sophisticated means to balance the ballast.

## *Lead Poisoning*

Another intriguing heavy-metal problem related to a brass factory that made fittings for several industries. The owner had left Germany before World War II because he was tired of European wars and started the brass factory in Duluth. He was very successful. He had a European mindset toward his employees. When he hired someone, he paid them well, much higher than starting wages in any other factories in Duluth. He ensured every employee had good health insurance, and he was very conscious of safety. It takes several years to train a craftsman, so he did everything he could to retain his employees.

The problem was that all brass has lead in it. He arranged for his employees to get serum lead levels every three months. He organized the factory so employees could not get to the lunchroom without going through the bathroom to wash their hands. The result of his safety engineering was that his employees' serum test results were always well below the safe level.

Then, he hired a new employee, a young man with a high school education who was impressed with the wages he could get at the factory. He was given an explicit orientation to the danger of lead. Coveralls were required, and they had to be left at the factory, not brought home. The literature documented toxicity to spouses who washed their husbands' clothes.

I checked his lead level before he started working. It was almost zero. Three months later, when I checked him, he was toxic. The employer was frantic, took the employee out of the workplace with pay, and sent him to me to figure out why his lead level was elevated.

"Did you wash your hands before entering the lunchroom?" I asked him.

"Yes."

"Did you wear your coveralls and leave them at the factory?"

"Yes."

Then I noticed that he was chewing gum. "Do you chew gum at work?"

"Yah, why? I put it in my coverall pocket and chew it to reduce stress. I'm still learning how to use that metal lathe."

So, he was taking the gum out of the wrapper inside the factory. The lead on his hands contaminated his chewing gum. He was laid off with pay until his lead level was back to normal. The other employees were instructed to warn him not to chew gum in the factory.

Three months after he returned to work, his lead level was still normal. He decided that chewing gum was not the correct way to relieve stress at work. He found the other employees supportive of his learning curve, as they had all been through it.

As a result of my experience with lead and mercury, the Minnesota State Department of Health asked me to set up a protocol for heavy-metal exposure. To do this, I worked with a pediatrician who had experience with hundreds of immigrant children with lead exposure and advised other physicians whose pediatric patients were exposed to lead. Her daughter had developed lead exposure when they moved to a historic house in the Twin Cities. The protocol she and I created identified dangerous heavy-metal levels and who should receive treatment. To my knowledge, the state is still using the protocol the two of us set up.

## *Coast Guard*

St. Luke's Hospital had a contract with the Coast Guard to provide them with primary care. It was decided I could fill that obligation. I did see some Coast Guard personnel for work-related problems, anyway, so it was a good fit.

One of the Coast Guard officers complained of a chronic cough. His chest X-ray was curious, demonstrating puffballs in his lung fields. He also had a cervical lymph node that was enlarged. Biopsy showed he had sarcoidosis despite being Caucasian. His cough and shortness of breath responded dramatically to low-dose steroids.

One year, the Coast Guard decided that smoking was not allowed on its property, so the commander told smokers they had to go off property to smoke. The problem was the Coast Guard owned over a square block on Park Point. That wasn't too onerous in the summer, but that winter, the temperature dropped to 40 below zero with forty- to sixty-mile-per-hour winds off the lake. I had twenty Coast Guard personnel requesting Nicorette gum; it required a prescription then. I met with them, and they decided to be their own support group. All quit smoking and stopped using gum in three months, except one high-ranking enlisted fellow. He was teased by the others who had quit, and his wife, who didn't smoke, had been harassing him to quit. He quit at work and even quit at home, but smoking in his car to and from work was a psychological barrier, partly because his car smelled of tobacco and that was the stimulus to light up.

I received a letter from him years later. "I finally quit smoking completely," he wrote, "when I bought a new car."

## Supraventricular Tachycardia

One Coast Guard man went into supraventricular tachycardia (SVT) while on the icebreaker. He had to be flown off the ship by helicopter. His EKG demonstrated Wolff–Parkinson–White (WPW) syndrome. I treated him with beta-blockers until he could be sent to Bethesda Naval Hospital, where they ablated his auxiliary conduction. He felt great on return, and when the icebreaker returned to a port on Lake Superior, he went back to work.

About a week later, his commander called me. He was back in SVT. Another expensive helicopter ride brought him back to Duluth. He had another auxiliary conduction system, and I had to return him to Bethesda, where they ablated his other conduction. Finally, he was in normal rhythm and returned to the icebreaker. This was the only patient I have ever seen with two congenital aberrant conduction systems.

## The Invisible Dog

The most curious Coast Guard case was a young recruit who had an invisible dog. His commander wasn't too concerned until the recruit became severely depressed and complained to his commander, "Someone threw my invisible dog overboard."

I saw him in my office, where I questioned him as to how he knew that his invisible dog had been thrown overboard. "Because he stopped eating his invisible food," he said. Further history revealed he was from a small town in Mississippi where he worked on a cotton plantation. He had never traveled more than ten miles from his home community. His high school sweetheart had told him she would not marry him unless he had some kind of uniform.

So, he decided to join the Coast Guard. He probably would have done well if he had been assigned to a station on the Mississippi River. But he was assigned to Duluth. He struggled with the culture. He told me, "People talk fast and funny here."

Then winter came and he was on the icebreaker. He had never even seen snow before. He was teased on the ship, referred to as a "cotton picker." Then he got a letter from his girlfriend that said she had married someone else. He couldn't handle all this stress and had to be admitted to the psychiatric ward at St. Luke's for acute depression. The psychiatrist whom I consulted felt he had a good prognosis. His depression and invisible dog disappeared. He was subsequently medically discharged from the Coast Guard, and returned home to find a new girlfriend.

### Degenerative Hip

A new female commander came to me complaining of hip pain. She was very athletic and had quickly risen in rank because of her inspiring personality. X-ray revealed that she had a destroyed hip socket. Maybe it had been congenital, but now it was hard to tell since it was so destroyed. I sent her to an orthopedist who was reluctant to do a total hip because she was so young, in her middle thirties. She loved the Coast Guard and had planned to make it her career. I then sent her to Bethesda to get a second opinion. I couldn't treat her pain with anything other than nonsteroidal anti-inflammatories (NSAIDs) because the Coast Guard doesn't allow narcotics while working.

She didn't return from Maryland. I hope they gave her a desk job or did surgery.

## *Developing Urgent Care*

I worked for St. Luke's Hospital for nine years. It was a dream job with excellent pay, limited hours (forty per week), good benefits, and no night call. St. Luke's asked me to develop two urgent care clinics because of my experience working in the emergency department. Many patients who went to the ED did not have emergencies but sought help with minor problems. The patients complained that the waits were intolerable. The vice president asked me how this could be resolved. I suggested an urgent care clinic with RNs triaging the patients. I toured the ED and found there were rooms next to the ED that were being used just as offices. It did not take much remodeling to make an urgent care (UC) clinic out of them.

I interviewed several physicians interested in working at UC; I found excellent physicians who were tired of their practices and schedules. I worked with the RNs to provide criteria for ushering patients to UC. We made a rule that patients were seen within fifteen minutes if they decided to go to UC instead of the ED.

The clinic was a dramatic success. I worked there temporarily to iron out problems. The community provided such positive feedback that St. Luke's decided to set up another UC on the other side of town in the Denfeld area. It was just as successful. The ED physicians even met to thank me. Now they did not have a waiting room full of patients complaining about not being seen in a timely fashion and they mostly cared for emergencies.

Ironically, within months of St. Luke's setting up a UC clinic, St. Mary's, the other hospital in town, was jealous and decided to do the same. I think it was the billboard ads claiming a fifteen-minute-or-less wait that caught St. Mary's attention. I had nothing to do with the billboards!

## Completing My Tour of Occupational Medicine

Dr. Kastamo had come to Duluth to care for her ailing mother. When her mother died, there was no further reason for Dr. Kastamo to stay in Duluth. Her father lived in Greece, and she had no other relatives in the area. So she left for Greece.

I was board certified as an internist, but St. Luke's wanted someone who was board certified in occupational medicine. I contacted the occupational medicine board to see if I was eligible for taking the certification exam. Initially, the board said that I was, so I scheduled the test. But then they decided that I needed a master's in public health to take the exam.

The University of Wisconsin–Madison offered an online degree that only required six months of mostly online classes and two visits to their campus. Since I was already board certified in internal medicine and had been working in OM for eight years, they agreed that a short master's in public health course would qualify me to take the occupational medicine board exam. I offered this to St. Luke's and asked for Wednesday afternoon to do the coursework in my office. They considered it but chose to hire another physician who was already board certified.

He was a pleasant physician, but despite his certification, he was not very sophisticated. He tended to be absolute in his assessments, did not relate well to patients, and did not want to see more than ten patients a day. At this point, I was seeing twenty to twenty-five patients per day. Some of our companies complained about his doctor–patient rapport. They informed our scheduler that they only wanted their employees to see "Dr. Roach."

Two things happened. First, St. Luke's decided they did not want to pay for my master's in public health or allow me work time to complete my certification. The vice president who hired me had retired, or else the decision might have been very different. Then in November 2000, I received a call from Kalamazoo asking me if I would work for Michigan State University's internal medicine residency program. I was fully vested with St. Luke's, so I would get a nice pension when I retired, and teaching residents full-time was what I had always dreamed of doing.

It was time to change careers.

# 17

## CMDA EDUCATION CONFERENCES

Since I had more time and income during my OM years in the 1990s, my former SWMC partner, Robert Schindler, MD, thought that I could take on a position as medicine stream coordinator for the Christian Medical and Dental Association (CMDA). The position involved finding speakers for the international conference sponsored by CMDA with credentialing through Indiana University. Many expatriate physicians working in developing countries needed continuing medical education (CME) credits to maintain their licenses in the United States; the CMDA / Indiana University conference allowed them to obtain CME credits without going to the United States. One year, it was held in Kenya, and the next year in Malaysia. As coordinator, I could serve for eight years: four years in Kenya, four years in Malaysia.

I oversaw the medicine-pediatrics stream. One of the pediatricians from Indiana University originally coordinated the conference, so I had a ready handful of pediatricians to give lectures. I invited my friend Dave Flagler, MD, from Kalamazoo to give neurology lectures. I would give a few lectures based on my experiences in Madagascar setting up an alcohol treatment program. Then I had to find speakers to fill in the rest of the week.

It was a great opportunity to meet some amazing people. Some of the speakers were nationally known as primary publishers on their topics. I contacted physicians from Boston to San Diego who were specialists in their fields. A Navy oncologist from San Diego spoke on Burkitt lymphoma. A medical statistician working with the Centers for Disease Control and Prevention (CDC) spoke on analyzing epidemics. She even had the opportunity to discern the cause of a diarrhea episode among physicians at the conference when about two hundred conference participants developed diarrhea. She figured out that it was a staphylococcal toxin in the salad dressing.

A U.S. military officer coordinating care for prostitutes in Mombasa spoke on sexually transmitted diseases; the military was concerned about soldiers contracting such diseases from prostitutes.[22] A delightful dermatologist from South Carolina spoke on diagnosing skin cancer and caring for albinos. Albinos in Africa are stigmatized and require special care. Francis Collins even agreed to speak for me regarding the Human Genome Project. We discovered that he was an accomplished guitarist; he performed in the evening after supper to rousing applause.

The first trip to Kenya, Priscilla came with me. We had a wonderful evening walking through the coffee plantation. The coffee trees were in bloom and smelled like gardenias. Later that week, Priscilla ate some of the contaminated salad and became quite ill. My friends Ken and Connie, who lived in Nairobi, offered to nurse her back to health. I think they bought her a whole case

---

[22] I fictionalized his story in my novel *Never a Woman*.

of Fanta to keep her hydrated from the staphylococcal toxin. We have been forever grateful for their intervention.

Equally amazing speakers volunteered to speak in Malaysia the next year. Some of those who volunteered in Kenya were willing to speak in Malaysia. We also had expatriate physicians speak. One speaker from Nepal had set up a psychiatric service in rural villages. A young Canadian woman physician had developed rural health care for northwestern China. Her trainees, called "barefoot doctors," were equivalent to nursing assistants based on the training she provided. An obstetrician from Lebanon spoke on developing health care for Muslim women.

Malaysia is a beautiful, green country. Our meetings were on the west coast, so I was able to swim at break times in the Strait of Malacca. The water was so warm that to do any vigorous swimming made me nauseated. It was refreshing just to plunge in the water and relax.

I learned that Malaysia is very prejudiced against the Chinese, whom I discovered are mostly Christians in a Muslim country. The Malaysian universities only allow 5 percent of students to be Chinese. WMU set up a branch university there, as did Oxford. These were two-year schools, and then the students must go to England or Kalamazoo to finish their degrees. This explained why there were so many Chinese Malaysians in Kalamazoo.

I learned another interesting tidbit when the cook for the conference offered to let me accompany him to the grocery store—that ketchup is soy sauce in Malaysia. I knew no one would believe me, so I bought a bottle of ketjup. It was soy sauce. I understand that *ketjup* is a Chinese–Malay word for the sauce, but Europeans wanted a tomato-based "sauce," which became *tomato ketchup* to distinguish it from soya sauce ketjup. But we just call it *ketchup*.

I was not in charge of surgery, dentistry, or obstetrics, which were separate CMDA streams. Those streams had their own coordinators, but if they knew someone who was a great lecturer in a medical field, they would share the information and I would contact them. It was helpful to fill all the slots. I was profoundly impacted to meet all these amazing people and coordinate their lectures over my eight-year term.

## SCAN Editor

At the same time, I was editor-in-chief of SCAN magazine. I would search for articles that had practical relevance to physicians working in countries with a lack of technology. The SCAN budget provided by CMDA also paid Renee Hyatte, my secretary, to format SCAN and to coordinate the requests to various journals for permission to republish their articles. Initially, we published in paper form, but some countries had poor postal systems, so the physicians didn't always receive their copies. Besides, the postage was expensive.

Most journals were excited to allow us to republish considering who read SCAN. The New England Journal of Medicine gave us carte blanche republishing privileges. The Lancet and British Medical Journal (BMJ) claimed that providing medical information to physicians in developing countries was part of their mission statement. They sent us a letter stating that any article in their journals, we were allowed to republish. BMJ published a pictorial of leprosy. For SCAN to reprint the colored pictures was financially prohibitive, but BMJ offered to pay for the colored reprints at no expense to CMDA. JAMA refused every request, so I canceled my subscription.

When the internet became available, we switched to an electronic version of SCAN, which saved postage. We had several thousand addresses to whom we mailed. We asked those who received our publication to send us email addresses. Most returned our request. Email, however, posed new problems. Some countries blocked emails with the word *Christian,* so we excluded Christian terminology from *SCAN.* This also required that we *not* share our email addresses with CMDA, our supporting institution, because if CMDA added our addresses to their database, our readers would receive all CMDA emails with no discretion to remove Christian terminology. Renee had to be very circumspect.

We also found we were limited to a certain number of bytes for the emails to be received with our readers' limited internet service. Certain countries blocked email that reached a certain threshold of bytes. This meant editing the articles so they were logical despite missing data. We added a note that if a receiver wanted full articles, and had good internet, we would send them a separate email.

We encouraged our readers to respond by email. Renee would pass on medical requests for my opinion. We were gratified when some of our readers told us examples of how our articles and responses had improved their patient care. One request I passed on to Tirzah, my veterinarian daughter. Our reader had been plagued with patients developing bovine tuberculosis contracted from an infected local cow. He requested information on treating the cow. My daughter replied, "Shoot the cow." Unfortunately, this was an unacceptable solution in the cow's country.

Of note, at CMDA's Kenya/Malaysia CME conference, I met many of my readers. Of the thousands of email addresses, I learned that some had multiple readers. One email to Kijabe Hospital in Kenya would be read by seventeen physicians. CMDA–CME was eventually suspended as CMDA focused on U.S. physicians. An offshoot of members formed a separate organization to continue meeting their need, but they had limited resources.

Expatriate physicians soon found online medical self-assessment programs that met state licensing requirements. Expatriate nurses had a similar problem. Most nurse licensing boards recognized our CME for physicians and allowed nurses CME credit. New online programs became available for nurses as well.

After twenty-five years of publishing *SCAN*, CMDA gave me the President's Heritage Award in 2006. I was honored to be given the award by Betty Elliot. I was truly humbled. Renee was also honored for her twenty-five faithful years. Then CMDA decided to focus on U.S./Canadian physicians. Our budget for *SCAN* was canceled. Renee and I were out of the publishing business.

# 18

## PROFESSORIAL CAREER

When Western Michigan University's physician assistant (PA) program was celebrating its twenty-fifth anniversary in 1999, the graduates were asked to provide the name of their favorite mentor. Robert Roschmann, MD, was chosen for specialty, rheumatology, and I was chosen for primary care. I had been a mentor for the PA program a decade before. The program flew me to Kalamazoo from Duluth and provided hotel accommodations for a celebratory dinner. It was a lot of fun, and it was great to see Robert again.

Dr. Loehrke heard about this, and neurologist Dr. Flagler recommended that he interview me about a job in university's residency program. So, we had breakfast together. My interview with Dr. Loehrke was remarkable. I really liked the job description he provided, but I told him that periodically, I would need time off to go to Madagascar, as I had initiated a training program for Malagasy physicians. In response, he asked, "Would you be willing to take residents?"

"Of course," I said.

"Then our program will pay for you to go."

I was in awe. The job would require that I accept a substantial pay cut, but if the university residency program would pay my expenses to Madagascar, it was worth it. But there wasn't a faculty opening yet.

A year after that interview, when St. Luke's decided they wanted a board-certified OM physician, and wouldn't pay for me to be certified, Dr. Loehrke called me. He had a faculty person suddenly resign, who gave him only two weeks' notice. I was ready. I always envisioned volunteering to work with residents when I retired, but this was even better. I would be getting paid to teach. I had retained my Michigan license from residency, but I had to apply with a Michigan address … again.

Teaching residents was the highlight of my career because I enjoyed teaching and sharing my varied clinical background. Dr. Loehrke was the best boss anyone could ever want. Because of my diverse experiences, he called me the "Swiss Army knife physician."

CEOs came and went, eventually becoming medical school deans when Western Michigan University (WMU) developed their medical school, but none of them was as insightful as Dr. Loehrke. Some of them thought the tropical medicine program we created was a waste of money. But it continued for almost twenty years, except for one year when we went to Kenya because there were two presidents in Madagascar, and that is one too many.

In addition to complaining about the expenses of the program, CEOs were opposed because they felt that there was no need for our residents to know tropical diseases. In defense, I published a series of cases of malaria in Kalamazoo. WMU had 130 countries represented in their student body. My published research demonstrated that there were, on average, six cases of malaria a year over the five years of the study. In addition, there was a delay in treatment because local physicians were unsure of the management.

One patient, a WMU student from Kenya, presented to the ED stating, "I have malaria." His malaria smear was reported as negative, so he was misdiagnosed and went into renal failure on dialysis.

One of the residents who had been to Madagascar consulted on his infectious disease rotation, and insisted that the patient did have malaria. The resident requested a pathologist's review of the technician's "negative result" peripheral smear. A pathologist who had worked in Kenya looked at the slide and said, "It's full of malarial parasites." The patient was treated for malaria, and two days later, he no longer needed dialysis, and his renal function returned to normal. Ten days of hospitalization and a myriad of tests could have been prevented if the physician attending understood malaria.

That quelled the CEO's argument against the program. But Dr. Loehrke still had the financial argument to contend with every year. Part of his defense was that since the program had been initiated, Kalamazoo had not had to scramble for residents. Our program competed with Grand Rapids and Lansing's internal medicine programs for residents. Our tropical medicine program was not duplicated by the competing programs. As a result, if a prospective resident was interested in international medicine opportunities, they chose our program. Several prospective residents claimed they did not want to go to Madagascar but wanted a program that had an international perspective.

For two decades, Dr. Loehrke promoted and protected the program until COVID-19 disrupted everything and finally stopped the program. I retired and no one was willing to continue it.

## *Occupational Medicine*

Our program had the opportunity to teach Michigan State University's students occupational medicine. The Lansing program sent their students to various locations to learn OM. Our site was chosen, at Dr. Loehrke's recommendation. He asked me to set up a program since he knew that I had been employed as an occupational medicine physician in Duluth.

Lansing's OM physician supervising the program required students to do an occupational history on one of their hospital admissions from any of their previous rotations and present it to their mentor with a literature review of potential occupational hazards. For example, if their patient was a truck driver, they were to search the literature to discover what occupational hazards truck drivers were prone to.

Based on my experience, I contacted several companies in Kalamazoo requesting to take students on a company tour. They were enthusiastic, so with permission from Lansing, I added this to the medical students' curriculum. We toured the Kalamazoo septic system, a printing company, a pharmaceutical company, an electronic manufacturing company, et cetera. The companies even provided histories of their employee injuries and how they dealt with workers' compensation. In addition, Dr. Loehrke allowed me to take the students out for lunch after the tours to discuss their case presentations. They had so much fun doing this over several years that the students gave our program excellent evaluations.

But that was the problem. The other sites could not or would not duplicate what we were doing in Kalamazoo. I was called to Lansing to meet with the other mentors and describe what we were doing and how they could set up the same kind of experience. I was sure they could do the same thing. I was wrong. Some mentors adamantly refused. Other mentors claimed it was too difficult.

The medical students who went to other sites complained that they didn't get the same experience as in Kalamazoo. They claimed the OM experience at the other locations was a waste of time. They all wanted to come to Kalamazoo. So, the medical school administration informed the director that he had to cancel the whole program. We would gladly have expanded our program—Dr. Loehrke considered it good promotion for our residency program—but mediocrity reigned.

## Racial Diversity

Another responsibility that I was assigned was to teach medical diversity to the medical students. Dr. Loehrke knew that I had worked in Kenya, Sierra Leone, and Rwanda. He was aware of my experience working with First Nation patients in Cloquet as well.

The medical school class was supposed to include an interactive aspect, so I presented some scenarios of patients I had cared for and had the students form groups to work out solutions to the problems (for example, a surgical patient who required permission from the family matriarch before their surgery permit could be signed, or the patient who refused to stay in the hospital because he wanted to go ricing, or the patient who complained of low back pain but thought nothing of the pain in his broken hand due to a fistfight in a bar). I was impressed with the students' solutions. Some were better than the solutions I had used on the actual patients. My favorite was preventing neonatal tetanus by vaccinating all pregnant women, which is what the Malagasy government eventually did, although I cringed at their methods.[23]

I enjoyed my interactions with the medical students, but when WMU developed their medical school, they hired professors to do most of the teaching. I taught a couple of classes until I was replaced.

## Precepting Internal Medicine Residents

My main professorial responsibility was working with the internal medicine residents. I supervised their interactions with the outpatients and six weeks of inpatients. It was exciting and stimulating. All my past experiences with patients became relevant to teaching the residents to care for their patients.

I laughed when a resident said, "How can you just walk in the room and know what's wrong with the patient?" I would often tell stories of similar patients for whom I had cared in the past. For example, in admitting a patient with cirrhosis, I knew how to manage the patient related to the seven hundred patients I had admitted to the drug and alcohol treatment program in Benton Harbor. Many of the residents claimed that they learned so much because my stories helped them remember medical principles.

Of course, some patient care was traumatic, especially when a resident diagnosed cancer or cared for a patient who died. As an attending, I had to model physician–patient–family interactions in these difficult situations. Some patients were obnoxious. Again, modeling interaction was critical to appropriate care. I was

---

[23] Soldiers with automatic rifles went to villages on market day and, at gunpoint, insisted that pregnant women be vaccinated. Later, it was a government requirement that any physician who diagnosed pregnancy vaccinate the patient. The women were not given an option.

disappointed when residents neglected to ask about the military service experience of a patient who was a veteran. I stimulated the residents to return to the bedside to obtain their history. Many times, it was clinically significant to the present illness.

We had a constant parade of patients with pneumonia, heart failure, and infections. What I will present are some patients who were unusual. Don't worry; their identities cannot be determined from my descriptions.

## Lung Mass

A middle-aged man presented with a cough. A chest X-ray revealed a mass in his left upper lung. It had the appearance of lung cancer. The ED physician informed him of the possibility, so he was admitted to academic medicine. Bedside conversations were strained because the patient was otherwise healthy, and now, he worried that he might have terminal cancer.

The patient requested a biopsy as soon as possible. Our team made the arrangements and waited for the pathologist's report. I've always insisted that I have the pathology report in hand before informing the patient of their diagnosis. But he was anticipating bad news and kept asking the resident. I cautioned the resident to resist.

When the report came back, we were stunned. The mass was a granuloma surrounding a dog heartworm. I had no clue what the clinical implications were, or how or if it needed to be treated. I called my daughter to get her opinion as a veterinarian. The residents and I listened attentively as I used my speakerphone. She knew of cases in which veterinarians had been exposed and developed such granulomas. "Don't worry, Dad," she said. "Nothing bad will happen because the worm is not able to attach to human membranes. It will just become a benign granuloma as his body walls it off."

Our academic team was delighted with my daughter's information. We marched into the patient's room. I asked him, "Do you have a very close relationship with your dog?"

"Oh yes," he said. "We often sleep together."

"You don't have cancer."

He smiled and then added, "But what is my lung mass?"

"Dog heartworm."

He jumped at hearing the diagnosis. "What do I have to do to treat that?"

"I called a specialist who has experience with this problem." I didn't tell him that the specialist was my daughter. "Your body will take care of it. Besides, your cough is just viral bronchitis. It has nothing to do with the mass."

He felt much better and planned to have his dog treated for heartworms.


## 9/11

I will never forget 9/11, but not for the usual reasons. I was making rounds in the intensive care unit. One of our residents had developed respiratory failure from an asthma attack. She was intubated and on the ventilator. That day, I assessed her condition and found that she was breathing better. Her oxygenation had improved, and I thought her ability to breath was sufficient for her to be extubated.

I stood beside her, explained what I was going to do. As I deflated the endotracheal balloon and prepared to pull it out, she suddenly became frantic, pointing at the television. I turned to see the plane crashing into the towers. I finished extubating her, and we watched the television in horror together.

She still sends me messages every 9/11, thanking me for extubating her from the ventilator.

## Pheochromocytoma

I have already described the pheochromocytoma that I diagnosed in the Benton Harbor patient. I have diagnosed three other cases that were more typical, as the tumors were found in the adrenals. Dr. Loehrke laughs when I say it, but the Mayo Clinic's advice about orthostatic drop is significant: no orthostatic drop, no need to test for pheo.

Another patient presented to Bronson Hospital with some nonspecific complaints but was admitted because of his high blood pressure. The team was confused because sometimes his BP was normal, and when it was high, it didn't respond well to medication. I suspected the blood pressures were taken in different postures. The night nurse taking the patient's BP while he was in bed reported high blood pressures. The day nurses checking when the patient was in his chair reported normal pressures.

I was curious, so I asked the medical student assigned to our team to check for orthostatic hypotension while we were having lunch. The student returned to the lunchroom to tell us that the patient's systolic pressure was 160 when lying in bed but dropped to 120 when standing.

I ordered an abdominal MRI scan, and sure enough, the patient had an adrenal tumor. I went to the patient's bedside and explained that he had a tumor in his adrenal gland. "This will require some extensive testing. I suspect that you have a pheochromocytoma."

I explained what it was, and asked, "Do you want our academic team to do the diagnostic assessment, or your primary physician?"

"I want out of this hospital. I'll see my own doctor," he said. His face was red as he shook his fists at me.

"Fine," I said as he erupted. "We will discharge you and I will send a note to your doctor."

I documented in the progress note what we had told him and his preference to be evaluated by his own physician as an outpatient. I had medical records send his discharge summary as a letter to his primary care physician.

Several months later, the hospital received notice of a lawsuit for "failure to diagnose a pheochromocytoma." The hospital lawyer requested that I meet with her. I laughed. "I documented the diagnosis in the chart, but the patient wanted his own physician to finish the evaluation."

The hospital lawyer laughed with me. She sent documentation to the patient's lawyer, and the case was immediately dropped.

So much for my fifth pheochromocytoma.


## Stevens-Johnson Syndrome

Stevens-Johnson syndrome (SJS) is a horrible phenomenon. It is related to a drug that causes a skin reaction. In mild cases, the patient has a total body rash, and if recognized early, massive steroids can result in a full recovery. I had a patient at SWMC who had a reaction to Dilantin. I diagnosed it early and treated her, and she made a full recovery. Some patients who delay presenting lose all their skin and are usually managed in a burn center.

This young lady had taken a large dose of marijuana and developed SJS. She was embarrassed, so she delayed seeking medical help. It was the worst case I ever saw in my career. She lost all her skin, including the lining of her mouth, esophagus, and vagina. When her father came to the burn unit, he did not recognize her. He wept when he saw her. She spent three months in the burn unit, and survived, but ended up in a nursing home for rehabilitation with severe burn-related contractures.

As an academic team, we researched SJS related to marijuana. There was not a single case in the literature. The allergist consultant suggested that the reaction was related to some contaminant in the marijuana, not THC itself, which is a small molecule. Allergies that cause SJS require large molecules or small molecules attached to a protein, like a penicillin allergy. Without a sample of what she took, we could not hypothesize to what exactly she had reacted. Her urine drug screen showed only marijuana. Maybe a forensic pathologist could have found something else, but we remained clueless. The senior resident did find articles about SJS related to heroin contaminants, but that was the best we could speculate since she had taken no other medications associated with SJS.

This was such a tragic case, with the patient losing all her skin. I felt completely devastated in compassion for the patient and her father, who came every day to see his daughter.

# 19

## KENYA

Dr. Loehrke encouraged me to take residents to Madagascar, which I did for almost nineteen years, minus one year when there were two presidents, one too many, which caused riots in the streets. Forty Malagasy were killed. The state department did not allow U.S. citizens to go to Madagascar that year.

Instead, we went to Kenya. I had a friend, Dr. Bruce Dahlman, who was the director of Kijabe Hospital in Kenya. He agreed to host our residents. The residents claimed that it was a good experience but not very tropical. I was disappointed because we saw multiple cases of HIV/AIDS and tuberculosis but few cases of parasitic diseases or malaria.

A pulmonologist who was almost ready to retire from Kalamazoo accompanied us. He was in pulmonary ecstasy. He claimed that he saw more TB in the month we were in Kenya than he had seen in his whole career in Kalamazoo. One night, he did not show up for supper. I asked the residents if they had seen him. Nobody had. He finally showed up late. When I asked about his tardiness, he said with a Cheshire grin, "I was taking pictures of all the chest X-rays." Later, he taught the residents about tuberculosis using those pictures.

One of my residents, Dr. Duncan, cared for a young girl with pneumonia. He was very concerned about her and checked on her multiple times a day. When she recovered, the family was so grateful and delighted with his care that they gave him a goat. He came to me and asked, "What am I supposed to do with the goat?"

"Just wait," I said.

Our housekeeper tied up the goat on the lawn of our guesthouse, moving it every day to "mow the lawn." Then the night before we were to leave, our cook said with a big grin that he had prepared a special dinner for us. We ate goat with all the trimmings. Dr. Duncan was chagrined.

One Sunday during our stay at Kijabe, Dr. Dahlman invited me to go to a church service in the Rift Valley with him. We went to the Maasai church. It was an anthropologist's dream. The pastor asked me to say a few words before his sermon, so I shared some scripture and explained about our residents' experience at Kijabe Hospital. Many Maasai understand English, but the pastor translated into Maasai anyway, as there were many children who had not attended school yet and didn't understand English.

Then they had "jumping and rejoicing" before the pastor preached. All the attendees stood and started jumping. I asked the pastor why this was part of the service. He laughed and said, "How do you expect them to sit still and listen to my sermon unless they have been jumping and rejoicing first?" I think our churches in the United States could learn from that.

After the service, Dr. Dahlman and I went outside the church. Since we were special guests, all the adults greeted us. Then the children lined up to be "blessed." I was told that I had to pat each one on the top of the head. What an experience to bless that parade of children.

Another weekend, Dr. Dahlman was invited to attend a traditional Maasai wedding. He invited me to come along. It started in the bride's village. She came out of her parents' hut dressed in her red finery. Her father spit a blessing on her and turned his back to her. Dr. Dahlman explained that after their marriage, the father was not allowed to have any contact with his daughter. They went to the same church, but the father would be careful not to acknowledge her. The bride walked through the gate of her parents' house with a sad countenance. She was then accompanied by her many bridesmaids, her groom standing off in the distance.

Since Dr. Dahlman was the only person attending with a vehicle, a white Land Rover, we were chosen to transport the bride, all her bridesmaids, and the groom to the groom's village. Somehow, all ten or eleven squeezed into our four-passenger car. When we arrived at the groom's village, there were almost three hundred women who surrounded the bride, singing to her. Her sad expression became more cheerful as they danced around her and sang. Dr. Dahlman explained that they were accepting her into their community and promising to help her adjust. The groom, who was standing outside the swirling throng of women, said he was so glad that his village accepted his new bride.

The bride, the groom, and both sets of parents were Christians, but I was delighted to experience traditional Maasai wedding customs, including a feast of a goat. It was incredible, laid out on a long table. Every part of the goat was included, although I sampled only the meat, leaving the brain and intestines to others. I don't remember what vegetables were offered. With full stomachs, Dr. Dahlman and I quietly left and drove back up the hill to the hospital. I felt lightheaded as I realized that I had just attended a Maasai wedding.

Dr. Duncan decided to do a fellowship in infectious disease, and all the residents gave Dr. Loehrke a positive report. They felt that they had learned a lot, especially about tuberculosis. But I was disappointed that they had not learned about tropical diseases such as malaria and schistosomiasis.

# 20

## MADAGASCAR

Despite the positive feedback from the residents about the Kenyan experience and the exhilaration of the pulmonologist, I felt that taking residents to Madagascar was a superior experience because they could learn how to diagnose and manage tropical diseases. As a result, and with Dr. Loehrke's encouragement, I took residents to Madagascar eighteen times. Of course, my memory doesn't allow me to relate the trips in order, but I will provide vignettes.

Madagascar is the fourth largest island in the world. It is as large as California (1,500 miles long, 500 miles wide) in surface area with a population of twenty million people. Two million people live in Antananarivo, which translates to "City of a Thousand." The soil is red and the large river that empties into the northwest Mozambique Channel flows red into the ocean, giving the appearance of bleeding, thus the nickname: the "Bleeding Island." There are basically three paved roads. The road from Mahajanga to Antananarivo was made by the French when they invaded in the 1890s, referred to as the French Road. The road to the south, called the Norwegian Road, ended at the Norwegian

Lutheran seminary in Fianarantsoa. The road from Antananarivo to the coast was developed by the Chinese—the Chinese Road. All other roads are under development and often impassable.

Stan Quanbeck, a missionary who grew up in Madagascar, created a health organization called SALFA, which staffed Malagasy Lutheran hospitals with nurses and physicians when the hospitals became independent of the American and Norwegian Lutheran Church mission organizations. Since I had worked with Stan at Ejeda, I was invited to bring residents and introduce them . to Malagasy physicians.

My focus was that the residents attend at least three different hospitals because tropical diseases tend to be regional. For example, Schistosomiasis mansoni is endemic in the highlands and northeastern Madagascar, but Schistosoma haematobium is endemic in the south. The reason, as research from the Institut Pasteur (IP) demonstrated, is the snails required are unique to that parasite and compete in any body of water. Therefore, there is never an endemicity of both.

## Institut Pasteur

We were invited to IP by the negotiation of SALFA. IP researchers had great respect for SALFA physicians, which generated good cooperation between the two. SALFA physicians referred their most challenging patients to IP. As an example, a patient in Mahajanga presented with Yersinia pestis pneumonia (pneumonic plague). The physician treated the patient with streptomycin according to the literature, but the patient was not improving, so he added Bactrim, which is not usually used, but the patient improved rapidly. The SALFA physician contacted IP, who sent an investigator to document the streptomycin-resistant strain, the first reported case in the world's literature, which was later published in the *New England Journal of Medicine*.[24]

Each time we went to Madagascar, we spent a day at IP to find out what they were researching. A virologist from Paris was asked to find out if polio had resurfaced because there were ten cases of viral paralysis in young children. He discovered that the polio vaccine had transferred genetic information to an enterovirus. Enteroviruses, not polio, caused the paralysis. Subsequent cases were reported around the world, including in California, all related to enteroviruses, not polio.

IP also had the polymerase chain reaction (PCR) technology for genetic testing of TB before the hospitals in Kalamazoo. They could determine TB in eighty minutes and grow the organism in ten days on a special medium. For U.S. health departments, this would take thirty to forty-five days. (Bronson's lab received TB-PCR in 2019.) In addition, IP had tested PCR for TB not only on sputum but on pleural fluid and spinal fluid. Pleural fluid is notorious for not growing TB because the organism lives in the pleura, while the antigen is in the fluid. IP tested PCR on one hundred cases of proven TB meningitis; ninety-eight showed positive PCR results. They demonstrated that PCR was far more effective at diagnosing pleural TB than culture.[25]

---

[24] I was disappointed that SALFA was not mentioned in the article.
[25] When Priscilla had a pleural effusion and the residents suspected TB, Bronson refused to do PCR on the fluid, much to the consternation of my resident who had been to IP with me.

## Malaria

Madagascar has four different kinds of malaria. Over the course of the residents' experience, they always saw patients with at least two types. Some years, the residents were able to see patients with all four. This is important for prophylaxis. CDC recommendations focus on Plasmodium falciparum, but those recommendations fall short for P. vivax, P. ovale, and P. malariae. Vivax, for example, is 50 percent resistant to the CDC's recommendations. I emphasized this in orientation and encouraged residents to follow my recommendations instead of the CDC's. Most of the time, they did.

## Plague

One year, there was a plague epidemic in Madagascar—a Yersinia pestis outbreak during a soccer match in the capital. The coach had been to a funeral, contracted the plague, and then spread it at the soccer game. Hundreds of people got the plague and many died.

I explained what was happening one morning at breakfast. "There is a plague epidemic here in Madagascar. But none of you need to worry because the malaria prophylaxis I recommended, doxycycline, will protect you from plague as well."

Two residents raised their hands. "We didn't take what you recommended. We followed CDC guidelines."

I cringed, biting my lip from saying anything critical or sarcastic. "Oops. Well then, we will have to ask one of the Malagasy physicians to prescribe the correct medicine."

I also had one surgical resident who brought in a bottle of gin and told me that she was taking gin and tonics every night for malaria prophylaxis. Of course, this was the British solution in the nineteenth century during the imperial days of India. But her thinking was archaic. That year, we mostly worked in urban hospitals where the incidence of malaria was very low. She did not get malaria, but I was concerned.

## *Orientation*

All the residents were required to attend three two-hour sessions of orientation. If their schedule didn't allow it, they had to meet with me privately to make up a session.

The first was an orientation to the history and culture of Madagascar. I made Malagasy food, which included rice, chicken cooked with peanut sauce and coconut milk, and a side of vegetables available in Madagascar. The vegetarians loved the side dish. We talked about taboos and the training of Malagasy physicians. I oriented the residents to the diseases they would encounter and assigned them homework to investigate management and treatment of specific diseases. I emphasized that this was neither a vacation nor a mission trip. They would be learning from Malagasy physicians who had expertise in tropical diseases.

The second orientation dealt with getting to Madagascar and their daily experience. Getting to Madagascar is a challenge, as there are no direct flights from the United States. You must go somewhere else first. In the 1990s, I had flown Alitalia, and there were flights from Kenya, where one could arrive by flights from London. The British Airways flight was all right, but the food was terrible—the only time I have ever vomited on an aircraft.

The best way for decades has been via Air France to Paris and then to Antananarivo. Air France is a very gracious airline. If you book the flight from Chicago or Detroit, then Air France takes care of you if there is a delay in the flight. For example, one time, they whisked us through security to make the next flight. Another time, we totally missed the connection because of weather problems and Air France supplied us with hotel reservations and meal vouchers until the next flight to Madagascar. If you fly in the same airplane but book United or Delta, none of that happens. I insisted that our travel agent book all the flights because she understood this phenomenon.

Of course, a few rare residents wanted to save the $50 our travel agent, Ms. Prom, charged and book their own flights. Two were successful. One resident, who spoke fluent Spanish, wanted to spend a week in Spain. She met us in Paris. Another resident flew from South Africa because she wanted to go on a safari first. All the rest who tried to book their own flights ended up with disasters: missing flights; spending their own money in Paris till the next flight; flying Air Madagascar, which is less than comfortable; or spending a long time in airports. For example, one resident who booked his flights independently arrived in Antananarivo a day late, which meant that I had to help him through customs and arrange special transport from the airport. He reported a miserable experience. At future orientations, he advised residents to use Ms. Prom.

The flight from Paris is ten hours. Air France has good food, and if you can't sleep, they serve ice cream at 3:00 a.m. The bar is open all during the flight for all beverages. The movies are in multiple languages, including English. In eighteen years, Air France lost a person's luggage once. It was quickly retrieved the next day.

I spent time in orientation discussing the chaos of the airport in Antananarivo—four hundred people jamming into a line to get visas from a single person authorized to sell them. I always had to email my friends in Madagascar to find out the cost. Sometimes, visas were free; some years, they cost $50 or less. The authorized person always smiled at me when I asked him the cost.

During the third orientation, we discussed where they would stay, including essentials such as how much it would cost, what each day's schedule would include, and what to pack. The mountain hospital gets cold at night, it rains every day at the rainforest hospital, the west coast is very hot, and we would stay near the ocean; therefore, the itinerary required packing for all these different environments. But perhaps more important was knowing what not to pack. For example, one resident brought a 110-volt hair dryer that she plugged into a 220-volt outlet. It promptly blew up.

The first week, we stayed in the capital at a hotel, Le Refuge, which had good security and was walking distance from the hospital. It cost $20 a night, which included coffee or tea and a baguette with butter and jam for breakfast. Some of the residents ordered an omelet.

The difficulty every morning was that they had to order their supper at breakfast, or else the cook wouldn't have anything at night. That was because they did not store any food in the kitchen. Whatever was ordered for supper, the cook would obtain it at the market that day, always fresh. Before we went to the hospital the first morning, I asked each resident, "Did you order your supper?" Some residents told Dr. Loehrke when they returned from the rotation that I was "hung up on food." He laughed when I explained the problem.

At the hospital, we made morning rounds with the Malagasy physician in charge of admissions; they reviewed the cases admitted during the night and any critical patient already hospitalized. Lunch, which was provided by the hospital cooks, was always delicious, served in three courses. In the afternoon, I assigned the residents to work with the outpatient physicians. They observed care of hypertension, diabetes, and skin infections, as well as children with parasites.

The first evening, we had dinner at Le Refuge, which had a limited menu since they only served what they could easily obtain at the market. Some evenings after that, the residents chose to go out for pizza. Malagasy pizza is very French, thin crust with sliced tomatoes or eggs on top with very little cheese or sauce. But at least it was different from Malagasy food at Le Refuge.

During that first week, as the residents resolved their eight-hour jet lag, I would make the arrangements to go to the other hospitals. Our travel agent in Kalamazoo tried to do this but found it impossible. So, while the residents were seeing outpatients with a Malagasy physician, I would go see my trusted Malagasy travel agent to plan the itinerary. Sometimes, this would require flights on Air Madagascar. Then I would need the residents to personally present themselves with their passports to obtain tickets.

That day, I took them out for lunch at the Colbert, which had a French chef and excellent food. Years later, Dr. Bannon, who went to Madagascar first as a resident and later as faculty, would salivate if someone mentioned the Colbert in the clinic.

Before going to the second hospital, I would plan a trip to Lemur Park. Madagascar has several areas protected from logging to preserve environments for the lemurs. The fifty-some species have specific environmental needs, so it was a surprise to most residents that they could only see certain lemurs in a given preserve. Much to my chagrin, the residents sent Dr. Loehrke pictures of the lemurs, which they saw only one weekend. I had to encourage them to send him pictures of seeing patients so he didn't think that they were just goofing off.

Dr. Loehrke understood our schedule in detail, but our CEO didn't. She decided the rotation was worthless based on the pictures shown at graduation. So, we quit submitting our pictures for graduation. Without interesting pictures submitted by the other residents, the administration stopped having the graduation slideshow.

The next week would be spent at a different hospital. SALFA has twenty-three hospitals and clinics, but I chose hospitals that were in different climates so that the residents would see different diseases. These included Vohemar in the northeast coastal area; Mahajanga on the west coast; Antsirabe in the mountains, which is more than five thousand feet in elevation; and Manambaro in the southeastern jungle. On rare occasions, we went to Ejeda in the southwestern desert. But there are no real roads there. One can drive there cross-country, but it could take one to two weeks. We went twice, but it required an expensive flight with a Mission Aviation Fellowship bush pilot, as there are no Air Madagascar flights to Ejeda.

## Making Arrangements

I would email my Malagasy contacts at least three to four months in advance. My travel agent in Madagascar arranged for hotels, which hospitals we planned to go to, and very important, our driver. Some hotels required a deposit, so I had to send money by Western Union. The WU person, after looking at the long Malagasy name, always asked, "Do you actually know this person?"

"Yes, he is a good friend," I would reply.

I always arranged the stay at Lemur Park and paid for it personally as a gift to the residents who were willing to take on this adventure. They always had a good time and were delighted with the guide I chose who knew the plants, medical uses of the plants, and local customs, as well as had an uncanny knowledge of where to find the lemur populations.

## Continuing Education Seminar

Email communication with the director of SALFA included requests for updates on certain diseases. Most of the requests related to common diseases on which the residents had expertise. As a result, the last week of the rotation, we gave a seminar to our hosts to update them on the latest treatments of diabetes, hypertension, management of strokes, et cetera. This was our way of thanking them.

During orientation, the residents were assigned to make PowerPoint presentations for the seminar. Half the textbooks used in the Malagasy medical school are in English; Malagasy physicians all read English, but only half speak it. Therefore, the residents' PowerPoint presentations did not require translation, but their talks did. I reviewed their presentations to remove aspects that were meaningless in the environment of Madagascar, such as medications or technological investigations that were unavailable.

What the residents discovered was that the Malagasy physicians understood pathophysiology very well, not only tropical diseases but also diseases common to our residents. What they wanted to know at the seminar related to novel treatment. Our residents were amazed by the quality of care the Malagasy provided with limited resources.

The last day of the seminar, the Malagasy physicians would present cases and ask for our input on treatment. One case that was presented to Dr. Bannon, I will never forget. They presented a twenty-three-year-old woman with rheumatic heart disease and asked how it should be managed. Dr. Bannon gave an excellent review. When she finished her discussion, they added that the patient was one-week postpartum and had postpartum cardiomyopathy. How should her heart failure be managed? Dr. Bannon reviewed the management of postpartum cardiomyopathy and heart failure. Then the physicians added that the patient also had tuberculosis. Dr. Bannon decided to let me answer that part of the question.

During orientation, I also invited past residents who had been on previous rotations to present their experiences. Priscilla had been to Madagascar a few times and added her female perspective on what to bring and what was not available. Every resident heard these stories and learned about the cultural aspects of Madagascar during the three sessions of orientation. Were they ready? Every resident claimed the orientation sessions were valuable. Some still experienced culture shock despite the orientation.

## No Normal Deliveries

One family medicine resident wanted to assist in deliveries. She had delivered several babies in Kalamazoo and asked if she could be involved in deliveries in Madagascar. I told her to ask the Malagasy physician to contact her when there was a pending delivery, which she did. But I warned her that there were no normal deliveries in SALFA hospitals. Normal deliveries were performed by midwives in the villages. Patients were sent to the hospital if their midwife felt that she couldn't handle some aspect of the delivery.

The Malagasy preceptor told her that there was a pending delivery with a woman who had an adequate pelvis and normal blood pressure. The resident was invited to do the delivery with the Malagasy physician. She laughed at my warning. "See, Dr. Roach, there are normal deliveries here."

"I'm happy for you. Enjoy."

When labor started, the resident was called to the hospital. The obstetric nurse ran to our hotel to bring her. I was not surprised when the resident did not show up for dinner, as I knew how important this delivery was to her. But by ten o'clock, she still had not returned. A nurse suddenly arrived by ambulance and said, "We need one of the pediatric residents right away."

A senior pediatric resident had come with our group of residents. He grabbed his scrubs and was whisked away by ambulance.

Late that night, the two of them returned. With tears dripping down her cheeks, the family medicine resident told me, "You're right, Dr. Roach. There are no normal deliveries here."

"What happened?"

She was too choked up to respond, so the pediatric resident responded, "The child was born with part of his skull missing."

Tears still dripping, she said, "I didn't know what to do."

He said, "We had a case like this at Bronson. I wrapped the exposed brain in sterile surgical wrap. They're taking the child to Antananarivo in the morning."

I spent time that night comforting the family medicine resident. It helped her to know the next day that the trip to the capital was uneventful and a neurosurgeon had a pediatric metal brain cover that fit the child. The baby did not develop an infection and had a positive post-op result.

### Rheumatic Heart Disease

Many residents experienced culture shock during the rotation because they were thrown into an environment of poverty, lack of technology, lack of medicines they were accustomed to using, and frequent fatalities of patients who might have survived in the

285

United States. The residents needed comforting. That was usually my role, but when other faculty professors were available, I asked them to help.

One pediatric resident wasn't showing up for meals and seemed aloof to the group. Our faculty included a woman who was a pediatric rheumatologist, so I asked her to see if she could counsel the resident, or at least find out why she was avoiding the group. After meeting with the resident, the faculty member told me that the resident was in shock because all through her pediatric residency, she had never had a patient die, and she was a senior.

We admitted a ten-year-old boy brought to the hospital by his father. The child was gasping for breath even at rest. Investigation revealed severe rheumatic heart disease, both aortic and mitral stenosis, with an echo ejection fraction of about 5 percent. He needed a heart transplant, which was available in Johannesburg, South Africa. I cautioned the residents that the usual treatment for congestive heart failure with his valvular heart diseases was contraindicated. The Malagasy physicians, meanwhile, assessed how he could be transported to South Africa. He died during the wait.

That experience troubled the resident. The faculty physician spent a lot of time comforting her privately. Eventually, she met with us for the next supper. Many of the residents shared their own shocking experiences with her. She was not alone. She then felt like part of the group. After that, we decided to have a discussion every night, sharing our experiences. Sharing time at supper became a regular routine of the rotation.

## Favorite Hospitals

The residents' favorite hospital was Vohemar because it was the only hospital for several days' travel in any direction, and therefore had plenty of patients with excellent pathology. The clinical director not only spoke English but was intellectually brilliant in presenting patients. Besides, the accommodations were at a French resort that charged us $40 a night, including breakfast with fresh fruit, which could be shared by two residents. The problem was how to get there.

One choice was a private bush plane, which we took on several occasions, landing on the dirt runway. That was not too expensive in the early 2000s flying with Mission Aviation Fellowship, but the Malagasy government forced them to increase their prices to match the competition, even though there was no competing Air Madagascar flight to Vohemar. Subsequently, we took Air Madagascar to Sambava, a town south of Vohemar, and had the hospital personnel pick us up and drive us four hours north to the hospital. Yes, there was another paved road called the Vanilla Road, paved by the vanilla companies to transport vanilla beans to the port at Sambava. It was well maintained but went nowhere else, as it did not connect with any other road.

The hospital at Antsirabe, built in 1890 by the Norwegian Lutheran Church, was on the Norwegian Road. It was an easy trip by Malagasy standards, four hours on winding roads. The residents liked that hospital because it was a referral hospital for surgery and obstetrics as well as infectious disease for the entire SALFA system. This is where we saw the most complex patients.

For accommodations, we stayed at the Norwegian guesthouse, walking distance to the hospital. It was more expensive—$40 per person a night each, and for a minimal charge, we could add breakfast, which included fruit, bread, yogurt, and eggs on request. The comic books in the bathrooms were in Norwegian. The extensive library was in Norwegian. However, most of the Norwegian managers spoke English, and the internet was excellent.

There is a French spa with a nice pool in Antsirabe. During the imperial age, French tourists would come to visit the therapeutic hot springs. The resort is of the Grand Hotel vintage. Our residents could sit poolside and swim for about $1. Tea and pastries were extra, but reasonably priced.

Antsirabe has several nice restaurants to choose from, and a well-stocked grocery store. My favorite place to visit was Chez Joseph, where semiprecious gems were cut. Often, the residents wanted to go to the Pizza Parlor, where the pizza was more American style and delicious. I preferred the Chinese restaurant. The food was delicious and always well cooked and presented. No resident ever got dysentery eating there.

I warned residents during orientation not to eat salad. Two residents said in the evening that they would meet us at the Pizza Parlor and left early. Their purpose turned out to be so they could eat salad against my recommendation. I found out when they spent all night in the bathroom.

Mahajanga is on the northwest coast. The hospital is primarily for poor patients who cannot afford to go to the government hospital, which is an extension of the Malagasy medical school. To reach Mahajanga is an all-day drive over the French Road.

During the day, Mahajanga is hot, with 100°F temperatures, but it has beautiful white sand beaches. Accommodations are nice. We stayed at the beach hotel called Eden. The problem was that the clinic and hospital were almost an hour's drive east of the center of town. And from the hotel, there was heavy traffic.

There is an inexpensive Malagasy hotel near the hospital, but it has no air-conditioning, which is important for two reasons. First, it is hard to sleep in stifling heat. Second, temperatures below 70°F kill falciparum in mosquitoes. Therefore, a lack of air-conditioning increased the risk of malaria exposure for my residents. Besides, the hotel had no screens on their open windows.

## Several Cases

Dr. Prashant Patel edited this section and suggested that I needed to describe a few more of the cases we saw in Madagascar. So here are a few vignettes.

## Endocarditis

We saw a ten-year-old girl who seemed to have pneumonia. She would get better with basic antibiotics but became feverish again when the antibiotics were stopped. We did an echocardiogram on her and found her mitral valve damaged by rheumatic heart disease with a vegetation. The treatment for bacterial endocarditis requires a prolonged course of antibiotics. She did well despite a lack of cultures to identify the organism.

## Vibrio Vulnificus

An alcoholic fisherman overturned his canoe while fishing and scraped his leg on coral. The wound would just not heal despite the Malagasy physician's adequate staph–strep antibiotic choice. In fact, the wound looked worse every day. I changed the antibiotic to ciprofloxacin presuming that he had Vibrio vulnificus. In two days, it was healed. The Malagasy physician applied this treatment whenever he obtained a history of exposure to coral.

An elderly man presented in the area where there was Schistosoma haematobium complaining of not being able to urinate. Ultrasound revealed a calcified bladder. He was catheterized, which improved his renal function, and then taken to surgery, where a small piece of ilium was sewed onto his bladder. The residents became familiar with the surgery invented by Dr. Quanbeck.

## Missing Penis

A farmer who had been wading in a flooded field was attacked by a Malagasy crocodile, which bit off his penis. Dr. Solo used a sharpened sound to pierce his bladder through his perineum and prostate, as the remnant of the urethra was impossible to find. He followed it with a Foley catheter preserving renal function. Seven surgeries later, he had formed a new penis from a transplanted scrotum. The track of the catheter even epithelialized, and the catheter was able to be removed.

The patient's intact prostate allowed him to control his urine. His complaint was that he couldn't have sex with his wife. Dr. Solo, therefore, took out a part of his chondral rib and placed it in his penis. Consequently, the patient reported that his wife was satisfied with his performance.

## Tetanus

When I was in Madagascar in 1976, I had set up a protocol for Malagasy physicians to treat neonatal tetanus. Vaccinating pregnant women eliminated the disease from the island, and most children received initial vaccinations for polio, measles, mumps, rubella, and tetanus. So, the tetanus cases the Malagasy physicians were now seeing involved teens and middle-aged adults. My protocol required initial treatment of 25 mg/kg a day of Valium and then decreased doses over three weeks, the time required for the toxin to be metabolized. I treated a teenage girl with almost 700 mg of Valium a day, then weaned her off. She did well.

A middle-aged man presented with tetanus. He had received his "baby shots" but nothing since. The Malagasy physician was giving him 75 mg of Valium a day for a week. The patient was able to breathe but unable to get out of bed because of muscle spasms, so I increased his dose to 125 mg. The next day, he was out of bed and walking when we made rounds. He said in English, "Thanks, Doc. I needed that."

I reviewed the treatment with the Malagasy physician, who thought the dose was extraordinary but saw the benefit. I told her to reduce the dose to 75 mg in five to seven days, then wait a week and reduce it again. He did well and went home walking. I have treated twenty-eight patients with tetanus with only the two deaths.

## P. Malariae

One evening in Vohemar, we invited two anthropologists to meet with us to describe their fieldwork. They were trying to find evidence of human occupation in Madagascar prior to the Polynesian arrival. We invited them to our resort for a cocktail.

The two, both professors from Oxford University, delighted us with their findings from their dig site in an ancient, abandoned village. They reported no evidence of human habitation of the island before the Polynesian Malagasy invasion. After a wonderful candid discussion, the older professor got up to go back to his hotel. He stumbled and I had to help him navigate to the hotel, which was next to ours. He hadn't had that much to drink, so I was concerned.

In the morning, his coworker appeared while we were eating breakfast. He was frantic. The professor had been delirious all night. He asked our team to check him because he was anticipating evacuating him to England, which would be very expensive and interfere with their research. The professor was brought to the hospital, where we examined him and did a peripheral smear, which was positive for P. malariae. We treated him with artemisinin-based combination therapy, and he recovered in twenty-four hours. The professors were so grateful they could continue their research that they gave us their cards and offered a tour of Oxford University should we go to England.

I also suggested a more comprehensive malaria prophylaxis. There is not much in the medical literature regarding P. malariae, as there are so few cases worldwide. I was glad that our residents were able to learn from the professor's experience and that he completely recovered. The residents also learned why I insisted on a different prophylaxis from the CDC recommendation and air-conditioned bedrooms.

## Peritoneal TB

Our team was asked to see a middle-aged man with a fever and abdominal pain. He had a small amount of ascites but had no alcohol history. His liver enzymes were only mildly elevated, and ultrasound did not reveal any cirrhosis. There was no evidence of schistosomiasis, as he had lived in the city his whole life.

We were perplexed. The Malagasy physician planned to do a

paracentesis. There wasn't much fluid, but he was quite expert in performing the tap. The fluid demonstrated acid-fast bacilli, peritoneal tuberculosis. I don't think that diagnosis was on our differential. The patient was treated for TB; his symptoms resolved within a week of treatment with four drugs following a protocol advised by IP.

Later, by email, the Malagasy physician informed me that the man was completely cured. We learned that peritoneal TB is not contagious.

## Tuberculosis

We had a pediatric intensivist, Dr. Bob Beck, with us on a couple of occasions. He gave our residents insights into inborn errors of metabolism, congenital anomalies, and treatment of children's diseases with expertise that I didn't have. We were presented with a child, only a few months old, whom we suspected had pulmonary TB. Medicine for TB treatment is free in Madagascar, but the glitch is that the diagnosis must be confirmed. The physician may not treat based on suspicion. How to make the diagnosis in a baby is a challenge; they do not cough up sputum for you. I suppose in Kalamazoo, a bronchoscopy could be performed, but we did not have a bronchoscope available. Dr. Beck suggested putting down a nasogastric tube and checking suctioned results for TB, since babies swallow their sputum. That was diagnostic, but the baby was so sick she died despite initiation of treatment.

I was frustrated when I saw a teenage girl with a high fever and obvious meningitis. I initiated antibiotics, but there was no improvement. The first spinal tap revealed many lymphocytic white blood cells and very low glucose, suggesting TB meningitis. But the tap did not show any acid-fast bacilli. Since treatment for TB could not be initiated without a confirmed diagnosis, I repeated the tap every morning. On the fourth tap, the acid-fast bacilli were seen, the diagnosis made. I rushed to the bedside to initiate TB treatment, but the young girl died that morning in my arms.

SALFA has been granted permission to establish a TB program. When a case is diagnosed, they send a team to the patient's village to check people who might have been exposed by the index case. The result is that the diagnosis is made earlier, and treatment begins before individuals develop a terminal disease. Often, the team discovers an elderly source who is exposing others but is considered too old to take to the hospital. IP is developing a drone system to provide medication to patients in distant villages to which there are no roads. The goal of these efforts is to reduce the endemicity of TB in Madagascar.

The residents had great experiences. They admired the Malagasy physicians, and for eighteen years, WMed graduated residents with an excellent knowledge of tropical pathology. Many chose to become infectious disease fellows; others set up travel medicine clinics. All reported that it was a worthwhile, though expensive, rotation.

One resident told me she now could never marry. "Why?" I asked.

"I used my dowry to go to Madagascar."

Years later, her brother told me that she still hasn't married, but is now a child psychiatrist.

# 21

## SIERRA LEONE

Ron Baker, MD, was my partner in Berrien Springs when home on furlough from the hospital his father had started in Matru, Sierra Leone. He invited me to visit his hospital and give some medical education talks to his staff. I was apprehensive but decided to coordinate the visit with a trip to Madagascar.

The first physician assistant (PA) I hired, Mark, was intrigued by Ron's description of Sierra Leone. Ron talked Mark into joining him at Matru. That left me without a PA. I therefore had another reason to go to Sierra Leone—to see if I could coax Mark to come back. That didn't work out. Mark enjoyed his experience so much that when he returned to the United States, he went to medical school and became a surgeon. I had to hire another PA, John Kittredge.

Matru is a long way from the capital, Freetown. In addition, England built the airport during World War II for defensive purposes and placed it on the other side of the river from the city. Following the roads from the airport east, we could find the first bridge on the road from Port Loko to Masiaka. That would be a seven-hour road trip just to get to Freetown. Not a good choice.

There are two other choices: the ferryboat from the airport to Freetown or the helicopter. Ron suggested the ferryboat might be a problem, as engine trouble was common and the previous ferry ended up thirty miles out in the ocean before the motor was repaired. So, the best choice was the helicopter. Ron told me it cost $50. I didn't consider that a big problem because when you entered the country, we had to exchange $300 of hard currency (Euros, British pounds, or U.S. dollars) to immigrate. When I did so, I was awarded a free bag into which to place all my leones (the largest bill was worth about $5).

I went to the helicopter pad and forked over $50 worth of leones to obtain my ticket. The cashier looked at me and shook his head no. He said, "The helicopter only *eats* dollars." Fortunately, I had enough extra cash to provide food for the helicopter.

Ron had arranged for one of the seminary professors to meet me at the helicopter pad on my arrival in Freetown. Unfortunately, no one was there. The backup plan was to go to a certain hotel, whose name and address Ron had sent me in an email. I gave the paper to the taxi driver and was blessed that the taxi ate leones.

By the time I reached the hotel, the whole hillside had lost electricity. I went to the front desk to get my room. There was a single candle burning. I carefully counted out my leones for the hotel bill. It took about thirty minutes because the receptionist had to count them out again, and then she called the manager, who counted them out again.

A young man with a candle appeared to take me upstairs. Ushered into my room, I discovered that there was no lock on the door, and it didn't shut very well. There was no glass or screen on the window, so it was a large opening onto the central courtyard. A concrete walkway went around the courtyard to every room on the second floor. The young man had given me his candle, but it did not provide enough light to even read by, so I was just stuck in this room with a large gaping hole to the courtyard, no locks, and a toilet that was beyond description. I sunk into the skinny mattress, holding my suitcase, wondering what the morning would bring.

An hour or so later—the exact time escapes me—there was a knock on the door. It was the seminary professor who was supposed to take me to the Methodist seminary for the night. We went to the front desk, and he asked if my money for the room could be returned. The receptionist smiled and said, "No problem." I thought there would be another half hour of counting leones, but to my surprise, she put a pile of money on the desk, patted it, and said, "That should be about right."

In the back seat of the professor's car, I sat counting my leones. She was only off by two dollars. Impressive. When we arrived at the seminary, I was given a beautiful, air-conditioned room with a wonderful toilet, shower, and sink.

The next day, while I was walking the grounds of the seminary, Ron arrived to take me to Matru. It was a seven-hour drive. Along the way, I counted seventeen military checkpoints. I was concerned that the soldiers at each would want to check my passport and visa obtained at the airport. But at each checkpoint, the grim-looking soldier carrying an automatic rifle would look in the window and smile; say, "Ah, Dr. Baker"; and motion us through. At one of the checkpoints, Ron added, "I did hernia surgery on that soldier."

On our arrival at the hospital, we made quick rounds, and then we went to Ron's for dinner. I forget exactly what we had, but Ron is quite a fisherman. When he has time off, he goes fishing in the river that leads to the ocean. There is no limit, so when he catches lots of fish, he keeps one and gives the rest to poor people in the village. So, I think we had fish and rice.

What I do remember is he had gotten milk from a local farmer, and as it settled in his gas-powered refrigerator, he skimmed off the cream to make ice cream as a special treat. To his chagrin, the old ice machine leaked so that when salt was added to the ice to freeze the cream, it leaked into the ice cream. As a result, the ice cream was so salty we couldn't eat it.

I enjoyed Ron's staff. I was invited to join them in surgery, and then have lunch—a massive bowl of rice topped with palm oil–fried chicken, which everyone shared. They ate with their fingers. I had no concern, as their hands were sterile from scrubbing for surgery. After the meal, I gave some lectures based on their requests to thank them for my visit.

## Hypertension and Diet

One remarkable ward had fifty beds, all full, for complicated obstetrics. Noncomplicated obstetrics were in another ward managed by midwives.

"What is the complication here?" I asked Ron.

"All these pregnant women have hypertension. Some may have preeclampsia, so we keep them in this hospital ward for nurse observation and treating their blood pressure. If they get into problems, we do an emergency C-section so they don't have seizures."

"How common is hypertension here in Sierra Leone?" I asked.

"Thirty to forty percent of the outpatients have hypertension."

"That is the same percentage as my African American patients in Benton Harbor. In medical school, our professors claimed that hypertension is related to the American diet."

"None of these patients have ever had an American diet," Ron said with a grin. "They eat rice and sorghum and add some vegetables every day. They have meat maybe once a week. One chicken might be shared among an extended family of a dozen people." That is quite a contrast to an American diet.

## Botflies

I was surprised when I saw Ron's housekeeper ironing his underwear. I thought that must be an imperial carryover. I know Ron well, and knew he had great respect for Sierra Leonean workers, so I asked him why he had his maid iron his underwear. "Because of the botflies. They lay their eggs on the underwear while they are drying on the clothesline. Then you put them on, and the larvae dig into your skin. If you iron everything that touches your skin, the eggs die and no skinworms or myiasis develops."

"Oh, how clever."

## Crises

I saw many patients with Ron, who speaks fluent Mende. Many of the tropical diseases in Sierra Leone I was familiar with from Madagascar, but some, like river blindness, were unknown in Madagascar because they did not have the required parasite.

Ron trained his staff well in protecting themselves. When Ebola hit Sierra Leone, his staff knew personal protective measures, which they taught to the village elders, who taught the villagers. As a result, there were very few cases in their district and no cases among his staff.

Another crisis was the invasion of the National Patriotic Front of Liberia, commanded by Charles Taylor. It was tragic that the rebels invaded the villages and cut off the hands of the village elders. The Matru hospital staff fled to the jungles to hide. But before they left, they dug huge holes and buried the hospital's X-ray machine, lab equipment, and other valuables.

When the rebels arrived, it seemed to them that the hospital had been ransacked. No further damage was done. When the rebels left, the staff dug up the equipment and informed Dr. Baker, who was back in the United States, that the hospital was saved. He returned to find the hospital fully functioning again.

When it was time for me to go, Ron drove me seven hours back to the heliport. I gave him all my leftover leones. Another helicopter ride required dollars for the helicopter to eat.

The airport was neat and clean. I waited at the gate for the nonstop flight to Ghana. Then I would transfer to Air Ethiopia for the flight to Kenya and then on to Madagascar. It seemed simple.

## Flying across Africa

First, the attendant at the gate refused to let me board. I sat and waited. Was there something wrong with my ticket or visa? The answer came when he asked me for a bribe. I laughed and said I was here in Sierra Leone to provide medical care for the people in Matru, and any extra money, I had donated to the hospital. Finally, he gave up and let me board.

Since it was booked as a nonstop flight to Ghana, I disembarked when the plane landed. Unknown to me, the plane had made an unscheduled stop in Liberia. When I went to immigration, they took my passport. It surprised me, but they do that in Madagascar and then stamp the visa and give it back as you leave. My luggage never arrived on the turntable, so I asked the young lad who was going to help me with my luggage to see what the problem was. He said, "This ticket is for Ghana. You are in Liberia."

"I'm in the wrong country. I need my passport to get back on the plane," I told him.

"Follow me," he said.

We went back up the stairs, and he looked in the back door of immigration. "I see it," he whispered. He ran in the back door, grabbed my passport, and yelled, "Come quick!" We raced back down to the baggage terminal and scooted through the opening in the wall. I followed as he ran around in the back of the airport, finally finding an exit to the tarmac. I gave him two U.S. dollars and he said, "Run fast."

The ladder to the airplane was still down, so I ran. Suddenly, two soldiers with automatic rifles started chasing me across the tarmac. I scooted up the stairs and returned to my seat, buckling my seat belt. I did my best to look innocent. The two armed soldiers came right to me, demanding my passport. I apologized profusely for getting off the plane in the wrong country. They talked between themselves; I did not understand them, as they were probably speaking a tribal language. It seemed to take forever. But they gave me back my passport and said, "OK," and left.

*Next time, I will ask what country I am in before disembarking, even if it is a direct flight,* I told myself.

The flight to Ghana went well. I did ask what country we were in at the time. The attendees smiled and assured me, "Yes, we are in Ghana."

"Is this where we transfer to Air Ethiopia?"

A well-dressed gentleman behind me said, "Yes. I'm flying to Kenya too."

We paraded into the Ghana airport. It was stifling hot. Those of us transferring to Air Ethiopia were corralled between four posts with chains surrounding us. One armed soldier was at each corner. I asked the nice gentleman, who seemed comfortable in the heat despite his three-piece suit, "What is this all about?"

He said, "Don't worry. Air Ethiopia is not ready to receive us."

We stood, no place to sit, chained into our square for almost an hour. Then a short, petite, handsome Ethiopian man in a three-piece suit arrived. The soldiers unlocked one of the chains, and the Ethiopian said to our group of passengers in English, "Follow me."

We followed down a hallway that eventually narrowed to allow only one person at a time to pass. There were two alcoves, one with a man and the other with a woman, who bodychecked us according to our sex. Then we arrived at a beautifully decorated, air-conditioned room with plush, comfortable seats for everyone. Free bottled water was available. When the plane was ready, we were escorted across the tarmac to the waiting plane.

I will never forget the captain's remarks as we buckled our seat belts, waiting to take off. After the usual instructions, he said in perfect English, "Have you all noticed that we have the most beautiful flight attendants in the world?" I admit they were attractive.

We flew to Addis Ababa. It was amazing to see the tropical jungle degenerate into the Sahara Desert from thirty thousand feet. As we circled the airport, I noticed many gray military planes with red tails. When we finally landed, we were informed that there had been a coup d'etat and the Russian military had arrived to stabilize the government. As we disembarked, we had to walk between two rows of armed Russian soldiers. Once in the airport, we were surrounded by armed military. My friendly gentleman seemed unfazed by it all. He helped me remain calm. I stayed right near him. Then we were once again paraded between the military guards to board our flight to Kenya.

The flight from Addis Ababa to Nairobi was uneventful. On

the plane, I became more and more relaxed as we neared the airport. I had been to Nairobi many times before, and it was like coming home. My good friend from UMD, Connie Shingledecker, was there to meet me. When we landed, I got down on the ground and kissed the Kenyan tarmac. I stayed with Ken and Connie for a while, until my scheduled flight to Madagascar. Spending time with them was very therapeutic.

Over dinner, Ken related going to Nigeria for a mission conference. He said the attendant would not let him on the plane without a bribe. Eventually, the plane took off without him; the attendant didn't care. Ken then met a fellow missionary who was traveling back to Kenya on a private plane because of his bad experiences in Nigeria. So, he was able to return to Kenya on a private flight.

Ken said that I was blessed the attendant finally gave up trying to extract a bribe and let me on the plane in Sierra Leone. Maybe he did that because I told him I had given all my money to the hospital.

After a nice rest with the Shingledeckers' hospitality, I returned to the airport to fly to Madagascar.

# 22

## RWANDA

When Temujin was ten years old and Tirzah was eight, we were invited by Al Snyder, MD, to go to Rwanda (correctly pronounced *Gwanda*, although news reporters have never figured that out and still pronounce it *Rue-wanda*). Dr. Snyder was a surgeon. The physician caring for the non-surgical patients had returned to the United States for a rest. For three months, I would be responsible for the medicine patients. We applied for a three-month visa and flew to Kigali on Air France.

Kibogora Hospital is on Lake Kivu, the western border of Rwanda. The drive takes about five hours. But along the way is a beautiful waterfall that allows a nice break from the twisting roads. Everything is green with flowers blooming, which is why Rwanda is called "the land of eternal spring." On the trip, we saw children playing soccer. Since there is almost no level ground in the entire country, even its soccer fields are tilted. Because of this, soccer is played in quarters so each team gets two quarters downhill. The scores are more reasonable that way; otherwise, one team would get a whole half downhill, and then when fatigued, the other team would get their half downhill. Quarters make more sense to Rwandans.

When we arrived at the hospital, Dr. Snyder explained that the hills are mostly clay, so when he arrived, he dug a hole in a hill and used the clay to make bricks. He put the hospital in the hole he dug. It's a beautiful hospital with sheltered walkways between the buildings since it rains every day at 11:00 a.m. and 4:00 p.m. for about thirty minutes. No wonder it is so green.

There is tension between the tribes of Rwanda. The problems between the tribes are complex. Hutus considered the Tutsis invaders from the north from prehistoric times. The Hutus and the Tutsis were tolerating each other when we were there. The holocaust killing almost a million people happened five years later. Lesser known are the Twa (Batwa tribe). They are small jungle people, less than 1 percent of the population. The government made a rule that every organization had to hire at least one Twa. A Twa appeared one day out of the Congo jungle. He had no education and did not speak Kinyarwanda. Dr. Snyder hired him on the spot to sweep the walkways, meeting the legal obligation.

A more serious problem is the difference in attitudes toward education. Even in the time of Livingstone (1840s) and the first European contact, Tutsis had a prolonged education system lasting years for both boys and girls. Hutus had only a two-week puberty ritual for each sex. Rwanda was under German rule in 1899. Unfortunately, the Hutus resented this and skirmished with the Germans. Germany lost control as part of the Treaty of Versailles after World War I. The Belgians and French then set up a school system. Tutsis enthusiastically accepted the schools and sent their children to attend. Hutus saw no benefit and did not send their children. As a result, when Europeans tried to nationalize the country, they required applicants to pass a civil service exam to qualify for government positions. Many Tutsis qualified; very few Hutus had the education to qualify. The result: a Tutsi minority government, which the majority Hutus resented because of lack of representation.

Despite speaking the same language, Kinyarwanda, the two tribes have quite different cultural values regarding social status, parental roles, and education. It took me only two weeks before I could look at a patient and tell which tribe they were from, but they have no problem. Interestingly, intermarriage between the tribes only occurs among college-educated people. I met some physicians and college graduates who had mixed tribal marriages, but no uneducated people. When one reads the holocaust stories, one comes to the same conclusion.

The Tutsis tried to stabilize the politics by appointing a Hutu president. That was effective for a while, but when the radio station initiated the holocaust (broadcasting, "Kill the cockroaches"), the Hutus started the war by shooting a missile that destroyed the plane in which the Hutu president was returning to the country.

Back to my story. We stayed in a nice ranch-style house about a block away from the hospital. We were up on a hill with a nice breeze off Lake Kivu. Marceline was our housekeeper and Bizimana was our cook. I was initially opposed to house help, but Dr. Snyder explained that to not hire house help, and therefore not share your income with Rwandans, was considered selfish.

Bizimana made sorghum porridge for us because that is what 90 percent of Rwandans eat for breakfast. It was bitter stuff despite adding raw brown sugar and butter. We decided to just have some of the luscious fruit for breakfast instead. He also made a delicious seafood lunch for us every day, and before he left, there was a nice supper in the oven. Dr. Snyder told us not to finish our food, as Bizimana would take leftovers home to his family. Rwandans do have a curious habit: they consider it taboo to eat when the sun is up, so they eat breakfast before sunrise, don't eat all day, and have supper after sunset. Seems to me that is a healthy habit, but remember the sun rises at 6:00 a.m. and sets at 6:00 p.m. in the tropics.

Marceline was delightful. She spoke English well but had a curious habit. She would capture spiders in the garden and bring them into the house. I asked why she did that, and she replied, "They eat mosquitoes. You don't want to get malaria, do you?" She encouraged geckos to dwell in the house for the same reason. One day, there was a particularly large spider in the bathroom that scared Tirzah. Marceline carefully cradled it in her hands and took it outside to the garden, unwilling to kill any creature that ate mosquitoes.

Priscilla enjoyed the house help and focused on the children. Tirzah and Temujin made fast friends of Rwandan children. I have a picture of them playing with a yard full of children who regularly visited.

My daily routine was to eat breakfast and then scurry down the hill to the hospital to make patient rounds. Charts were simple. Just a note of progress was needed every day. There were several patients with liver abscesses, which I drained percutaneously since I could feel the fluctuance of the abscess on the physical exam. Once treated with Flagyl (metronidazole), the palpable abscesses resolved, and the patients did well. One exception, a man presented with multiple liver abscesses, all too small to drain. His fever resolved with Flagyl, and I was delighted. Then we ran out of Flagyl. Dr. Snyder sent a courier to Kigali to get more. That took three days. Meanwhile, the patient became febrile, septic. I tried other antibiotics, but he died before additional Flagyl could be obtained.

An interesting aspect of caring for the patients was when they needed an X-ray. We had no X-ray machine at the hospital, but the Catholic clinic down the road did. If we wanted an X-ray, for TB or a fractured limb, we sent the patient to the Catholic clinic, and they returned with their film.

## Diarrhea

An innovation I designed, having learned it from Dr. Fekety, was to give cholestyramine to patients with diarrhea. The hospital had a diarrhea ward with half of a wall down the middle. It was intended to be two wards, but the builders ran out of bricks. Dr. Snyder was skeptical, so I gave cholestyramine to patients on one side of the wall and the usual treatment to the others. Since patients were randomly assigned to available beds, it constituted a randomized trial.

It didn't take long to see the dramatic difference between the cholestyramine treatment and the usual treatment. The reason was that the drug, which tastes like mud and is used for treatment of elevated cholesterol in the United States, adsorbs many things, including medicines, cholesterol, and toxins. The treated patients recovered in half the time of those who received the usual treatment. I even gave cholestyramine to cholera patients, who recovered much faster than usual.

One comical incident occurred. A patient admitted for diarrhea was ready for discharge and asked the nurse, my translator, for more of that "mud" medicine. I asked him if he still had diarrhea. "No, all gone," he replied.

"Why do you want the medicine, then?"

"It tastes better than what my wife cooks for breakfast," he said with a smile to entice me to give him more cholestyramine.

My nurse translator explained that it was for diarrhea, and if

308

he should get sick again, he could return for some. He seemed disappointed.

## Measles

Measles was epidemic in Rwanda when we were there. Hundreds of children across Africa died. Mass vaccination programs were initiated, but the rumor that the vaccine caused male sterilization prevented parents from vaccinating their sons.

One mother brought three sons to the hospital, all critically ill with measles. Over the course of supportive treatment, the youngest died, but the two older boys survived. When they were ready for discharge, my nurse said the mother wanted to talk to me. I assumed she was upset that the one son had died. When I arrived on the ward, she got down on her knees and kissed my feet. I asked the nurse why she did that. My nurse explained the mother had assumed all three of her sons would die because that is what she had observed in her village. She was kissing my feet to thank me that she had two healthy sons to take home. I was heartbroken.

## Water

The hospital had a well, and Dr. Snyder provided an outdoor spigot for washing. I observed patients washing their feet. One woman I watched spent almost a half hour washing her feet. I asked Dr. Snyder why. He claimed Rwandans were very paranoid about anything that affected their feet. He explained that if you can't walk to work your garden or obtain water or food for your family, you might die. That experience made me more aware of washing my own feet and gave me insight into the care with which Jesus washed the disciples' feet.

309

The German government decided to donate wells in Rwanda. They made a grid of the country, and where the grid lines crossed, they placed wells. Dr. Snyder claimed that the German wells decreased child mortality more than the hospital had in twenty years.

## Rwandan Church

Kibogora is a Christian hospital, and the church was nearby. Of course, the sermon there was in Kinyarwanda, so we would stay to listen to the singing and sneak out the back door once the sermon started. The music was always accompanied by impressive, melodious drumming. It always featured three different synchronized drums, unlike American drumming, which mostly sounds like noise to me. When we got home and went to our own church, we missed the drumming during the singing.

We attended a remarkable event that year. The Old Testament had just been translated into Kinyarwanda. The New Testament had been translated for almost a hundred years, and the four gospels were translated in 1904, so there was quite a celebration for the completion of the Bible translation. After reading the Old Testament, many Rwandans said they related to the tribalism of Israel in it much more than to the New Testament. "Why wasn't this available sooner? Why didn't they translate this first?" were the complaints that I heard. So many people attended the church service the day the Old Testament was handed out that the church could not accommodate them all. The church building was always full every Sunday, but so many attended the distribution of the Old Testament that they met on the hillside beside the church. There must have been over a thousand people.

I met a young lady at church that day who spoke fluent English, so I spent time talking to her. She related her story of being kidnapped for the sex trade before she finally escaped. Part of her experience is presented in my book *Never a Woman*.

## Response of My Children

Rwanda had a profound effect on our children. When we prepared to return to the United States, they gave away their few toys and their clothes to their playmates. Temujin had even gone to one of his friend's homes to see how he lived. It was just a mud hut with an outdoor firepit. Back in the states, this caused some problems. Tirzah could not understand her school friends' hang-ups with clothes and makeup. Temujin could not relate his experience because the other boys teased him. He even got in trouble with a teacher. She was teaching the geography of Africa, and unfortunately, she put her finger right on Rwanda and said, "These are the flat planes of Central Africa."

Temujin raised his hand and said, "I've lived there, and it isn't flat. What other lies have you been telling us?" He probably shouldn't have added the second part.

## Need for Rwandan Physicians

Before we left, I had a talk with Dr. Snyder. "You need Rwandan physicians at your hospital. If you are ever forced to leave the country, national physicians will continue the work you've started. Otherwise, it will fall apart."

"I agree with you, but they're hard to find," he stated.

The Methodist bishop's son, John, had just graduated from medical school, so Dr. Snyder hired him. During the five years leading up to the holocaust, he hired several more Rwandan physicians. When the slaughter started, John, a Tutsi, escaped to Kenya.

Dr. Snyder put a Hutu physician in charge when the U.S. military[26] came to escort him and his wife, Louise, out of the country. In his book *On a Hill Far Away*, he writes the Hutu physician admitted more than a hundred Tutsis to the hospital. When the gangs appeared, he told them not to go into that ward because of lethal contagious diseases. They left. That saved them all.

## Illegal Aliens

Leaving Rwanda was a problem. We went to the airport and checked our luggage, but when we went through immigration, we were informed that our visas had expired. I couldn't understand it. We had been in the country less than three months, and I had requested a three-month visa. The official explained that our visa said *onze jours*, "eleven days" in French. I did not speak or read French then.[27] I had not realized that when we arrived, we had eleven days to renew our visas for the three months I was to work at the hospital. We were informed we were under arrest.

A miracle happened. One of the baggage workers found out about our plight. He was a friend of the Methodist bishop's. He called the bishop to come to the airport. He also took out our luggage, except one suitcase, which was already on the plane, so that we would have clothes to wear. When the bishop, who was highly respected in the government, arrived, he negotiated house

---

[26] A med-peds resident in Kalamazoo was part of the special forces that escorted Al and Louise Snyder out of the country. He gave me a vivid description of their evacuation.

[27] I took classes when I got home so this wouldn't happen again.

arrest for us. Otherwise, we would have been stuck in some cell at the airport.

Under house arrest, we went to the bishop's home. It was spacious and he was quite gracious. He arranged two things. First, the next day, we went to the immigration office. We sat in the lobby for over an hour. The official was getting ready to go for lunch, which is usually two to three hours, but the bishop informed him we were not leaving until he resolved our problem. The bishop explained my lack of "French understanding" and that we had spent the time working at the hospital: "They were not tourists. They were saving Rwandan lives daily." The resolution the bishop negotiated was that we would pay an $80 fine and leave the country within four days. I wanted seven days because the Air France flight only came once a week, but the official refused. The next flight was on a Belgian airline, Sabena. It cost $4,000 but took credit cards. I still have our illegal alien certificate.

Second, the bishop arranged for us to go to Akagera National Park. We hadn't done any tourist things except visit a tea factory with Dr. Snyder, so it was a fun time for the children, as we went on a safari to see giraffes and hippopotamuses. We stayed at a nice hotel where monkeys, gazelles, and even elephants came to a water hole just outside our window in the evening and morning.

Back at the airport, everything went smoothly this time. We didn't get to spend four days in Paris as planned but flew directly to Boston, where we had a reservation at the Marriott Long Wharf hotel. It was August 19, Priscilla's birthday. She said, "Flying with the sun resulted in the longest birthday I've ever had, about thirty-two hours."

RICHARD R. ROACH, MD, FACP

## Boston

Friday, we arrived at the Marriott Long Wharf bedraggled, tired, and needing showers. The receptionist said that they lost our reservation made six months before. "We're full." She fiddled with her computer and then looked up at us. "I have one room left, but you will have to check in the morning to see if we have any rooms for the weekend." Our flight home was on Monday. We profusely thanked the receptionist and shuffled off to our room, showered, and fell asleep.

During the night, the fire alarm went off. Priscilla said to me, "I'm too tired. I don't smell smoke. Go see what it's about."

I found everyone gathered in the lobby. A couple of firefighters were scurrying around. There was no smoke. Later, we were informed that someone had thrown a cigarette in the garbage, which caused a fire. Within an hour, I and the other guests were released to return to our rooms.

The next morning, I dutifully went to the front desk to see whether my family and I could stay for the weekend. The clerk said, "Because of the fire, a lot of people left. We have plenty of rooms." While I was at the reception desk, I signed us up for the Sunday brunch with the concierge.

Saturday, we hiked the Freedom Trail, went to Faneuil Hall, and toured the ship the *Constitution*. The children lacked enthusiasm, but in retrospect, they have great memories of the adventure.

Sunday brunch was a heavenly feast. Recall that we had been eating Rwandan food. As great as the fruit was (the sweetest pineapple ever cost $0.11), we hadn't had any variety to our diet. Sunday brunch at the Marriott Long Wharf was a sight, smell, and flavor treat to behold. We stood paralyzed by the choices

314

at the multiple tables. I think we spent three hours at our table, sometimes just gazing at the food.

About that suitcase, we hadn't given it up for lost. We called Air France and explained the situation. The woman on the other end said, "Oh my God, you'll never see that suitcase again."

"Right person, wrong conclusion," I replied. She didn't respond.

We prayed for the suitcase. Three months later, it arrived on our doorstep. The only thing missing was one of Priscilla's favorite dresses. "Perhaps someone needed a nice dress," she said.

We will never forget our adventure in Rwanda. The bishop arranged that we could return one day. The government official was initially against it, but the bishop persuaded him. We have never had the opportunity to return to the country.

## Learning French

After we experienced house arrest for our visa, I decided to learn French. I had a patient who requested home visits for her invalid mother. My receptionist told me that this patient taught French at Andrews University, so I asked Dr. Runion if she would teach me when I checked on her mother. We struck up a deal: I would not charge for the home visits if she would spend an hour each time teaching me French. It worked well.

Paulette, who owned the French restaurant in town, would come into my office telling my receptionist her problems. Julie could not understand her, so Paulette would yell. I discovered that she was speaking English using French pronunciations. She had been a Parisian French teacher in Algeria. So another deal was struck. I went to her house on Thursday afternoons and she would tutor me. On my trips to Paris, I discovered that my pronunciation was well understood.

## *Holocaust Aftermath*

Five years later, we learned that Bizimana had been hacked to death in front of his wife for having a canoe. Marceline was commanded to stand along the wall of the church since she was the youth Bible study leader. She and other church leaders were executed by firing squad.

# 23

## CHINA

While I was in Kalamazoo working for Michigan State's Kalamazoo Center for Medical Studies (KCMS, before WMU took over the program), we had an internal medicine resident from China, Nathan Benning, MD. KCMS allowed residents one away rotation during training. Most residents interested in fellowships would take the rotation at the place where they were applying for fellowship. Nathan requested an away rotation in China, where his father was a physician, specifically an anesthesiologist.

Dr. Loehrke proposed Nathan's request at a faculty meeting. None of the faculty was particularly opposed to the idea, as he had outlined seeing patients for two weeks at the gastroenterology hospital and two weeks at Beijing Emergency Hospital. The faculty agreed that he could go. Dr. Loehrke qualified the decision, saying, "I wish someone would go with him so that this is not just a family vacation for Nathan."

After some thought and discussion with Priscilla, I volunteered to go with him. Priscilla suggested that Temujin go with us. Nathan was delighted and informed his father, who set up a gastroenterology conference at which he asked me to speak on evidence-based medicine in gastroenterology.

We flew over the North Pole. The pilot told us all to look out the window. There were sheets of snow and ice with debris from those who made it to the pole. What an opportunity. I never in my life expected to see the North Pole.

The landing in Beijing was uneventful, but there was some kind of problem at the airport as we tried to get on the plane to Xinxiang (Chongqing, variously spelled). The commotion was settled when Nathan's father showed up. He is a four-star general in the Chinese military, so whatever the problem was, he quickly resolved it. He escorted us to our next plane without further incident.

We stayed at a four-star tourist hotel. It was grand. It even had a small pool. My and Temujin's room had a balcony, so we were able to watch the early morning people gather for Tai Chi exercise on the front lawn. Our room included a breakfast buffet, much of which we had no idea what it was. I did recognize the chicken feet, and they were tender and delicious.

We were escorted to the conference at the gastroenterology hospital by a white-gloved military driver. At the conference, the general sat next to me and translated the talks of the other gastroenterologists. It was quite remarkable to hear about their management of hepatocellular carcinoma. They described the cannulation of hepatic arteries to give toxic chemotherapy to the specific artery feeding the cancer. The imagery was impressive.

I was introduced, and Nathan translated my talk into Chinese. This was in the Szechuan area, so I think it might have been translated into that dialect. In any case, when I was done speaking, the general said, "Your talk received an A from the audience. Nathan's translation received a C+." Then I understood that many physicians in China understand and read English, but are hesitant to speak it because of problems with pronunciation.

The next day, we went to the hospital and made rounds with several of the gastroenterologists who had been present at the meeting. There was a whole ward, the fourth floor of the hospital, just for patients with liver cancer. We saw selected patients and then went to the conference room to review their histories and progress with treatment.

During the conference, we ate with the attendees at a massive round table. An amazing collection of delicacies were served. Temujin and I had no idea what most of the offerings were, but they were delicious. However, there was no rice. I was surprised and asked our host about this. He said, "Rice is for cleansing the palate. Besides, it's for poor people. We are not poor."

The night after the two-day conference was completed, the director invited us for dinner. Hot pot was served in elegant fashion, boiling water on one side, boiling oil on the other. We were served probably fifty small dishes of meat and vegetables to boil or fry. I often lost my vegetables in the boiling water. Our host said that was all right because after we were full of meat, the water with the missing vegetables was served as soup. No rice.

Temujin suggested the rule that we not ask what we were eating. We just tried the delicacies and ate them if we liked them, and didn't finish what we didn't like. It was a good rule. But for one dish we both really enjoyed, we decided to break our rule. We should not have done that. After eating two servings, we asked about the particular dish. "That's a cow tendon cured in lye," our host explained.

The next day, we toured the emergency department hospital. I learned that if a physician admits a patient from the ED, they are responsible to care for the patient for the first thirty days.

Therefore, the ED physician becomes a primary care physician for admissions. After that, if the patient still needs hospitalization, they are transferred to the care of the appropriate specialist.

We also toured a military hospital because our four-star general host gave permission for such a tour. I doubt that many visiting physicians have that opportunity. The hospital was well supplied with the latest technology.

On the weekend, we set out to tour a Buddhist monastery. The general explained that the four-lane highways are tollways for everyone but the military. Our white-gloved military chauffeur just waved at the tollbooth. The road was beautiful, but there were no other cars on it. I didn't understand why the general wanted us to see this monastery, but it became clear once we started touring it. This monastery was an ancient alcohol treatment facility. The mountain walls displayed relief carvings used for teaching the disaster befalling a patient if they continued drinking as well as the glories of sobriety. I was impressed by how modern the psychological treatment was, it being a two-thousand-year-old twelve-step program, with each step carved into the mountain wall.

While there, I needed to use the facilities. I was directed to what appeared to be an outhouse. Very thankful, I entered to do my business, and found the facility was perched precariously on a cliff. The urine and feces dropped hundreds of feet into the abyss.

After our tour, we were invited to have lunch at a local restaurant. Of course, nothing was in English. The general ordered for us as we sat around a large circular table. After ordering, he asked me if there was something Temujin and I would like. I thought some chicken would be nice since it would be something I would recognize. Nathan's father called the waiter and put in an order for chicken. I expected something like the chicken in vegetables available at Chinese restaurants in the United States.

As we waited for our food and sipped our fruit juice drinks, an attractive teenage girl ran across the room and out the door with a large knife. I asked, "What is that all about?"

The general explained, "She went out to get your chicken." I felt humiliated that I had sent the teenager on such a mission.

We were then served multiple delicacies, none of which Temujin or I recognized. When we were satisfied with our food, the waitress brought out a cooked chicken. I felt obligated to try it. That was the toughest chicken I have ever tried to eat. It was then Temujin added a new rule: we should not order anything other than what our host orders.

The last day, we met Nathan's brother, who spoke perfect English, and his family. Nathan's brother had one daughter. The rule there is if a child scores in the top 5 percent, the parents do not need to pay the child's tuition. Otherwise, tuition equals an adult's annual wage, requiring both parents to work. This young lady scored in the top 1 percent, so her tuition was free.

Our last night at Xinxiang, we were invited to the general's home for dinner. It was a comfortable apartment, more than I expected. There, the general related his story for us. Before the revolution, he had trained as an anesthesiologist. During the revolution, it was determined that he needed retraining. So, he was sent to a pig farm to shovel pig dung, which he did for five years.

One day, while he was busy shoveling, a black limousine appeared at the farm. A communist official approached and asked him, "Are you an anesthesiologist?"

"Yes, I am a physician trained as an anesthesiologist," he replied.

"Come with me."

He didn't even have time to change his clothes. He was driven to the military hospital, where he showered and changed into scrubs, and put in charge of anesthesia for the hospital. The communist committee met and decided that, as head of the department, he should marry the head of the nursing department. They were allowed two children, Nathan and his brother. The problem with the marriage was that he was Cantonese and his wife was Szechuan; they spoke different dialects and preferred different foods.

As we sat down at the long table for dinner, the general sat at one end, his wife at the other. Nathan and his brother sat in the middle opposite Temujin and me. There were a multitude of dishes on the table—Cantonese on the father's end, Szechuan on his wife's end. Nathan explained that he and his brother liked both styles of food. But when his parents were first married, his mother had to learn to cook Cantonese because his father could not tolerate the spices of Szechuan food.

It was an entertaining evening highlighted by animated conversation and intriguing stories. Nathan's father explained he was trained in acupuncture as well as chemical anesthesia. He shared some of the surgeries performed with acupuncture, but I was impressed when he added, "It doesn't work with children. I've tried it but always have to resort to general anesthesia."

We received warm hugs from the general and his wife as we departed. We were chauffeured back to our hotel with happy, full stomachs.

The next morning, Temujin and I went to the front desk at the hotel to pay for our room. The clerk smiled at us and in perfect English said, "Your room is already paid for."

"Who paid?" I asked.

"The army."

Nathan and his parents met us outside the hotel. We thanked the general and proceeded to the wharf to take a cruise down the Yangtze River. This was a cruise boat for Chinese people; it had none of the amenities like Carnival Cruise ships have. We did have a private room, of which there were very few. Our toilet had a shower nozzle over it, so it was both a toilet and our shower. It smelled of sewage, so we kept the door closed. Most of the people on the ship rolled up in blankets on the deck.

Food was available at the galley, an open-air affair with massive pots and open-flame stoves. Nathan's mother had packed us food, so we did not sample any of the ship's. We spent most of our time on the bow deck, as it smelled better than the aft deck. While scanning the scenic riverbanks, we met a young couple there who had made millions of dollars selling their IT company. They were taking a year off to travel.

I saw a massive sign along the river that showed four Chinese characters. I asked Nathan what the sign said. "It's hard to explain," he replied.

"We've got time," I said. "Go ahead."

He went on to explain the phrase was something a powerful military general had said long ago. It was to remind people how great the Chinese civilization was. It took Nathan a half hour, and still, he did not exactly translate the phrase.

The dam at Sandouping had not been completed, so we were able to see the beautiful gorges and towns along the river before they were flooded. Of interest were the signposts showing how far up the banks the water was expected to rise. Several towns along the banks were built above the signposts. These new cities had identical layouts to the old ones. People who owned homes in the soon-to-be-flooded cities had matching homes built for them in the new cities.

An excursion was included in our tour. We went up and down the Three Gorges tributary in small boats. Seeing the rock formations and tributary rivers was magnificent. This area is now flooded, so I am sure it is not nearly as picturesque as when we saw it. An article in *National Geographic* showing the gorge after the flooding from the completed dam made it look quite ordinary. I'm glad we saw it in its pristine condition.

We got off the cruise ship at Wuhan. It was quite commercial, with little shops scattered along the road into town. From there, we flew to Beijing. Nathan was starting a rotation at a large ED hospital. He needed no further supervision, so Temujin and I had time to visit the Forbidden City.

There, we met a young woman who was selling her artwork to pay for further art education at the Sorbonne in Paris. Her English was excellent, and she was fluent in French. We bought some of her art to encourage her. In addition, at a museum with glassware and bronze dating back as far as three thousand years, I bought Priscilla a museum replica of a two-thousand-year-old bronze sheep.

We spent a day at the garden built for the princesses, a huge city park with its own lake. The corridor to the palace was lined with artwork. I don't think our whole day of walking allowed us to see even a quarter of the park.

We did poke our heads into several gift shops. One had beautiful carvings at very reasonable prices. I really liked a dragon, but it was so large it would not fit in my suitcase. As I walked out of the store, the wood carver said, "Did you not like dragon?"

"Yes, I did, but it is too big."

"How big you want it?"

I sort of showed him with my hands the approximate size. He replied, "Come back tomorrow, dragon ready."

We returned the next day, and he had carved an identical dragon to fit my measurements. Amazing!

We wanted to see the Great Wall. Nathan had introduced us to a tour guide to make the arrangements. The part of the Great Wall we saw was not the part Nixon visited with wide walkways and nice walls on each side. We visited a part that had just been opened to the public the week before. It was steep and narrow. There were eleven guard posts along the wall to which we were allowed to walk. I think we went to only four because the wall became very narrow, and the side walls disappeared into a hundred-foot drop on both sides. This gave us a much more realistic understanding of the construction of the Great Wall. We were the only tourists that day.

Back in Beijing, we treated ourselves to Peking duck at a restaurant at the end of Tiananmen Square. The ducks were hanging in the window, so we had no trouble finding a place to eat. It was outstanding. The restaurant also featured seafood. The fish, octopi, lobsters, and shrimp were live, enclosed in huge tanks along the wall. We were entertained watching them swim while we ate our duck.

Right outside the restaurant was a woodworking store where I bought a Forstner drill bit. The store had wonderful hand tools as well. I would have liked to spend a day in there, but I had to consider the weight of my luggage. The Forstner bit was a good choice; I have used it frequently.

Nathan got us to the airport to fly home. I think Dr. Loehrke had negotiated my time off to half vacation and half business, because I gave that lecture and went on rounds at the hospital the first week, and I gained new insights into Chinese culture and medical care as well.

# 24

## GERMANY

The first time I visited Germany, I think in 1998, I was on my way back from Madagascar. My brother-in-law, Steve Hasskamp (whose last name means "hates war"), is an electrical engineer, and he and his friend had helped repair electrical equipment while I worked at the hospital in Manambaro. On our way back to the states, they wanted to see Neuschwanstein.

We landed in Paris. The train station is in the airport, so it is convenient. There, we scheduled a trip on the train to Munich (*München*), arranging a sleeper compartment to avoid a hotel stay. The train left Paris in the evening and would arrive in Munich at about 9:30 in the morning. The porter who checked on us on board said, "*Bonne nuit.*" I had been thinking in French during my work in Madagascar.

That evening, as I lay in the sleeper bed, I tried to remember German vocabulary. Only a few words came to mind. I was concerned about helping my friends with the language once we arrived in Munich.

In the morning, the same porter greeted us with, "*Guten*

*Morgen.*" Outside the train station, we found a concierge to help us with accommodations. Suddenly, my German came back to me, and I had no problem arranging a hotel stay myself. It's very odd how our brains work.

The bed-and-breakfast was great and inexpensive. We had a great time in Munich, toured the ancient part of the city, visited the Hoffbräuhaus, and arranged a guided tour of Neuschwanstein. Steve and his friend appreciated my language skills when ordering food and planning. I was amazed how my vocabulary returned to my brain once in Germany.

Subsequent visits to Germany were because of a strange thing that happened. Dr. Gupta, who had been one of our residents and become an interventional cardiologist, had invited a German medical student to do a rotation with his cardiology group in Kalamazoo. He called me in a panic, as his partner who had agreed to house her in his home was out of town, and she was arriving the next day. "Would you be willing to have her stay with you?"

"Of course," I said. "We would be delighted."

That was how we met Lisa. Priscilla and I were empty nesters, and Lisa was a delightful young woman. I could easily read her German medical school textbooks, so I would review the patients she had seen with the cardiologists and discuss the principles in a mixture of English and German. She enjoyed our Michigan fruit and Priscilla's and my cooking. She loved our indigenous wild rice. I made coffee every morning. One day, she took a sip and said, "Oh, this is good. My father said that Americans don't know how to make good coffee."

We had a delightful time together. She left with an invitation for us to visit her in Germany. Priscilla and I were excited by the possibility.

On a return from Madagascar, Priscilla was meeting me at the

Paris airport. I was unsure of how we were going to meet, but we had arranged a place, Priscilla's favorite patisserie at the stairway to the train station, since we had to take the train to Freiburg, where Lisa's medical school was located. The planning was unnecessary. Her luggage carrousel was right next to mine. We arrived at almost the same time.

We enjoyed the train, as we had a beautiful view of the countryside. Lisa met us with warm hugs and housed us. The next day, she arranged a tour of Freiburg, including Munster Cathedral; the Martinstor, the ancient gate of the city; and the ornate Neues Rathaus. We finished the tour at the very modern medical school. Lisa and I had lunch in the medical school cafeteria while Priscilla got over her jet lag.

The next adventure was to meet her parents, Sylvia and Volker, who lived in a small Bavarian town not far away from Freiburg. Volker speaks fluent English and Sylvia understands a lot of English, so meals were animated and delightful. They arranged for us to stay in a reconditioned barn that was becoming a bed-and-breakfast. Priscilla and I had breakfast on our own at the local pastry shop but had lunch and dinner with them. They love cheese, so we had some delightful Bavarian cheeses and sausages for lunch. One of Lisa's sisters joined us for dinner one evening.

Both of Lisa's parents are ordained ministers. Volker is semiretired but preaches as needed at various churches. I attended a sermon of his and was delighted that I could understand most of it. During the congregational singing, I was afforded a hymnal so I could sing along.

Sylvia is the chaplain at a psychiatric hospital. She laughed saying, "I have a captive congregation."

Volker treated us to a tour down the highway that parallels the Rhine, stopping at several lookouts. He and I stood on top of the Lorelei rock and sang Wagner's chorus together, which I had learned in German class. Lisa and Priscilla, embarrassed at our antics, left and told us to meet them in the restaurant.

Volker took us to several stores. We had lunch at a pastry shop that served the best Black Forest cake in Germany, according to Volker. At a nearby bookstore, I was looking for a *Max und Moritz* book because I had studied the cartoons in German class. I found one, but on close inspection, all the words were spelled oddly. Volker saw my consternation and laughed. "That is in Palatine, a local dialect." He pulled me aside to tell me, "My wife speaks Palatine to our daughters when they don't want me to know what they are talking about. I can't understand a word they say."

So, Lisa speaks English, German, French, and Spanish[28] as well as conversing with her mother in Palatine. What a woman!

Our last evening, Volker took us to a restaurant down a dark alleyway. I was apprehensive. At the end of the alley was a small door. Entering, we found a grand German, Gothic-style restaurant. The food was beyond imagination. I had caramelized wild boar meat. I have never tasted any meat so rich, tender, and tasty. Priscilla said her food was amazing as well, but I don't remember what she ordered, as I was in ecstasy over mine.

After hugs, Priscilla and I returned to the United States. Lisa went back to school. That Christmas, I received a package from Volker: *Die Klassiker*, a collection of German tales, including *Max und Moritz*, in German, not Palatine. I can understand it and enjoy reading and laughing through it periodically.

We still receive emails from Lisa, who is a psychiatrist in Zurich, Switzerland, and married a Swiss engineer, Phillipe. During the five hundredth anniversary of the Reformation (2021), on returning from Madagascar, she invited me to stay with them

---

[28] She did a medical school rotation in Spain.

for a week. It was great fun. I bought some groceries and made meals for them, as they were both working full-time. Touring some of the churches in Zurich, I was able to see some of Martin Luther's letters, which he sent to the Protestant Reformers in Switzerland. He had nice, legible handwriting; therefore, I could read some of them.

From a cardiology rotation that almost ran amok, Lisa and I have developed a delightful, meaningful relationship. Priscilla and I have kept in touch with her, receiving pictures of Lisa and Phillipe's children, Christmas letters, and the like. Their third child is due in January 2025.

# 25

# MY PARTNER LEE BRICKER

While working for WMed, I had an influential partner whom I highly respected: Lee Bricker, an endocrinologist. Our clinics were right next to each other. Our window looked out over the parking lot. He would watch his patients coming for their appointments and say, "Physical exam begins in the parking lot." He was a tremendous observer and diagnostician.

Once, he diagnosed a molar pregnancy over the telephone. The obstetrician asked for an endocrinology consult regarding a young woman who had received no prenatal care because she had been raped and was ashamed to go to the doctor. Her thyroid-stimulating hormone (TSH) was extremely high. Dr. Bricker suggested that he do a quick ultrasound because the hCG produced by molar pregnancies interferes with the TSH test. He was right. There was nothing wrong with her thyroid. The patient, who was ashamed of her situation, was delighted to have a molar pregnancy, which was evacuated, and not a baby.

Lee and I developed a close relationship because he was the oldest on the faculty and I was the second oldest. He was a Russian

Jew whose family had immigrated to Denver to avoid World War II. He had always yearned to see Russia, especially where his family had emigrated from. I kept telling him he should go. One day, when he came into my office, I showed him a Viking Cruises brochure describing a trip down the Volga River. I reviewed it with him and said, "You should go."

"I won't go without you."

I looked at the prices and said, "Lee, I can't afford this trip right now."

"Don't worry about the expense. I'll pay for you. You can pay me back if you want to, but you don't have to."

Arrangements were made. Priscilla and I joined Lee and his wife, Marilyn, on the cruise. When Steve and Marilyn Terranella, MD, another WMed partner, heard about the trip, they joined us too. We toured St. Petersburg and Moscow and cruised down the Volga. We toured Czar Peter the Great's gardens and palace, Catherine the Great's Hermitage collection, Stalin's hideout during World War II, and many towns along the river, including the Orthodox churches.

On the ship, we were served Russian fare. The food was great. We had the same waitress for the entire trip; she spoke excellent English as she described the available entrees. She was taking graduate courses in hospitality and hotel management. She always laughed because the six of us never ordered the same thing, until the last dinner, when we all ordered the same dessert. Her eyes went wide, and she said, "Amazing." We all laughed.

We even had a vodka demonstration. I had never tasted vodka I liked, but I went with Lee to the demonstration anyway. We had tiny sips of several different vodkas. I only liked one. The others tasted bitter to me. The one I liked was $500 a bottle, so I am still immune to vodka.

The guides Viking hired lived in the small towns we visited along the river. That made each tour very personable. People in Russia don't move much, so each guide lived in the town they guided us through. They would explain where they grew up, where they went to school, and where their parents lived during the war.

Visiting the Jewish cemetery brought tears to Lee's eyes. Names and the Star of David were engraved on the stones. Most of the Russian soldiers were buried in mass graves with no names. Our guide explained that the Russian soldiers would throw away their own dog tags so their families wouldn't know they had been killed, but the Jewish soldiers wanted their names remembered.

Moscow's synagogue was also an emotional visit for Lee. It was beautiful with engraved woodwork panels. There was also a library of ancient manuscripts.

The Hermitage was astounding. Our guided tour oriented us to the design and architecture. Then we had free time to explore the museum.

The rooms of the Hermitage are as fabulous as the artwork displayed. Each room is different, an artist's dream world. I had studied art in high school and college, so I recognized the artists, but many of the pieces I had never seen before, even in books. The guide explained that Catherine the Great would send her agents to France to investigate estate sales. They would buy the entire estate, not focused on what they were buying. As a result, the Hermitage presented many unknown works of famous artists when it first opened to the public.

Somehow during our free time, we lost Lee. When we gathered at the appointed place to board the bus to take us back to the ship, everyone except Lee was present. I knew that he loved sculpture, as he had apprenticed with a sculptor in Kalamazoo, so I volunteered to find him. I went to the sculpture exhibit on the top floor. There was Lee, standing like a statue. "Everyone is waiting for you," I said.

His hand roamed across the room of sculptures. "This is like trying to take a drink from a firehose."

I laughed at his comment but insisted that he follow, as the bus was ready to leave.

Another curiosity was visiting the World War II cemetery where the statue of Mother Russia stands taller than the Statue of Liberty. It was another emotional moment. What surprised us was the tour of brides. We must have seen a dozen brides and bridegrooms touring. We were led to understand that it is a custom for bridal couples to visit the cemetery as part of their wedding ceremony to honor their forebears.

When we were back in Kalamazoo, Lee would periodically come to my office to thank me for suggesting the trip. About a year after our return, his wife died of metastatic breast cancer. He came to my office several months after her death, shut the door, and with tears streaming down his cheeks said, "I'm so glad we went on that trip. Marilyn and I were so happy. I'm glad she got to experience that before she died." Hugging me, he told me, "You are my favorite *goy*."[29]

I think it took two years of small allotments, but I finally paid him back.

---

[29] A derogatory term for a non-Jew

# 26

## RHINE—FINDING THE MAUSETURM

I wanted to traverse the Rhine River to see the Mauseturm, the castle tower I had studied in high school German class. When the Tarranellas suggested going on a Viking river cruise down the Rhine, Priscilla and I were instantly interested. I shared my excitement with Kalamazoo friends, Gary and Marilyn Petzhold, who agreed to go, and they invited some of their friends to join us. The result was that ten of us from Kalamazoo went on the trip. I think we got a discount for having a party of ten.

The cruise was magnificent, as we viewed the vineyards along the riverbank, visited some of the wineries, and observed numerous castles. All along, I was searching for the Mauseturm. I knew the tower castle was in the middle of the river. The story, which I read in German, is that a rich miser refused to share his voluminous grain supply with the starving townspeople. He stored his grain in the tower so the townspeople couldn't steal it. When a riot ensued, he fled to the tower. But the mice and rats also fled to the storage tower since they could find nothing to eat in the town.

They found a way to float to the island tower to feast on the grain and in the process attacked and ate the miser in his own tower.

While searching for the Mauseturm, we saw many wonderful castles. We toured several of them. I was fascinated with the kitchens, which were often in a stone structure separated from the main castle to avoid fire danger. Pots and pans hung over huge fireplaces. Swinging spits allowed the servants to put the pots over the fire and then swing them back out. Often, the tables were arranged with original place settings or recreations based on archaeological finds.

We took the opportunity to visit several vineyards along the river, which winds its way between France and Germany. The vineyards were always on the east- or west-facing banks to take advantage of the morning or evening sun. The wine tastings were great.

The most interesting vineyard produced *spätlese*, which means "late arrival." The guide explained that the vineyard, a monastery, was bought by a rich merchant who lived in Vienna. When the grapes were ripe, the monks had to get the merchant's permission to harvest them, so they sent a young monk to Vienna. This young monk decided that he needed some time with the local prostitutes first. Later, he did find the owner and received the permission he sought.

When he arrived back at the monastery, the grapes were covered in white mold. But since the owner had given his permission to harvest them, the monks did. Despite the mold or because of it, the taste of the wine was extraordinary. Ever since, the winery has allowed 10 percent of the grapes to develop white mold. Sometimes, it fails; the mold doesn't arrive or the grapes spoil first. But when it succeeds, the wine is amazing. We were treated to the regular wine, which was excellent, and then they gave us a small taste of the late, moldy wine. The rich flavor was incredible. I have never tasted such a complex white wine. But it cost $300 a bottle. (Interesting sidenote: Thomas Jefferson enjoyed the wine and managed to take some cuttings of the vines back to Monticello, but alas, the mold didn't grow in the United States, so he was disappointed.)

We finally came around a bend in the river, and there was the Mauseturm. I almost cried, having labored so hard in German class to translate the whole story. Now I could see it. Unfortunately, no tours were provided. The concierge on the ship said that the inside was not much to see, anyway—no bones, rats, or mice.

The weather was pleasant during the entire cruise, so our Kalamazoo crew mostly spent time on the deck, watching the castles go by. We did have some fun tours of towns along the way, which added to our joy. The chef produced good German treats for our meals, which made the trip even more satisfying. There was even a demonstration of how to make *apfelkuchen*. It was a great cruise and especially meaningful for me.

# 27

## First-Class Flight

In all my trips, over a hundred flights, I have never chosen to fly first class. Even with points, when I could have upgraded, I stayed with my residents who were in regular seats. But one time, I did fly first class, by accident. I spent a few days in Paris, staying at an inexpensive hotel. I had a small room with a tight shower. When I dropped the soap, I had to step out of the shower to bend over to fetch it. But it was pleasant, and besides, I didn't spend that much time in my room.

I had a wonderful time in Paris. When it was time to leave, I had all my bags packed and went to breakfast, which was provided. It included croissants and other pastries, strawberry jam, and excellent coffee with real cream. I savored every mouthful. On returning to my room, I found that the key didn't work. I went downstairs and explained to the owner-manager that I could not open my door. He said, "That is because you are an American and it is a French lock."

I gave him my key, and he went upstairs to fetch my bags while I sat in the lobby. He was gone a long time. Meanwhile, I heard a persistent drilling noise. I checked the time, as it was getting late. I was afraid that I would miss my flight. He came down with a smile, saying, "You can get your bags now."

I ran upstairs. There was a huge hole in the door where he had drilled out the lock. So I grabbed my bags, thanked him, and ran for the Metro. I had to change trains at the Gare du Nord to arrive at the airport. Jumping off the train, I ran through security and then to my gate.

Everyone had already boarded the flight. I showed the Air France lady my ticket. "The hotel manager couldn't get my room door open," I explained.

She said, "We sold your ticket, but just sit down." I sat right in front of her desk, barely three feet away.

After a long pause, during which she was working on her computer, she picked up the microphone and said, "Monsieur *Roche*, please come to the desk."

I stood up. She smiled. I think she was giggling. She was probably required to use the microphone even though I was just in front of her. She gave me a new ticket.

I boarded the plane and found myself in first class. What an amazing experience. At mealtime, I dined on a linen tablecloth, spread out on my tray. My meal was served on porcelain plates, with refills of Pays d'Oc wine and a delightful, sweet dessert followed by a cheese tray. I was able to stretch out in the extra-large seat to have a nice rest across the Atlantic. Breakfast was equally extraordinary. I was well rested when I arrived in the United States.

# 28

## A FEW THOUGHTS ABOUT BEING A PHYSICIAN

I loved being a physician. I loved my patients as family. I loved the intellectual stimulation of medicine—the mystery, problem solving, and science. There were only a few things that upset me during my career.

### Questioning Medical Decisions

While staffing New Horizons, the drug and alcohol treatment center, I had a patient I wanted to admit to our thirty-day program. When I appeared on the ward, my nurse informed me the patient's insurance had denied admission. She asked me to call the insurance company.

I explained to the agent, "The patient tried outpatient treatment and failed. Furthermore, his parents were both alcoholics, as well as his siblings. The addictionology literature recommends in-patient treatment for patients with that history."

The young woman on the other end of the line explained in a monotone, canned speech, "We can't authorize his admission."

"Why not?"

"Because."

So, I asked, "What is your education?" I didn't think that I was talking to a nurse or a physician based on her vocabulary.

"I have my GED."

I was furious. Someone with a high school non-diploma, a GED, was telling me that I couldn't admit my patient. I asked to speak to a physician, and she hung up.

I apologized to the patient that his insurance wouldn't allow admission and sent him to outpatient. He failed.

## Thumb Splint

The only time I became angry in Kalamazoo was when a healthy young woman presented having fallen at work with an outstretched hand to break her fall. An X-ray revealed a fracture of her thumb, but it was nondisplaced. She wasn't in too much pain. After reviewing the X-ray with her, I suggested a thumb-spica splint. She claimed that the splint would allow her to return to work.

My nurse called the insurance company for prior authorization. They denied my nurse, who turned the telephone over to me. I explained to the person on the phone that the woman needed a thumb-spica splint so she could return to work.

"All right, your patient can get the splint in seven to ten days," I was told.

I couldn't believe it. I yelled at her, "If your CEO fractured his thumb, would he have to wait seven to ten days to get a splint?" She hung up.

I have experience as an orderly, as a medical student, and as

341

an ED physician putting on casts, so I took the patient to the orthopedic clinic, which was across the hall, and manufactured a plaster thumb-spica splint. Then I referred her to the orthopedic surgeon for consultation in a week.

The orthopedic surgeon was impressed. He manipulated the insurance company out of a thumb-spica splint, but charged a hefty consult fee, so the bill to the insurance company was hundreds of dollars more than if they had just paid for the splint in the first place. The consulting orthopedic surgeon, who was a close friend, got quite a chuckle over the situation.

## FDA Drug Approval

Part of the dilemma for physicians is the medical literature is way ahead of the FDA. There can be a plethora of articles regarding an effective medical treatment, but it takes time for the FDA to approve it. The most horrific example is the treatment of gout with colchicine. Colchicine has been used for gout since 1820. There is even evidence that the ancient Egyptians used it. However, a glitch in the system meant the FDA had never approved the indication for gout.

An unscrupulous, unethical CEO of a pharmaceutical company discovered this glitch. He sent the medical literature to the FDA and asked for the indication. It was readily approved. The CEO then raised the price of colchicine 500 percent! Eventually, he ended up in prison for security fraud, but the price didn't return to what it had been. As a result, physicians used steroids with many more side effects instead of colchicine because most patients couldn't afford its unethical price. A prescription for colchicine in Madagascar costs $0.06. Unfortunately, there are other examples of such snafus.

Medicaid does not like paying for medicine, so if there is a medicine that is being frequently prescribed, Medicaid proposes that the FDA make it over the counter. That way, Medicaid patients must pay for it out of pocket. Examples include Motrin, Aleve, and Lotrimin (a vaginal antifungal cream). This happened multiple times in my forty-year career.

## Vioxx

The Vioxx story is sad. Vioxx is a COX-2 receptor inhibitor, which inhibits inflammation. We have others such as meloxicam, which inhibits COX-2 receptors by a 1:300 ratio. Vioxx inhibited COX-2 receptors by a 1:15,000 ratio. Patients loved it. I had at least ten patients who had tried other arthritis medications without benefit; Vioxx gave them new, pain-free lives. Unfortunately, a runner in Florida had a heart attack while taking Vioxx.

When I first read the article, I fumed because the runner didn't have any indication for taking the drug. Also, the *British Medical Journal* (*BMJ*) said the company had informed physicians that Vioxx had no antiplatelet effects. Therefore, if there was a concern about coronary disease, the patient should take aspirin in addition to Vioxx (1999).

The wife claimed her husband had been in perfect health. (Really? Had they done an autopsy?) She sued the manufacturer, claiming Vioxx *caused* the heart attack. So the FDA required a study to see if there was an increase in myocardial infarctions *associated* (notice I did not use *caused*) with Vioxx.

Sure enough, there was an increased risk of three myocardial infarctions per ten thousand patients. The FDA claimed the company had hidden the data. Didn't they read the *BMJ* article? The drug was taken off the market. That day, we had ten patients in the clinic who were in tears because other drugs they had tried never worked. Meloxicam is the best we have now.

Some curious researchers decided to check other NSAIDs and discovered the same increased risk of three myocardial infarctions per ten thousand patients occurred with both naprosyn and ibuprofen. Naprosyn received over-the-counter status because Medicaid got tired of paying for it, not because it was safer than other NSAID drugs. Vioxx's manufacturer won all subsequent lawsuits when this medical research data was available. But the manufacturer considered applying for Vioxx's reintroduction to be too expensive.

## Narcotics

Narcotics are a problem for physicians. I always told my residents that narcotics are a bad choice, only to be prescribed if they are the only choice. The side effects are horrible, even discounting addiction. Unnecessary narcotics are the worst part of the problem. I had an elderly patient with severe, deforming rheumatoid arthritis. He came to see me every three months for his narcotics. Looking at his hands, any physician would agree to prescribe narcotics in addition to NSAIDs for his apparent pain. But one day, my receptionist told me, "I don't like the car he came in."

"What do you mean, Dorothy?"

"I've seen that car before; the owner is a drug dealer."

I asked the patient, "Are you taking your narcotics?"

"Oh, yes, every day."

"Did you take them this morning?"

"Oh, yes, Doctor."

I did a urine drug screen in my office and found no narcotics.

When I confronted the patient, he said, "The guy that brings me to the doctor always takes my medicine. I don't really need it."

I didn't give him a refill. This phenomenon is called *harvesting*, an abuse of the geriatric population.

A middle-aged woman requested Tylenol #3 (acetaminophen with codeine) for pain. She seemed to have an indication, so I prescribed it on that Thursday. She called on Monday, stating she had a painful weekend and had taken all her pills. That much acetaminophen would cause liver failure, so I requested an emergency blood draw for acetaminophen level and liver enzymes. The Tylenol level was zero, and the liver enzymes were normal. I told her, "You did not take the prescription."

Her husband presented to the clinic very angry. "Are you calling my wife a liar?"

"I am telling you," I said in a firm voice, "that she did not take the medication, or she would be in liver failure. She has no Tylenol in her blood and her liver enzymes are normal."

Further investigation revealed that he was a contractor and was giving the Tylenol #3 to his workers who complained of backaches. I said, "Should I call the police for these felonies, or will you cease doing this?"

He said he would quit prescribing without a license and left. It was documented in the chart so that none of my partners would give her a prescription either.


### *Administration*

Some administrative problems are aggravating. The hospital wants to discharge a patient as soon as possible because of payment. And the administration encourages the physician to discharge patients who shouldn't be discharged. This often results in readmission, for which the hospital loses reimbursement. It is a tug-of-war. Hospital administrators who listen to physicians explain the complexity of patient care fare much better.

Outpatient medicine has become a specialty. But often, clinic managers design a fifteen-minute appointment for patients' multiple ongoing problems. We studied our internal medicine clinic and found our average patient had ten problems that needed addressing each visit. Fifteen minutes is not enough time to assess all ten. When managers control the office instead of physicians, it causes great consternation. When managers see their role as promoting patient care rather than office efficiency or wealth management, clinics run much better.

These are some of the frustrations of medical care. Notice that I did not mention patients vomiting blood on me, me crying over patients who died in my arms, or psychiatric patients with hallucinations and personality pathology. These patients cause only compassion, not frustration.

# CONCLUSION

Looking back at forty-some years of medical practice, I see the frustrations do not compare to the immense joy of my experience as a physician. I still rejoice, thinking back on the many patients I served in the hospitals and clinics. In addition, my experiences in Africa, Asia, and Madagascar were so enriching. Some nights, I'm awakened in ecstasy over a patient who survived but should have died by textbook statistics, or a one-in-ten-million diagnosis that was confirmed, or an alcoholic who thanked me after years of sobriety, or an intravenous drug abuser who found a new life.

I loved canoeing. To me, the BWCA and Quetico are amazing environments that need protection. Wilderness experiences change attitudes and change lives. May there always be a wilderness available to each generation.

I initiated a Facebook presence because many of my former residents and Malagasy physicians change their addresses and locations. I do include family, but most of my Facebook friends are physicians, nurses, and the rare patient. I rejoice over their contact. When I became professor emeritus for the Western Michigan University School of Medicine, the privilege allowed me to keep my email. Even though my residents and Malagasy physicians change their locations, my email is available to them. It is a delightful surprise to hear from them. I have even been invited by a former resident and faculty to give seminars in Kalamazoo and San Francisco. How exciting for an elderly physician!

My spirit is constantly strengthened by the still, small voice of one who told me that he used one untrained jackass, and he could use another. I don't steal anymore but have used my hands to give to others. Out with joy!

Printed in the United States
by Baker & Taylor Publisher Services